# CERTAINTY

## ~ A Place to Stand

### Critique of the Emergent
### Church of Postevangelicals

# Dr. Grant C. Richison

*Foreword by*
## Dr. Norm Geisler

Copyright ©2010 Dr. Grant C. Richison
All rights reserved
Printed in Canada
International Standard Book Number: 978-1-894860-62-8

Published by:
Castle Quay Books
1307 Wharf Street, Pickering, Ontario, L1W 1A5
Tel: (416) 573-3249
E-mail: info@castlequaybooks.com
*www.castlequaybooks.com*

Executive editor / producer: Diane Roblin-Lee
Design and production: byDesign Media, *www.bydesignmedia.ca*
Cover art: Elma Eidse Neufeld, *http://www.chateauroc.com*
Technical assistant: Candace Morgan
Printed by Transcontinental, Louiseville, Quebec, Canada

Scripture quotations, unless otherwise indicated, are from the New King James Version of the Bible.
Thomas Nelson Publishers ©1984, 1982, 1980, 1979

Scripture quotations from The Holy Bible, English Standard Version® (ESV®),
copyright © 2001 by Crossway, a publishing ministry of Good News Publishers are used by permission.
All rights reserved.

Library and Archives Canada Cataloguing in Publication

Richison, Grant C., 1936-
    Certainty : a place to stand / Grant C. Richison.

Includes bibliographical references.

ISBN 978-1-894860-62-8

    1. Evangelicalism. 2. Emerging church movement.
3. Christianity--21st century. I. Title.

BR1640.R53 2010          270.8'3          C2010-906704-5

CASTLE QUAY BOOKS

*To my wife, Joyce, who faithfully supports me in ministry.*
*And to my sons Grant (Heather and children),*
*Blake (Kristin and children), and Ross.*

## In Appreciation

Deb Elkink, a professional editor, is a long-time friend and editor of my website Verse-by-Verse Commentary *www.versebyversecommentary.com*. As a significant editor of this book, she poured countless hours into its preparation.

I am honored that Norm Geisler, a friend of many years and author of more than 50 books, wrote the Foreword.

Finally, I am thankful to Jack and Carol Klemke for encouraging me to write this book.

# Table of Contents

**Chapter One** ......................................................... *13*
Loss of Certainty Among Evangelicals
*A Sad Story*

**Chapter Two** ......................................................... *23*
The Great Evangelical Disaster Fulfilled
*Accommodating the Message to Culture*

**Chapter Three** ......................................................... *41*
Fraternities Living in Isolation
*Conciliation and Capitulation to Culture*

**Chapter Four** ......................................................... *77*
Renouncing Certainty
*Rejecting Certainty via Philosophical Assumptions*

**Chapter Five** ......................................................... *99*
Preference for Perspective
*Perspective of Self Precludes Certainty*

**Chapter Six** ......................................................... *129*
Let Your Yea be Yea
*Correlation Between Truth and Certainty*

**Chapter Seven** ......................................................... *161*
Is There Certainty Anywhere?
*Relationship of Propositions to Certainty*

**Chapter Eight** ......................................................... *193*
There Is Certainty Somewhere
*Source for Certainty—a Watershed Issue*

**Chapter Nine** ............................................................ *217*
A Place To Stand
*A Pou Sto*

**Chapter Ten** ............................................................ *229*
Source of Certainty
*Extant Statements from Scripture about Certainty*

**Chapter Eleven** ............................................................ *269*
Evangelical Identity Crisis
*Redefining Evangelicalism*

**Chapter Twelve** ............................................................ *287*
Reaching Those Without A Place To Stand
*Reaching Postmoderns*

**Conclusion** ............................................................ *307*

**Endnotes** ............................................................ *309*

# *Foreword*

In a day when the evangelical trumpet is making an uncertain sound, every Christian leader needs to read this book. It shows the need to be anchored to the Rock in our efforts to be geared to the times. At no time in our generation has there been a greater need and a clearer call to return to a surer foundation than that which is laid for our faith.

Dr. Norman L. Geisler
*Professor of Apologetics*
*Veritas Evangelical Seminary*
*www.VeritasSeminary.com*
*Murrieta, CA*

# Preface

I have not written this book for theologians or scholars but for broad-spectrum leaders within evangelicalism. For that reason, heavier theological or philosophical concepts have been relegated to the endnotes. While this is not always the case, hopefully the context will help the reader to decipher concepts that are more difficult.

I would like to recommend three books to the more general reader that expose the postconservative movement for what it is: *The Evangelical Left* by Millard J. Erickson (Baker Books, 1997), *Becoming Conversant with the Emerging Church* by D. A. Carson (Zondervan, 2005), and *The Courage to be Protestant* by David Wells (Eerdmans, 2008).

A heavier book, *Reclaiming the Center: Confronting Evangelical Accommodation in Postmodern Times*, edited by Millard J. Erickson, Paul Kjoss Helseth, and Justin Taylor (Crossway Books, 2004), critiques *Renewing the Center* by recently deceased Stanley Grenz. Bob DeWaay wrote one of the best books that I have read on this subject called *The Emergent Church, Undefining Christianity* (Bethany Press International, 2009). *Evangelicals Engaging Emergent: A Discussion of the Emergent Church Movement* (B&H Academic, 2009) is a balanced book critiquing the emergent church movement.

*Why We're Not Emergent (by Two Guys Who Should Be)*, by Kevin DeYoung and Tel Kluck (Moody, 2009) is an easy-to-read book that challenges the paradigm of emergent thinking.

Prior to launching into a discussion on evangelical postmodernism, a caveat is in order. Philosophical and functional postmodernism differ. Philosophical postmodernism is a belief in a system; the function of postmodernity manifests itself in how people live their normal lives but without a clear understanding of the philosophy. Philosophical postmodernism gives no direct extrapolation to functional postmodernism; we find functional postmodernism in television, movies, and business. Not all postmodernity (the function) comes from postmodernism (the philosophy)

# Loss of Certainty
# Among Evangelicals
## *A Sad Story*

### Denial of Certainty

Two centuries before Christ, the Greek mathematician and inventor Archimedes experimented with the lever. He declared that he could "move the earth" if he had a place to stand somewhere in the cosmos. People need a certain place to stand, a point of reference beyond the self.

I was surprised to hear a fellow staff member make glowing comments about a book that assails certainty of biblical truth. He even recommended that book to our leadership, yet possessed little perception of what that book taught. This staff person assumed it was a book about congenial relationships, but it had to do with lack of certainty about truth.

Some forms of the emergent church reject certainty of truth. This group reacts with skepticism towards evangelicals who assert certainty. These people feel betrayed by the belief that we can know something for sure. They want to distance themselves from what they deem to be judgmentalism that comes from certainty. They believe in a more "generous orthodoxy" devoid of discernment. For them, coming to belief is a quest for truth rather than arrival at truth. These people want to be non-judgmental about truth, so they blur such ideas as eternal punishment and homosexuality. They cannot assert that homosexuality is wrong by going to extant statements of Romans 1. Thus, their thinking lands on the ash heap of relativism; that is, truth is relative to the individual but does not stand independent from individual perspective. This becomes a serious problem in presenting the gospel.

Adherents to this movement curb their generosity toward evangelicals who hold to final truth. They tolerate almost any movement except evangelicalism. They are cynical and condescending toward those who think they have certainty about truth.

The greatest problem with this type of the emergent church is that it accepts a philosophy (postmodernism) that runs rampant through academic and pop culture. This philosophy rejects the idea that anyone can come to ultimate truth. Those who hold to this view assume that because general culture does not accept the idea that someone has the truth, they themselves cannot be perceived as having the truth either. Instead of *critiquing* this culture from a biblical viewpoint, they *adopt* the viewpoint. In other words, they have bought into the assumptions of this belief system, which is ironic in that this belief system claims certainty of sorts—that is, the certainty that nothing is certain! In one sense they cannot critique this assumption about reality because they do not have anything certain by which they can evaluate it.

The Word of God refutes the idea that people cannot come to ultimate truth. The Bible presents universal and absolute truth; it positions itself as mutually exclusive with other beliefs. There is no middle ground on this issue. Christianity places itself in conflict with the idea that humanity does not have a place to stand in the universe. The belief that "man is the measure of all things" (Protagoras) is a polar opposite to the Bible. If we say "everything is relative" and "there are no absolutes," then those statements themselves become absolute.

Absolute truth is what is true of God and his creation. He and his Word are immutable (Hebrews 6:17–20). Truth does not begin with the individual but with revelation from God. That is the Christian's place to stand. Holding to this conviction is no more arrogant than belief in uncertainty. Christian revelation rises above finite man to God, who transcends culture. He existed before the universe and culture. He speaks with clarity and certainty. God knows exhaustively. Humans cannot know exhaustively.

The Bible itself makes no claim for exhaustive knowledge. It allows that other sacred books such as the Koran can make accurate statements, but they do not contain ultimate truth. The Word of God is as inerrant as God is; it, therefore, makes accurate claims to truth. Both academic and pop beliefs hold that it is impossible to come to certainty about truth. This skepticism denies ability to come to absolutes. Those who hold to uncertainty replace truth with pluralism, pragmatism, relativism, and other current popular philosophies. A subjective view of life is paramount in these days. But these people are certain about doubt! Because self is subjective, doubt pervades all knowledge. To know that one does not know is a universal fact; one has to know that he or she does not know in order to doubt. Subjective thinkers, who start from the premise of the self, believe there is no universal truth that all can accept. To them, no objective truth outside the self exists, and eternal truth is not an option. They preclude transcendent truth. They also abandon the principle of contradiction (that is, that A does not possess the predicate of B). But doubt, to be meaningful, presupposes the absolute validity of the principle of contradiction. Either there is truth or there is not. Both cannot be true. If both were truth and its contradictory opposite, then doubt would not make sense. Most skeptics can see that a thing cannot be and not be in the same sense at the same time.

Unending doubt is at the core of many modern evangelicals. They will not assert some things as true and other things as false. Second Timothy 3:7 nails the fallacy of those who are always learning and never able to come to the knowledge of the truth.

## Issue at Stake

In this book I hope to appeal to those committed to Scripture to take heed of evangelicals who try to domesticate the gospel. The Word of God requires that we gain great discernment about this issue. Scripture does not arbitrate its approach to false doctrine. It declares exclusive truth in no uncertain terms. We need leaders to reach those around them without denuding a straightforward approach to the message in evangelism.

We do not want to set contending for the gospel (Jude 3) in opposition to contextualizing the gospel (1 Corinthians 9:19–23). The purpose of the emergent church in contextualizing the gospel is a worthy end but not at the cost of the gospel itself. Accommodation of the message to current widespread ideas in culture weakens the gospel message. We cannot equate being humble about what we know personally with being uncertain about truth. However, we do need to approach people on their approachable side.

## Certainty ~ A Place to Stand

Christian leaders need to speak truth with confidence out of a sense of certainty about the gospel message. The gospel message itself is at stake because some today water down its truth. Effective evangelism is also in jeopardy. The reason Paul said, "I am not ashamed of the gospel" is that it is the gospel, not a method, that wins people (Romans 1:16). He did not proclaim the testimony of God in "lofty speech or wisdom [philosophy]." Paul decided to know nothing among the Corinthians "except Jesus Christ and him crucified" (1 Corinthians 2:1–2 ESV). Paul was clear about his message, and he would not allow methodology or philosophical, theological ideas move him off that focus.

It is clear that the most aggressive evangelistic success, whether in local churches or in large parachurch movements, comes from a burning conviction about the certainty of the truth of the gospel. Method does not bring passion for the gospel; only the gospel message itself impassions people to share the claims of Christ.

Conviction about the certainty of what we believe motivates Christians to share the gospel. Believers who do not share the gospel are indifferent and nonplussed about giving out the gospel because they do not engage with the reality of its message. The perspective of belief and the conviction of certainty about that belief are two different things. Certainty brings contagious conviction about distribution of the gospel. This brings courage to share when otherwise we would stay in our evangelistic shell. Certainty means there is no tentativeness or ambiguity about presenting the gospel. Those who are uncertain about truth do not disclose their faith boldly.

Recently I spoke to over 900 pastors in Canada about the hidden dynamic behind church growth, which I believe is strong certainty and conviction that Christ and his finished work is the answer. The positive response among pastors to that presentation was huge. Many pastors had not given serious consideration to that issue. Paul made the powerful point that Christ's love for us motivates us to live for him (2 Corinthians 5:14–15 ESV):

> For the love of Christ controls [constrains, motivates] us, because we have concluded this: that one has died for all, therefore all have died; and he died for all, that those who live might no longer live for themselves but for him who for their sake died and was raised.

I identify with and understand the contextualizing issues that concern those who want to reach this generation for Christ. We surely want to present the gospel in approachable and understandable terms to our generation. However, method should never overcome message. We can find methods appropriate for our times and still keep the message central and foremost. The message is what motivates Christians to boldly share their faith.

## Certainty Comes from Clarity of Scripture

The doctrine of the clarity (perspicuity) of the Bible has been a longstanding foundation of evangelical belief. If we read the Bible in a normal sense as we read any other literature, we can know what it says. God makes his Word essentially clear. Obviously there are isolated unclear passages but, as a whole, God communicated the Bible clearly. All people are accountable to that clarity.

Certainty comes from clarity. Where the Bible is unclear, there is uncertainty. If the Bible is essentially unclear for the most part, then there is no certainty in much of what it asserts. That is why this new type of evangelical (or, better, postevangelical) always seeks after truth but never arrives. They can never be sure that what they assert is true. This has a significant impact on evangelism. Why ask people to trust Christ's death for their sin if that central fact is not certain? One person who has made such thinking popular among evangelicals is Brian McLaren, whose book *A New Kind of Christian* was, sadly, honored with an award of merit by *Christianity Today*. The "new kind of Christian" he talks about is unsure and uncertain of what to believe (except for a few basic beliefs). With that tentativeness, such a Christian will not be forceful in sharing the gospel.

Diminishing doctrine to opinion or personal perspective carries unintended consequences. Reducing truth to personal perspective has devastating implications on the authority of the Bible. If we reduce every opinion to subjective equivalence, then no one possesses authority in message. All opinions hold equal validity. The central assumption is that tolerance is central to every viewpoint. Tolerance is central except for those who are certain about a universal truth claim. What appears as charitableness or being civil toward others leads to assault on the claims of Scripture.

Truth-claims of Scripture are exclusive. Jesus said, "I am the way, the truth, and the life. No one comes to the Father except through me" (John 14:6). That is an exclusive statement. The Holy Spirit makes another exclusive truth declaration in Acts: "Nor is there salvation is any other" (4:12). That excludes Mohammed or Buddha; it also excludes secular assumptions. Exclusive truth runs counter to the prevailing idea among postevangelicals.

Propositions of Scripture are sinister to those who claim that the Bible is unclear and without certainty. These people criticize those who claim certainty as having "truth captured, stuffed, and mounted on the wall."[1] Certainty to them is "downright dangerous."[2] They redefine humility as willingness to accept doctrinal uncertainty. Tolerance is equal to humility and is their ultimate doctrine. By establishing such a doctrine, they have no way to define heresy.[3]

Avoiding heresy demands separation of truth and falsity. The text has authority over the interpreter, not the interpreter over the text. How can we "avoid vain babblings" and contradictions if there is no clarity to distinguish between the two? Paul challenges Timothy to guard the faith:

> O Timothy! Guard what was committed to your trust, avoiding the profane *and* idle babblings and contradictions of what is falsely called knowledge—by professing it some have strayed concerning the faith. Grace *be* with you. Amen. (1 Timothy 6:20, 21)

If relativism were true, then the universe would hold contradictory conditions. This is impossible if there is a God. Opposites cannot both be truth; this denies the law of non-contradiction. We cannot be both right and wrong at the same time. We cannot be both completely dry and wet at the same time. It is impossible to have a stick with one end. We cannot say, "I am absolutely certain everything is relative." It is no longer relative if there is something certain. God cannot exist and not exist at the same time. We can only find something wrong if something is true. God's Word is the ultimate standard by which we measure truth.

The idea that we need air to breathe is true to all people everywhere at all times. Gravity works the same way everywhere on the planet. If I claim that 2+2 is 5, it would not be consistent with reality or truth. For something to be true, it must be true at all times. Mankind cannot arbitrarily establish what is right or true. Truth is always conformity to fact and what truly exists. God functions in the realm of absolute, total truth all of the time. That is why Jesus said, "Your word is truth" (John 17:17).

## Definitions

We need to understand important terms as we address this issue:

*Certainty* is lack of doubt about some state of affairs. Certainty admits degrees. Evangelicals do not affirm certainty about all things exhaustively. A proposition is certain if no other proposition has greater warrant than it does.

*Absolute certainty* is lack of any doubt. The Bible presents its thoughts with certainty, not tentatively (Luke 1:4; Acts 1:3). God's Word is the criterion for truth. Certainty comes by an act of God through the Holy Spirit (1 Corinthians 2:4–16; 1 Thessalonians 1:5). Absolute certainty is the supernatural foundation for knowledge.

*Postmodernism* is a catch-all term that covers many ideas. At its base, postmodernism is belief in plurality: no one can come to ultimate truth because people come to truth from their own perspective.

*Postconservatism* is belief in postmodernism by evangelicals who are sometimes called "postevangelicals." This is the belief system behind those in the emergent church who want to soft pedal truth.[4]

*Emerging church* is a broad term describing churches that seek to contextualize the gospel by method to postmodern philosophy. Not all emergent churches are postconservative in philosophy but are what we call "doctrine-friendly" or "truth-friendly" churches.

*Emergent church* is a particular term for an official network of contextualizers committed to postmodern Christianity. All their thinking is emerging; they do not claim certainty of truth. They deconstruct previous evangelical thinking about certainty and other essential doctrines of Scripture. They emphasize narrative theology rather than propositional truth. Presentation of Christianity is by missional living rather than by statements of the gospel. They presume that historic evangelicalism is non-authentic, not involved with non-Christians, obsessed with doctrine, and not operating by Christocentric living.[5] This group is not "truth-friendly."

*Coherent truth* is the basis of the emergent approach to reality, wherein facts and objective truth are not necessary and only a general coherence of an idea is needed.

*Correspondent truth* is the view that truth must correspond to facts, objectivity, and reality.

*Missional* is the term used for attempting to incarnate the gospel with personal and community testimony rather than presenting the gospel through propositions. Postconservatives use the word "missional" in the sense of "improving society now." It is a way to correct society's evils.

*Proposition* is that which corresponds to truth; it is the meaning of a declarative sentence. It is not an encounter, event, or personal experience. Biblical propositional assertions correspond to facts and reality.

*Spiritual formation* is not what evangelicals call sanctification, but it is rather the means whereby emergents use disciplines such as mysticism to make them feel closer to God. This is a non-biblical, extra-biblical idea. Many evangelicals use this term for sanctification and confuse terminology in doing so.

*Foundationalism* is an approach to reality that builds beliefs on givens. In the case of the Word of God, Christians build their beliefs on givens in the Bible. Emergents want to "rethink" everything. They do not operate on givens. It is important to distinguish the foundationalism of the Enlightenment from the foundationalism of the Bible. Biblical foundationalism does not rest on rationalism or empiricism but on the law of non-contradiction, the validity of the law of causality, and the reliability of sense perception. Without foundationalism we cannot establish truth by categories. Without the law of non-contradiction, it would be impossible to communicate adequately with others. Certainty does not require total understanding to know something for sure. To reject foundationalism is to reject rationality.

## Summary

Some in the emergent church believe that absolute truth exists but that we can never secure certainty about it. They claim that we cannot possess exhaustive personal knowledge of it even by the Bible. However, no honest evangelical claims to hold to exhaustive knowledge. There is a difference between exhaustive knowledge and certainty about an aspect of knowledge. The Bible affirms that humans are capable of distorted knowledge, but it also assumes we can know something for sure.

Many forms of Christianity deny the substitutionary work of Christ on the cross. Postconservatives seek to affirm all forms of Christianity including the Orthodox and Roman Catholic versions; they want to break out of the "evangelical ghetto." This is an attempt to be irenic rather than elitist and critical. I suppose postconservatives would preclude writers of the Bible who thoroughly attacked false doctrine.

The radical form of the emergent church is a church of conformity, not transformation. True transformation requires going against the prevailing opinions of culture. The gospel has the power to transform any "post" idea. It is truth of Scripture that sets distinction between ideas. To reject the substitutionary death of Christ for our sins, inerrancy of Scripture, or forensic justification will eviscerate the power of the gospel. This has enormous implications on the nature of evangelism in our day.

# The Great Evangelical Disaster Fulfilled
## *Accommodating the Message to Culture*

### Describing Emergent

Emergent churches are not fond of defining themselves theologically. They want to be clever, coy, and provocative rather than understood. The emergent church defies definition. It defines itself more through practice. This type of church wants to placate the most prevailing secular movement today (postmodernism). That movement denies that we can arrive at certainty about anything: no religion has the right to declare its belief correct. All religions hold parity with each other, even in the face of the fact that they hold mutually contradictory ideas. The only absolute is that there are no absolutes. We must tolerate all viewpoints as equal in value. All beliefs are arbitrarily assembled by opinion and prejudice. All beliefs are subjective. There is no such thing as heresy.

At heart, this is unadulterated skepticism about all beliefs. The idea of absolute truth is abhorrent to the present generation, which boils down every idea to consensus, as if all truth were equivalent. The emergent church has lost its appetite for asserting itself, with its loss of objective truth and prevailing subjectivism. The last impression it wants to give is that it holds exclusive truth.

Because practice takes priority over theology, emergent church adherents go to people to find a practice that fits their needs. This is what they mean by "missional." Their mission determines their theology. They begin with mission, and a theology emerges out of it. Definitely their mission is not bringing people the substitutionary death of Christ so that people can avert judgment from God. Practice takes priority over doctrine. This is a reason why they cannot come to certainty. By rejecting the idea of certainty, they put the Bible into oblivion without clear communication from God. They can know truth only at some point in the future. Ideas are in the process of emerging.[6]

The emergent church introduces remarkable softening of its message to the world. Preachers today build their messages with felt needs in mind rather than with the God who talks. It is one thing to keep felt needs in mind, but it is another to eliminate what God says in his Word. The Word of God insists that certain things are false and others true. It warns of a wrath to come. The emergent preacher has to blunt the hard edges of the Bible. How far can these communicators of the gospel religion go before their message is no longer distinctively Christian?

These people must retreat to the idea that their belief is independent from reason (fideism). They allow prevailing culture to effectively engineer their message. Emergent church leaders have not come to terms with the idea that they undermine their own faith in doing so. Adherents tolerate varying views of truth rather than adopt an attitude of forbearance toward persons. What used to be civility toward people has become civility toward truth. Instead of seeing truth as the basis of what they believe, tolerance toward truth governs their sense of what is important. They have employed what used to be known as "civility"—an openness in listening to others—to define their mission and have consequently denuded their message. They diminish the merits of opposing ideas by adopting this new form of tolerance. Avoiding criticism of other ideas results in little thoughtful discussion of important ideas revolving around truth. This brand of tolerance is muddleheaded, and their sense of what is significant biblically is lost. Instead of seeing truth as the basis of what they believe, mere tolerance governs their sense of priorities.

Increasingly, people in the general public are not offended by new religions, no matter how off the wall they might be. The media and people in general will pursue the novelty of these religions. Society views the attempt to win people to Christ from other religions as an intolerable idea. Exclusive claim to one's belief is the only religious proposal that they cannot tolerate. Tolerance sets the "rules" for playing the game of ideas. This is a dogmatic opinion that rules out all other dogmatic opinions. By this attempt to transcend all other ideas, they prove to be enormously intolerant and dogmatic. Political correctness is the new absolute. This political correctness is intolerant of intolerance, not of substantive ideas. This form of open-mindedness does not identify with open discourse but with the conclusions of skepticism. It wants to own its own premises while denying other ideas the right of certainty. It reinstates certainty by denying it!

Yet the media loves to depict evangelicals as "intolerant." Postconservatives committed essentially to emergent thought are intimidated by this attitude, so they adopt the culture of complaint as their own and adjust their message to the relative and subjective. They hold the idea that their beliefs arise out of their associations and communities, not from the transcendent Word of God. Their view is that the finite individual cannot possibly come to the conclusion of absolute truth.

This view's assessment of reality thwarts the vitality of vibrant Christian conviction. Christian witness then has no basis for exclusive claim. The gospel becomes no more than the subjective opinion of a group called evangelicals. Why should people share their faith if they are not certain that it is true? This move away from a propositional presentation of the gospel will have enormous impact on how the public perceives our message. Emergent adherents bulldoze the gospel into the nearest landfill of relativism. They blow the uncertain sound that all ideas come from pre-understanding and opinion. They believe contingent interpretations without objective truth. The text today might not be the same for me tomorrow. Final certainty is impossible; sheer subjectivity is all that remains. They bind knowledge to the knower rather than to the objectivity of the Word of God. If truth resides in the interpreter, all that remains is as many meanings as there are interpreters. Objective truth disappears in this method. All we have in the final analysis is skeptical nihilism.

Knowledge and belief are different. Knowledge rests on what is self-evident, whereas belief rests on opinion and is only probable. We know knowledge with certainty. Because God revealed the Bible, we know that with certainty.

## Conciliation and Capitulation to Culture

The evangelical church must face this new and ominous challenge. There is cancer within the camp. We live in a day when evangelicals attempt to denude the Word of God. They believe little that it contains. Skepticism reigns in their thinking. They care little for clarity, certainty, or logic. They have been seduced by society. They cut the evangelical ship from its moorings to drift in a philosophical wind that blows wherever it will. We call this movement postconservatism. Evangelical postconservatism manifests itself in the emergent church and imposes a system of philosophy upon Scripture—the system of postmodernism that is skeptical about truth, wherein no one can come to certainty. Everyone has a personal perspective, but no one has the truth.

Evangelical postconservatives want Scripture to accommodate the prevailing culture of tolerance toward all viewpoints. They accommodate Scripture to philosophy rather than philosophy to Scripture. They reject certainty and give heed to ambiguity and doubt; in other words, they live by a philosophy of skepticism. Postconservatives equate "authenticity" with doubt, skepticism, and uncertainty. They want to redesign evangelicalism into another image. No wonder they have lost confidence in the sufficiency of the Word of God. This doctrinal deviation changes the basis on which evangelicalism stands.

The issue is not about method in approaching people who do not believe in truth but about the adoption of skepticism itself. The exclusiveness of the gospel or of Christ himself is no longer objectively true to postconservatives. They implicitly ignore the Bible for the purpose of contextualizing the gospel to society. They offer sentimental twaddle in place of sound biblical preaching. Their message is horizontal rather than vertical. They sell out to prevailing paradigms. By doing so, they gut the essence of evangelicalism.

Evangelical postconservatism today is feckless, frail, limp, and spineless. It cares little about truth but gives much heed to the prevailing opinion of culture. There is a core value problem in their thinking—culture prevails over truth. This is what the Bible calls "worldliness." Worldliness is the love of values other than God's values. In the name of keeping up with the Joneses of postmodernism, some evangelicals adopt assumptions of pluralism and relativism. In doing so, there is great defection of faith in the land.

The last book that Francis Schaeffer wrote was *The Great Evangelical Disaster*. His book predicted that the evangelical church would so accommodate its truth to culture that it would diminish the essence of Christianity and rip away the foundation of Christianity. This is exactly what evangelical postconservatives are doing to evangelical Christianity today in the form of the emergent church.

There is a growing chorus of evangelical leaders speaking against this pervasive iniquity. R. Albert Mohler, Jr., president of Southern Baptist Theological Seminary, adds his warning about the sad state of affairs among evangelicals: "Evangelicalism is in big trouble, and the root problem is theological accommodation. Compromise and confusion stand at the center of evangelicalism's theological crisis."[7]

Richard J. Mouw, president and professor of Christian philosophy at Fuller Seminary, says that he is "troubled by extravagant claims made by various evangelical scholars about the nature of the 'postmodern' challenge." Postconservatives attempt to redefine the center of evangelicalism and thus the very nature of evangelicalism itself.

Justin Taylor, editorial director of Crossway books, warns that this postconservatism is a significant shift from evangelicalism.[8] Most evangelicals committed to truth (with few exceptions) sit on their hands and watch in wonder what is happening to their faith. Seminary professors, pastors, and other leaders appear inept to do anything about this absconding from the faith.

There is a need to sound an alarm about so-called evangelicals who are currently leading the church astray. The evangelical church is in the process of turning from verities of the truth to fables and false doctrine. Postconservatives accuse those who sound this alarm of being alarmists who reason under rigid belief systems. Their loss of distinctive biblical Christianity and the inability to define themselves theologically takes them down the same road as their liberal predecessors. They have fallen into a pool of subjective experientialism without any doctrinal arms to swim to safety. This results in the loss of hope of valid certainty. It is a philosophy of unending doubt that even the one who believes it may be wrong and that clarity is overrated.[9]

Postconservatives are not certain about anything because they are "always learning and never able to arrive at a knowledge of the truth" (2 Timothy 3:7 ESV). They are not sure about anything. Objectivity is impossible, they say, because evangelical prejudices skew truth. All knowledge is relative, so we cannot come to certainty about truth. Because postconservatives begin with the self and stay in the self, they miss out on the certainty that is available only to Christians who begin with God's revelation of himself.

David Wells, distinguished senior research professor at Gordon-Conwell Theological Seminary, indicts current evangelicals who want to accommodate truth to culture by making the faith relatively true:

> Even among those who seek to guide the Church in its belief, many are of the mind that Christian faith is only relatively true, or they think, against every precept and example that we have in the New Testament, that Christ can be "encountered" in other religions—religions that they view not as rivals but as "interpretations" with which accommodation should be sought. What would have happened over the ages, one wonders, if more of the Church's leaders had been similarly persuaded?[10]

## Following a Perverse Path

The compromise of the postconservative emergent church follows a very similar path to that of the modernists of the late nineteenth and early twentieth centuries. Church leaders of that time accepted the philosophy of modernism, so they rejected the inspiration of Scripture, the deity of Christ, and miracles. Postconservatives have so accommodated themselves to postmodernism that they reject certainty, mutually exclusive truth, and objective understanding of the Bible. All that remains is cultural, random opinions and personal perspective. All beliefs are legitimate only to those who embrace them. With this view, it is impossible to distinguish truth from heresy, for there is no longer any doctrinal foundation for doing so.

Some evangelicals no longer have confidence in what they purport to believe. They mute their beliefs both to themselves and to the world at large. These postconservative evangelicals are now taking the same alleyway that tumbled liberals doctrinally and emptied their churches by the middle of the twentieth century. Liberal churches and theological seminaries became hollow shells by the end of the twentieth century because they first accommodated their beliefs to culture, then ultimately renounced those beliefs. There are many indications that evangelicals are beginning to walk down that same dark corridor of minimizing truth.

Speaking of the way churches are doing church, David Wells says that "those who once stood aloof from the older liberalism are now unwittingly producing a close cousin to it. By the time this becomes so evident that it will be incontrovertible, it will be too late."[11] This deviation occurs because postconservatism is cutting loose from the moorings of biblical structural understanding and has lost its way in a cultural and pragmatic morass, leaving muddled wanderers in the wilderness. This produces our "new kind of Christian."

A number of media outlets, such as CNN, do not like to use the term "terrorist" because "one man's terrorist is another man's freedom fighter." Imagine, these people do not have the capacity to make a distinction between those who purposefully kill innocent people and those who kill innocent people by accident or collaterally! This thinking reflects the essence of why people reject certainty, absolutes, and conclusions about the validity of Christianity. Today, evangelicals and postevangelicals buy into this thinking.

## Accommodating Truth to Culture

The emergent church is postconservative in presumption and culture-bound in its view of truth. The emergent worldview is an attempt to move beyond modernity (presuppositions of philosophy and science). It believes there is no single worldview (metanarrative), so truth is not absolute. This view is a form of cultural relativism in relation to truth, reason, and value. Experience takes predominance over reason. Secular postmodernism readily accepts spirituality and gods by syncretism. The evangelical emergent worldview follows closely on the heels of the secular emergent worldview in that it prefers syncretism to truth and spirituality without biblical content. Postconservatives believe they need to deconstruct the fallacy of evangelicalism in its culture-bound interpretation and view of Christianity. Some question every essential doctrine. All history of doctrine and scholarship is open to review in light of postconservatives' assumption of postmodern methodology.

Postconservatives hold that, given that people cannot know absolute truth, we can only experience what is "true" in our religious communities. Truth, to them, is culturally relative, although some deny this. Universal truth that communicates across cultures is not possible. There is only narrative, not metanarrative. They deem it not possible to be dogmatic about the pre-eminence of Christianity over other religions. Because we cannot know absolute truth, we cannot carry certainty about Christianity. They do not posture themselves as having the answer, but they deem themselves in dialogue with others who have input into the conversation with their beliefs. Doctrinal preaching must give way to dialogue. Postconservatives have no clear message, and all they have to offer is dialogue or conversation with non-Christians.

## Arriving at Truth and Certainty

The question of how we know what we know to be true is crucial to the issue of mutually exclusive truth.[12] How do we know that Christianity is true as over against other religions or philosophies? Is revelation just a matter of taste or preference? Is sincerity a Christian virtue? I don't think so, for it is possible to be sincere but wrong. The biblical idea behind the word translated "sincerity" is "genuineness"; this means that both intention and action are right in fact

Biblical Christianity flies in the face of pluralism, subjectivism, and relativism. Public schools expose our children to every belief except Christianity, whether it is witchcraft, Native American animism, or Eastern religions. The supposed justification for this is secularism, as if secularism were autonomous or neutral. This amounts to brainwashing and an exclusive closed shop in education. True liberal thought allows all viewpoints to be presented openly. Today's form of liberalism is establishment at its worst, resulting in awful political correctness.

Humanity's autonomy from God has disastrous social effects. Abortion and divorce are rampant even among evangelicals. AIDS, crime, single-parent families, and political corruption are now normal in society. The church adds to this new standard for society by its weakened view of truth, for it does not fancy exclusive truth as all-pervasive influence on its thinking. Postevangelicals want to set forth a "new kind of Christianity" that baptizes the believer into a relativistic culture, denying the inerrancy of Scripture and many other verities of biblical truth.[13] All this is a revolt against truth, against God, against the Word. It is an attempt to put self at the center of reality, to deify self through a fragmented viewpoint without ultimate coherence or purpose. Perhaps the postevangelical shift from personal responsibility to groupthink—to becoming "a village" for one other—comes out of seeking to find reality in the self rather than in the Creator.

The church stands at a crossroads of either adapting to culture or having the courage to stand up to culture. If the church is true to its message originating in truth from God, it will be powerful because the gospel has inherent power (Romans 1:16). We need to understand our culture (acculturation), but we cannot accommodate the message of truth to culture's proclivity to minimize truth. Hitler bought into Friedrich Nietzsche's super race forty years after Nietzsche's death in 1900. Nietzsche proclaimed, "God is dead." With this, absolutes began to die in the West. Nietzsche's philosophy was not the direct reason for postmodernism but a condition for its development. Modernism since the Enlightenment undermined the authority of God's revelation, and God's Word became less suitable to meet the needs of people. Rationalism marginalized God but did not meet the epistemic needs of humanity, so postmodernism rose up in skepticism against philosophy and science. Man's attempt to play God did not solve his problems.[14] The twentieth century did not fulfill the promises of modernism, so postmoderns lost hope in attaining any sense of certainty. To postmodernism, all viewpoints are relative, and any claim of absolutes creates intolerance. Relativism allows for openness and is the zenith of postmodern values. This controlling feature influences postmoderns' entire worldview. Truth is not a priority because truth divides.

Younger evangelicals grew up in the dialectical system of thinking that any viewpoint is as valid as the next. Some no longer believe that the Bible is inerrant and that it sets forth a system of absolutes. They flow with the flotsam and jetsam of current thinking, not believing that God is absolute and reveals a system of absolutes through his Word.

The cultural mindset against absolutes prohibits this age from believing the claims of the Bible about itself. Postmodern cultural thinking has no truth except the absolute that there is no truth. It claims that there is no absolute truth or universal truth but holds an absolute nevertheless, contradicting the very premise of postmodernism. By accepting postmodern belief systems, postconservative postmoderns can no longer draw truth from universal principles. Each situation shifts with subjective value judgments. Postmoderns attribute no objective meaning to language; therefore, no conduit of understanding can endure between viewpoints.

Some institutions, such as Fuller Theological Seminary, changed the meaning of "inerrant" to mean "reliable" or "coherent," so they argue that the Bible can no longer claim to be factually without error. To them, the Bible has historical and scientific error. Words no longer have objective meaning but only "interpretation." Words cannot communicate propositions of truth, so postconservatives have to "deconstruct" the Bible into "interpretations" of fluidity of meaning. This produces a form of nihilism among evangelicals that will leave them without fixed norms and beliefs. Evangelicalism will end in collective uncertainty.

Evangelicals today rationalize sin because it "meets my need." Therefore, evangelical young couples can live together without marriage. Businessmen can rip off their customers because "everyone does it and I have to do it to survive in the corporate jungle." Seminary students can cheat in class because this is part of culture. Pastors no longer proclaim truth from the pulpit because they know that objective truth sounds strange to the ears of their congregations. Seminaries shift from truth orientation to experience, therapeutic counseling, and practical orientation.[15]

## Loss of Certainty in Dialectical Method

Philosophers of the twentieth century came to a sense of despair in coming to ultimate truth; they found no rational basis for certainty of truth, and they saw people moving from non-meaning to whatever meaning can be found by irrational leaps of faith. They believed that faith and reason do not have anything to do with truth. They held that truth is paradoxical, and faith is an irrational leap at significance. This is unadulterated mysticism.[16] Many people attribute the shift from antithesis to synthesis to George Wilhelm Friedrich Hegel and the dialectic model to Soren Kierkegaard. However, Hegel did not hold to dialectic model. It was his students, such Schopenhauer, who reinterpreted Hegel. It was these young Hegelians that developed the dialectic, not Hegel.[17]

Emergent thinking is integrative or integral thinking, and it rests on a dialectical approach to truth as opposed to the biblical didactic/narrative approach. Because God deductively revealed himself in the Word of God, he did not leave truth open to be constantly put in the tension of thesis/antithesis/synthesis without the possibility of coming to certainty about truth.

"Transformational" and "managed" change is the postconservative method for retooling the evangelical church. This is a dialectical method of group consensus and the polar opposite of the biblical idea of didactic truth.[18] The dialectical approach flies in the face of the Bible because the Bible is *a priori* revelation (deductive), not *a posteriori* (inductive).

In a *Leadership Journal* article where Brian McLaren calls himself a poste-vangelical, he states that "instead of an exercise in transferring information so that people have a coherent, well-informed 'world-view'. . . preaching in the emerging culture aims at inspiring transformation."[19] This accommodation of truth and change of worldview shows lack of confidence in the sufficiency of Scripture through the power of the Holy Spirit to change lives. McLaren hopes that "post-evangelicals and post-liberals will begin finding one another in this common ground of spiritual formation, welcomed and hosted by our Catholic and Orthodox sisters and brothers. What is *terra nova* for us has been their native soil for a long, long time."[20] McLaren's baptism into postmodernism fails to distinguish evangelical from non-evangelical and blurs the message so that it is no longer distinctive. This, in turn, will make the evangelical church irrelevant because it no longer carries a biblical message. It is amazing how thoughtlessly many evangelical leaders hop aboard this postconservative bus going nowhere.

We now witness a sea change of enormous proportion in evangelicalism, but most evangelicals are blind to this fast-moving heterodoxy. Brian McLaren and Stanley Grenz and their ilk negotiate away essentials of biblical truth, and hardly anyone takes notice. This is philosophical adaptation of the message of the Bible to culture and is a far cry from the Apostle Paul's change of method to convey an unchanging message (1 Corinthians 9). Note David Wells's view of this situation:

> There is a yawning chasm between what evangelical faith was in the past and what it frequently is today, between the former spirituality and the contemporary emptiness and accommodation.[21]

This new thinking is not propositional and linear but circular, or web-like, associative thinking.

## Differentiating Tolerance of Attitude and Truth-Equivalence

Embedded pluralistic viewpoint is so pervasive in culture that few are willing to assert something as truth as over against something that is not true; that is, that Christianity is true and any other belief is false.

There is significant confusion between a pluralism of attitude and a pluralism dealing with truth. Christianity respects all viewpoints and the people who hold them, which is not the same as saying that all viewpoints are equally valid. If a person who holds that all truth is relative claims that a pedophile does not have the right to engage in sex with a child, the moment he makes that claim, he asserts a certainty. There is then a difference between tolerance in attitude and tolerance of truth. The biblical value is that Christians are to portray a tolerant attitude toward all people. That is not the same as saying that all perspectives on reality are valid. The way to truth, certainty, and reality is found in the Word of God that stands mutually exclusive from other viewpoints. The Christian does not hold to truth-equivalence.

Christians who assert that we cannot be dogmatic are inconsistent in their contention. They want to hold that "Jesus is the answer" but do not want to hold to it dogmatically. They undermine their own fundamental belief system like a dog that bites its tail. If they claim there is no absolute, they undermine their own belief that Jesus is the only Savior. Where do they get the unmitigated gall to assert that Jesus is the Savior of the world? Is that not just a preference? Worse, why would they assert a triune God? Coming to that conclusion requires theology. No extant statements of Scripture formulate Trinitarian doctrine.[22] These timid so-called evangelicals are left with a probability gospel: To be honest, we cannot assert that Jesus is God and Savior; we have maybe a forty percent chance of this being true.

They cannot have their cake and eat it too.

## Accommodation to Uncertainty

We are in a war of worldviews where postconservatives leave certainty homeless. People change viewpoints as quickly as they change channels. Evangelicals perplexed by the postmodern condition create a vacuous condition for themselves. Postconservatives haul into the court of public scorn anyone who has the audacity to claim certainty.

The desire of the emerging church movement is to reach a generation that does not believe in absolutes, that does not hold to certainty of truth, but looks askance at those who do. Postconservatives use accommodation of message to address skepticism toward certainty; however, by doing so they compromise fundamental belief in the verities of the Word of God.

The prevailing viewpoint of our age (postmodernism or the belief that there are no ultimate answers) shapes the context of modern evangelicalism, whether it means how we live out our lives or how we share our faith.[23] Those who do not accept the gospel view Christianity as narrow, obscure, and biased. To a generation that does not believe in absolutes, the gospel or Christianity is not plausible.

The widespread philosophy of our day says that all truth is equally valid and that no single truth can claim advantage over any other truth. This intimidates evangelical pastors and their people because they judge that it is arrogant to claim finality or certainty of truth. They think that dogmatic people have fallen out of phase with the times and are obscurant with regard to the culture and political correctness of our day.

After all, has anyone examined all truth of all times both qualitatively and quantitatively equally? Has anyone searched for truth everywhere in creation and examined it for all time? Has anyone done this with complete dispassion and absolute objectivity? Obviously, this is a pragmatic impossibility, so according to postconservatism no one can claim certain truth.[24]

This entire thinking rests on the idea that finite mankind can find the infinite God autonomously, but this is a particularly unwarranted assumption.[25] If we begin with finite man, there is no hope of coming to certainty about universal truth or of finding God. We will look at this fundamental flaw among evangelicals throughout this book.

The trend in thinking today is that people cannot find truth and that we live in a hopeless morass of viewpoints and opinions. Each opinion or viewpoint is just as valid as the next. No one has the answer, but everyone has "viewpoints."

People portray these answers in stories (narratives). No one has a total or final answer to the universe (a metanarrative: a narrative that explains all other narratives). The postmodern approach to reality is not linear or logical. Its mode of operation is via stories, images, and relationships.

Evangelical pastors and leaders today jump on this bandwagon to the detriment of the evangelical movement itself. They run pell-mell toward a type of thinking that accepts certainty about hardly anything. This will rip the heart out of the evangelical movement because it will destroy its mutually exclusive message that Jesus is the only way and that there is no salvation in any other than the Lord Jesus Christ (John 14:6; Acts 4:12).

Our society holds Christianity more tentatively than ever. As North America moves toward greater pluralism, the number of options for belief multiplies. The consumer can choose a menu of religions or philosophies at will. None can claim mutually exclusive truth. Because of this influence of pluralism and its extenuating postmodernism, Christians now prefer a cafeteria approach to Christianity: No one has the truth for sure, so pick and choose as you prefer from your individual perspective.

Evangelical belief is coming to accept truth as religious preference, private opinion, or personal preference. In doing so, evangelicals lose certainty from God's Word. This results in vulnerability to cultural relativism. According to a Barna poll, in 2001 sixty-eight percent of evangelical adults and ninety-one percent of evangelical teens believed in cultural relativism.[26] David F. Wells, speaking of the astounding growth of evangelicals and the attenuating loss of biblical convictions, said,

> There has nevertheless come a hollowing out of evangelical conviction, a loss of the biblical Word in its authoritative function, and an erosion of character to the point that today, no discernible ethical differences are evident in behavior when those claiming to have been reborn and secularists are compared.[27]

## Accommodation to Provisional Belief

Postevangelical postmoderns believe in constant, chaotic revision of doctrine and interpretation of the Bible.[28] They come to little more than provisional belief. They view past evangelicalism as a dogmatic and intolerant viewpoint that produces disputes within the evangelical community and insults the pluralistic world around them. Their challenge is to strip the Bible of its aura of infallibility so that people can live in tolerant and amorphous belief. They want ambiguity because categories and clarity cause division. This is the motivation behind postevangelical, postconservative postmodernism. If our beliefs are nebulous, vague, unstructured, fluid and formless, we can avoid dogmatism and definition of truth.

All this downgrades the inspiration of Scripture, especially the inerrancy of Scripture. Fundamental re-evaluation of how the Bible operates as the Word of God will lead to a different perceived status that evangelicals give to Scripture. The task is to "deconstruct" the Bible into a disparate, non-coherent collection of writings packed with error. There is little call for an inerrant Bible in a post-modern world because of the need to move away from ideological belief. The postevangelicals' approach is to commit to Jesus Christ historically in a grossly general way. They want to go back to a pre-Constantine time, when doctrine was less developed and more general, so that Christianity is not offensive to the postmodern world.[29]

Postevangelicals want to draw a dichotomy between the "religion of belief" and the "life of faith." They do not allow faith to elevate Scripture above perspectives on truth. Evangelicals, they say, define identity by belief. Postevangelicals define themselves by historical experience of imagination.

This is especially true with salvation. In postevangelical opinion, evangelicals developed a highly complex view of salvation that has taken on a life of its own. This resulted in the "myth" of justification by faith alone, according to them.

## Accommodation to Story Telling Rather than Truth Telling

Non-Christian postmodernism views the holding of a universal truth (metanarrative) as an attempt to control thought. Postevangelicals want to maintain a metanarrative of sorts, but they have no objective reason for doing so. They find themselves in a dilemma between truth and the denial of universal truth by rejecting absolute, objective truth.

Postevangelical postconservatives must readjust their reading of Scripture to something creatively interpreted by a community of believers. Interpretation comes from narrative rather than propositions and systematic thought. The narrative way of interpretation puts understanding of Scripture outside formulas of orthodoxy. Objective truth is not possible in this process.

We can see the postevangelical, postconservatives' dilemma in their desire to own the postmodern rejection of objective truth, universal truth, and yet hold onto a metanarrative (a broad perspective of belief). They believe in the relativity of all narratives; they also want to believe in a generalized Jesus that covers all religions and is an answer for non-believers, but they have no final message to unbelievers. All they have is provisional possibilities. In a desperate attempt to placate postmoderns, they void the exclusive message of the Bible.

This tramples principles of the Word of God. We have no criterion to distinguish truth from error with this view. D. A. Carson says that postmodern evangelicals like Stanley Grenz raised the "fine art of sidestepping crucial questions to an annoying level."[30] Instead of talking about the possibility of objective truth, Grenz chooses to deem that question "improper and ultimately unhelpful."[31] In other words, he does not want to deal with the most important question to evangelicals—the exclusive truth of Christianity. Grenz evades the issue in favor of his postmodern bias. He has no biblical basis to rest his philosophy of a community-established worldview. A sociological assumption about Christianity places it on very precarious grounds. Maybe a Muslim jihad assumption would be preferable. Who knows? There is no proper ground of belief. If evangelicals did not possess objective truth, every wind of doctrine would blow them about where it willed, and the opinion of the Christian community would have no greater validity than any other view.

Brian McLaren, in *The Church on the Other Side,* and others in the emergent church movement made a break with historical evangelical belief. William M. Easum wrote an "otherside" book on leadership titled *Leadership on the Other-Side.* The end of modernity apparently requires new church thinking and new leadership in the era of postmodernism. Leonard Sweet and Stanley Grenz are much-read authors in this movement. Purportedly this movement is not anti-modern, although in function it is anti-modern; for example, Brian McLaren challenges leaders to change not only their method but also their message. This message change rests on philosophical pluralism. Under modernism, truth was one. With postmodernism, truth is many. Each community has its own truth. Everyone has input into truth.

Postevangelicalism is an accommodation to postmodern thought and devaluation of objective truth. Postevangelicals place experience over reason and logic. The community discovers truth through consensus in commune. This is a change from objective truth to group-consensus truth.

## Accepting Informal Pluralism

Postevangelicals have gone so far as to deny "exclusive" claims to truth and call the gospel a "perspective" on truth. To them the term "exclusive" is pejorative, and they fear that it carries negative overtones to a relativist generation. But truth is truth, so we cannot mediate God's truth through other approaches to reality, that is, through acquiescence and accommodation to relativists. Postevangelicals find themselves in a place of undermining the essence of their truth claim.

Postevangelical arbitration of truth is an attempt to appear inclusive to an unbelieving world. This pluralistic accommodation rejects the idea that there is something ultimately authoritative or exclusively unique about God's revelation. This leaves every approach to truth up to consumer choice; therefore, postevangelicals hold religious commitments lightly. Passionate conviction that evangelicals hold the truth has waned. The church is losing its power and conviction. It acquiesces to the idea that it is just one of many perspectives out there and thus does not have exclusive truth. Belief is just a perspective of evangelicals.

Postevangelicals believe that Christians should affirm other cultures and respect differences of thought other than Christianity. That is not the issue at hand. The issue is whether Christianity is valid above all opinion, theory, or religion. Can Christianity access absolute truth in an unlimited way?

Have postevangelicals come to accept an informal pluralism where evangelical beliefs are no longer normative for all people, in all cultures, at any time? Have they surrendered the idea that other religions or philosophies are not true? Is it appropriate to judge other beliefs, because all judgments are relative?

## Certainty ~ A Place to Stand

Maybe all roads do lead to Rome after all. If this is true, what a waste of energy in the attempt to evangelize the world! We could divert great amounts of money from evangelism to meet the social needs of the world. Christians should not have the temerity or audacity to tell others about Christ. What gall, disdain, conceit, and superciliousness that is! Tolerance should be the name of the game. Any kind of spirituality, such as mysticism or Buddhism, is just fine because the purpose of "religion" is to meets the needs of humanity. These people get along fine without Christ, so why rock their boat? It appears that Schaeffer's "great evangelical disaster" is well under way. Many have already stepped into that disaster.

# Three

# FRATERNITIES
# LIVING IN ISOLATION
## Conciliation and Capitulation to Culture

David Wells captures the problem of postmodernism thought breaking into fragments as over against overarching meaning: "The single universe of meaning has dissolved, and the single field of discourse that flowed from it has dissipated." Meaning has moved from metanarrative to narratives, from universal meaning to finite perspectives of the individual.

## Rejecting the Core of Certainty—Absolutes

Brian McLaren, caught in the jaws of postmodernism, rejects absolutes because he deems the postmodern evaluation of the possibility of an absolute too overwhelming and persuasive to allow absolute truth to stand. He rejects at the same time the absolutism of philosophical pluralism and relativism, as well as the absolutes of evangelicalism. He cannot accept philosophical pluralism and be true to Scripture. Because he cannot accept absolutes in evangelicalism, he supposes that evangelicals need a measure of relativism that corrects rigidities in the movement. We, therefore, need to live with a fragmented world of evangelicalism where we accept radical differences among us. D. A. Carson shows the fallacy of McLaren's fragmented view of pluralism:

> If absolutism is not the answer and absolute relativism is not the answer, what is the Christian way ahead? Here McLaren finds himself heavily indebted to the short work by Jonathan Wilson, *Living Faithfully in a Fragmented World: Lessons for the Church* from MacIntyre's

*After Virtue.* This is surely what we want: we want to learn to live faithfully in a fragmented world. Absolutism plays by one set of rules. Real pluralism is like a large field where many games are being played, each game observing its own rules. This sort of pluralism is coherent. But we live in a fragmented world: we are playing golf with a baseball, baseball with a soccer ball, and so forth. This is not real pluralism; it is fragmented existence.[32]

Postconservatives hold that no evangelical lives in truly coherent truth because there is no coherent argument for postmoderns. We live in fragmentation, so the direction for evangelicals should be "transforming mission." This transforming mission accepts coexistence with different faiths and dialogues with them in the presence of God. Our story might not be the true story, so openness to dialogue and living with paradox will enable us to grow in our understanding of varying viewpoints.

McLaren's overwhelming criticism in his books is against modernism, not postmodernism. Postmodernism is the presuppositional matrix from which his theology flows. Carson asks a devastating question:

Is there at least some danger that what is being advocated is not so much a new kind of Christian in a new Emergent Church, but a church that is so submerging itself in the culture that it risks hopeless compromise? Even to ask the question will strike some as impertinence at best, or a tired appeal to the old-fashioned at worst. I mean it to be neither. Most movements have both good and bad in them, and in the book from which this article is taken I highlight some of the things I find encouraging and helpful in the Emergent Church movement. I find that I am more critical of the movement because my "take" on contemporary culture is a bit removed from theirs, partly because the solutions I think are required are somewhat different from theirs, partly because I worry about (unwitting) drift from Scripture, and partly because this movement feels like an exercise in pendulum swinging, where the law of unintended consequences can do a lot of damage before the pendulum comes to rest. [33]

## The Vital Issue of Certainty—Epistemology

The issue of certainty hinges on the subject of epistemology (how we know that what we know is true). This is the central issue in the debate between evangelicals and postevangelicals. The book *Stories of Emergence,* **by** Mike Yaconelli (editor), has the subtitle "Moving from Absolute to Authentic," betraying a false antithesis between holding absolutes and being authentic. The real issue is the battle over certainty. Hidden presuppositions lie beneath all beliefs.

McLaren wants believers today to be "a new kind of Christian," that is, a postmodern Christian; he wants to dismantle certainties that control much of the church today. He qualifies this attack on certainty by rejecting philosophical pluralism that also rejects the idea that any particular viewpoint can explain reality. On the other hand, if evangelicals perceive they have the answer, he maintains, they must account for the range of differences among evangelicals.

McLaren also qualifies relativism by rejecting philosophical relativism that denies absolutes and claims that truth is relative to culture and individual groups who embrace particular beliefs. He does not seem to associate relativism with postmodernism but thinks of it as an extreme conclusion of postmodernism. Yet he claims that evangelicals have differences that are relative to groups within evangelicalism.

Postevangelicals equate evangelical thought with modernism. They associate modernism with rationalism, absolutism, linear thinking, and mind over emotions. Modernism is inflexible, controlling, and arrogant. This new kind of Christian associates postmodernism with what is more flexible in belief, more connected with tradition, and is not concerned about being right or wrong in truth. Postevangelical postconservatives view modernism with scorn because it concentrates on truth and error while postmodernism centers on relationships and integrity.

The emergent church grew out of postmodern thinking. Though not everyone in this movement holds to pure postmodern thought, they nevertheless associate closely with a movement that undermines the essence of evangelicalism. Many in the more moderate emerging church simply want to form churches that reach postmoderns. It is important to distinguish postconservatives from those who attempt to reach postmoderns. True biblical viewpoint has unity of truth, not fragmented beliefs.

## Undermining Certainty by Preference for Perspective

Brian McLaren refuses to identify with particulars of Scripture because of his postmodern appetite for preference and perspective. This is the new norm—preference rather than certain truth. In other words, he attempts to draw people to Christianity by undermining the essence of biblical truth in lieu of the perspective. This mentality buys into the next great philosophical thought despite the existence of eternal truth revealed in propositional form in Scripture among other methods such as general revelation.

McLaren is more concerned about what liberals and postmoderns think of him than he is concerned with how the Word evaluates his positions or how evangelicals might assess his viewpoints. Although he might not be rationalistic in the philosophical sense, his system is full of rationalism and justifications based on the bias of postmodernism (i.e., the belief system of postmodernism).

In another book, *A is for Abductive: The Language of the Emerging Church*, Leonard Sweet, Brian D. McLaren, and Jerry Haselmayer give their dialectical system for finding truth. They promote abductive reasoning as that as that which seizes people

> by the imagination and transports them from their current world to another world, where they can gain new perspective. Abductive reasoning has powerful implications for preaching—and all communication, really! To go Abductive, get rid of your inductive/deductive outlines and points and make your sermons pointless! In other words, don't build your sermons around analysis, but instead, build them around *Abductive experience*.[34] (p. 31, italics mine)

Carson exposes manipulative machinations of postconservative postmoderns by this statement:

> Many postmoderns channel the discussion into a manipulative antithesis. The antithesis is this: Either we human beings can know something

absolutely, perfectly, exhaustively—one might say omnisciently—or we human beings can at best glimpse some small perspective on something or other without any mechanism for discovering whether our perspective is an important part of the whole, a distorted view of the whole, or a skewed view of the whole, and so forth—precisely because we have no way of knowing what the whole is. The antithesis is designed to drive everyone into a postmodern view to truth. . . . The antithesis demands that we be committed perspectivalists—i.e., those who say that human "knowledge" is never more than the perspective of some finite individual group, without any means of grasping any perspective's relative importance, since none of us can compare our perspective with ultimate reality.[35]

Perspectivism lays the basis for the postmodern view on the failure to reach certainty. It is true that finite humans will always have an incomplete perspective rather than a complete understanding; however, it is not necessary to have exhaustive knowledge in order to have true knowledge. It is possible to have objective knowledge, propositional knowledge with logical consistency. Biblical truth is more than a mere paradigm, even a reigning paradigm. It is universal truth for all people of all time and is not subject to paradigm shift.

## Authority as Communal

Robert E. Webber has an ecclesial (church) understanding of the Bible as over against individual understanding. But this belief—that the individual cannot perceive truth accurately—is an abandonment of God's ability to effectively communicate his truth. Evangelicals believe that interpretation of Scripture can transcend issues of time or culture. To put it another way, evangelicals believe in the perspicuity of Scripture. As over against Webber's ecclesial and consensual approximation method, evangelicals believe each person is able to understand God's Word. Ecclesial rejection of the individual believer's ability to know truth as it is produces despair, lack of confidence, and unassertiveness in one's convictions about what one believes. This is an issue of certitude. It delimits God's Word as authoritative and renders inoperative doctrine and systematic theology.

Authority for postconservatives is communal and disparages the individual's autonomy in reaching truth. This corporate concept of authority rests in the presupposition of democratic community, as if the community had more authority than an individual. It is a subjective approach to truth and is the result of abandoning the propositional approach to truth. If we bypass the objective Word and logic, then all that is left is corporate and personal experience. There would be no warrant to determine whether feelings are valid or not. By ruling out objective content, all that is left is subjective sentiment. Somehow, postconservatives know through feeling.[36] Feeling leads invariably to a subjective and fluid definition of truth. Consensus is arbitrary belief in pre-Constantinian ideas and deconstruction of evangelicalism in lieu of reconstruction of an ancient-future faith. It is a new construction of faith built on past traditions, and it is important for these people to hold to ambiguity, mystery, and multi-dimensional faith and worship.[37] To do this, they must enter into a narrative way of thinking and present the gospel in narrative form. This is dialectical assumption. The church fathers are not as sure or stable as the Scripture. If authority does not rest on propositional truth statements, then we will have an uncertain message. In-house authority will produce ambivalent opinionism peculiar to the "in" group, resulting in a religious malaise inviting skepticism at its root. It cannot make for committed Christians but cowardly, wobbly believers without something solid upon which they rest their case.

Dialectical thought and dialogue process result in assimilation of God's Word with human thought, producing an uncertainty about what the Bible teaches. This viewpoint believes that we cannot know truths of Scripture without contaminating meaning with some perspective or reference from our experience. By approaching Scripture from a multiple-meaning viewpoint (polyvalent), we put ourselves at the mercy of a plurality of viewpoints. There is no doubt that an interpreter of Scripture must be careful not to bring personal experience or opinions into the Word of God (interpolation). However, it is patently obvious that it is possible to divorce oneself from personal bias, prejudice, and culture preconditions to interpret Scripture. We do not have to constantly dialogue with other traditions to come to truth (although it is wise to seek wisdom from others).

## Universal Truth

There is a correlation between postmodernism and eclecticism (which is the rejection of the possibility of a single meaning or order). Postmodernism cannot escape the dilemma of modernity's rationalism.

Brian McLaren has a problem with holding to a metanarrative when the essence of postmodernism is denial of the metanarrative (universal truth that applies to all people of all time); however, he resists using the term "metanarrative."[38] He would rather talk about a "larger narrative," the "story of emergence," because he wants to avoid truth except as it emerges from community.[39] For him, ethics comes before doctrine, which is the exact opposite of how the Bible presents the sequence. Compare the argument of Romans (the first eleven chapters present doctrine, chapters 12 through 16 application of doctrine); the same is true with Ephesians and Colossians (Ephesians chapters 1 through 3 are doctrine and 4 through 6 application; Colossians chapters 1 and 2 doctrine, chapters 3 and 4 application). Doctrine according to McLaren is "a practice of the church—a practice of reflecting, discussing, articulating, critiquing, rethinking, rearticulating, and so on."[40] This, again, is dialectical process. McLaren writes,

> Orthodoxy isn't a destination. It is a way—a way on which one journeys, and on which one progresses, even if one never (in this life) arrives. Paul put it this way: "Not that I have already obtained all this. . . I do not consider myself yet to have taken hold of it (Philippians 3:12–13)."[41]

McLaren's use of the latter verse shows a misunderstanding of the passage, a passage dealing with maturity based on the content of God's Word. McLaren blindly accepts the dialectical and instrumental approach to truth and puts an interpolation on the passage.

To McLaren, there is no clear set of laws for determining universal knowledge. Premodern narrative knowledge has conventions about who may tell the story. This is a tautology; that is, it legitimizes itself. By contrast, modernity separates narrative and autonomous vindication of knowledge. This is blind faith in autonomous objectivity. For example, philosophy or science must verify its claims by objective examination. Self-assertion of authority became no longer valid under modernity. Postmoderns now view philosophy and science as having narratives of their own. This is a new authoritarianism based on a metanarrative (ironically) of postmodernism. Thus, we are left with a plurality of narratives of postmodernism—with fragmented knowledge and no hope of universal truth. Cynicism becomes the name of the game.

We conclude from this that neither modernists nor postmoderns have a universal place to stand. The biblical Christian has a transcendent place to stand and a universal basis as a foundation for truth. There is no other way than for God to reveal himself in an *a priori* manner. Human beings are finite and can never find infinite truth finitely. Postmodernism finds itself caught in modernism's essential presupposition—autonomous man has the answer for humanity. Postevangelical postmoderns appeal to the very viewpoint they reject. This dialectical labyrinth is at the heart of the problem. Postevangelicals have a metanarrative universal of another kind—a veiled absolute of fragmented "truths." This is an attempt to relativize the straightforwardness of Scripture.

## Perspective on Truth versus Universal All-Encompassing Truth

It is one thing to state that we all carry assumptions from our culture and experience and that we are all perspectivalists, but it is another thing to say we cannot justify one perspective over another.

Another fallacy in McLaren's postmodern thinking is that "there is no such thing as interreligious dialogue in general, rather there is dialogue between this Christian individual or community and that Jewish or Buddhist or Hindu individual or community."[42] In other words, there is narrative dialogue but not metanarrative dialogue. Dialectical dialogue "prepares one for the next" dialogue but with no certainty, no finality.[43]

McLaren constantly confuses true biblical love and humility with his view of tolerance. He gives birth to false humility when it comes to truth, for he constantly confuses truth with pragmatism.[44] A generously orthodox Christian, he says, does not "claim to have the truth captured, stuffed, and mounted on the wall" but rather chooses "to be in a loving (ethical) community of people who are seeking the truth (doctrine) on the road of mission . . . and who have been launched on the quest by Jesus."[45] He has little to say to the non-Christian; he does not know what he believes for sure because he is always on a quest for truth, lacking a biblical view of truth, love, or humility. His definition of humility eviscerates the biblical idea of humility; he confuses biblical humility with humility toward certainty. He would rather pursue truth than find it.[46]

It appears that McLaren has not sorted out the influence that William James's instrumentalism has had on his own views: "Orthodoxy will mean not merely correct conclusions but right processes to keep on reaching new and better conclusions, not just correct ends but right means and attitudes to keep on discovering them, not just straight answers but a straight path to the next question that will keep on leading to better answers."[47] Again, this is essential instrumentalism and dialectical process. Is this orthodoxy? How can one live a confident Christian life based on mere possibilities? McLaren even puts Jesus into this realm.[48] His views are very close to liberal progressive thinking.

## Exhaustive Truth versus Some Truth

McLaren sets up another straw man by implying that evangelicals believe they can come to absolute truth exhaustively.[49] It is one thing to know some absolutes and it is another to know all reality absolutely. The Bible everywhere presumes we can know truth. This is not to say there is no progress of doctrine; there is progress in doctrine, but that is not his point. McLaren warns at the end of his book *A Generous Orthodoxy* that we "shall always be discontented with our portraits of orthodoxy, but we must never, in frustration, throw the Subject of our portrait out the window."[50] Why not? Why hold to the person if the content of the person is in doubt?

## Perspective versus Objective Truth

Grenz and John R. Franke do not view Scripture as authoritative in itself. For them, Scripture is not objective apart from the faith of the church and means of the Holy Spirit; it is the vehicle through which the Holy Spirit speaks. The Bible is not authoritative in itself but because of the community experiencing power and truth of the Spirit through its writings. The community preceded Scriptural texts, so there is an authority anterior to Scripture, although to them the message of the Bible is the "norming norm." They are afraid to establish a one-to-one correspondence between the message and the text. They see the Word of God and the words of Scripture as two different things. The meaning of a text to them does not necessarily tie into the biblical author's intention in writing a book of the Bible. The text takes on a life of its own. According to these people, the factor that keeps them from falling into subjectivism rests on the community. Their view of Scripture does not justify what the Bible says of itself. They move ultimate authority from Scripture to the community and the experience of the individual. The Bible, for them, is not a self-authenticating text.

However, the Bible affirms for itself authority in the text because the Spirit inspired it, whether or not it is experienced by the reader. Note Stephen Wellum's summary of the communal approach to Scripture: "In the end, I am convinced that their proposal leaves us with a hermeneutical subjectivism that will not sufficiently ground a normative evangelical theology in a pluralistic and postmodern world."[51]

## Emergent Vacuum of Truth

*A Generous Orthodoxy* creates a massive vacuum of belief. It is a mixture of pragmatic liberalism and diluted, eviscerated evangelicalism. The book is an attempt to placate the unregenerate, degenerate minds of fallen man (1 Corinthians 2:14), but the entire construct of the book looks nothing like how the Bible presents itself.

Brian McLaren is a founder of the U.S. emergent movement. This movement is integral or integrative in its thinking. In other words, it is dialectical in belief system and modus operandi. He claims that emergent thinking is an "unspoken assumption behind all my previous books."[52] He says that Christianity is not the kingdom of God, but ultimate reality is the kingdom of God.[53] Christianity is here to lead people to the kingdom of God, "calling them from smaller rings, smaller Kingdoms."[54] Christians need to emerge out of denominational and doctrinal rings of confinement. But McLaren presumes that no one has come to truth with any certainty and that we are on an instrumental road through the dialectical process of discovering this kingdom. How does he "know" that this kingdom exists? He uses propositions and presuppositions to come to this deduction! Yet, on the other hand, he avoids much of biblical revelation about the kingdom.

McLaren seems to recognize the implication of his emergent philosophy when he says,

> Perhaps this sounds to you like heresy, not orthodoxy. Perhaps
> . . . this seems to present you with only two options: a non-
> emergent gospel that is definite, clear, sure, and certain, or a
> 'radically indeterminate,' anything goes that means anything
> and is worth nothing [gospel] . . . like a heterodox compromise
> with pluralistic relativism.[55]

He denies pluralistic relativism because it does not accept universals, but he still maintains the need to negate absolutes or anyone who claims to have the "final orthodoxy nailed down."[56] McLaren wants to deny relativism, which deems one idea as good as another idea. He probably wants to assert that Christianity is more viable than other systems. However, this premise places the choice of truth upon the judgment of the individual's construct of belief for determining truth.

Modern thought has its own presupposition that limits certainty to the empirical and the scientific method. Postmoderns rightly attack this presupposition. However, by denying any indubitable foundation for truth, postconservatives bite the hand that feeds them. By this, they lose a universal claim to truth and live in fragments of truth. They find themselves in the same predicament as secular postmoderns, with little authority to help people with no hope.

McLaren defines emergent Christians as postliberal and postconservative.[57] This viewpoint supposedly holds the "balance" because this theory "sees beyond pluralistic relativism and 'exclusivism/absolutism.'"[58] He wants to move beyond mutually exclusive truth. (His assumptions indicate that he has a problem with such statements as Acts 4:12 and John 14:6.) Somehow, by a massive logical leap, by inferential logic, by a leap in the dark from subjectivism, by dialectical thinking, he asserts that he has found the truth of something "above and beyond"—"the way of Jesus, which is the way of love and the way of embrace."[59] This is his kingdom of God. He says that this is the "more narrative approach to theology."[60] "Rather than trying to capture timeless truth in objective statements systematized in analytical outlines and recorded in books and institutionalized in schools and denominations, narrative theology embraces, preserves, and reflects on the stories of people and communities involved in the romance of God—always beginning with and always returning to the treasury of stories in Scripture. . . ."[61] "These stories (narratives) seek to understand the "larger narrative" (the story of emergence) that these individual stories constitute."[62] Narratives, then, lead us to a kind of metanarrative, but evidently he cannot concede that we do indeed arrive at a metanarrative (a word he intentionally avoids)

Postconservative theology begins with "ethics," not doctrine,[63] but how does one resolve which ethic or virtue is right? McLaren's answer is that we develop it in "community." Community is more essential than good theology and scholarship or logic![64] This is obvious because he violates logic, scholarship, and theology throughout his works. According to him, doctrine is a "practice of the church—a practice of reflecting, discussing, articulating, critiquing, rethinking, rearticulating, and so on."[65] McLaren's thesis is again both dialectical and instrumentalist, a "dynamic cycle that spirals upward."[66] For him, orthodoxy is not a destination but "a way" on which one journeys. He supports this thinking with a patently false interpretation and implication of Philippians 3:12–13. The issue in this passage is maturity of the believer, not some postmodern philosophical system based on instrumentalism and dialectical thought.

McLaren thinks that evangelicalism is the "historical accumulation of precedents"; in other words, the progress of dogma needs to be negated.[67] All that we need is a "right attitude toward Jesus."[68] If this is not minimalist, what is? Scriptures are full of propositions and didactic truth (as well as narratives). The progress of revelation is abundantly clear in Scripture, and development of doctrine in history (progress of dogma—such as the development of the doctrine of justification in the Reformation) holds the great value of teaching us from past doctrinal issues.

## Capitulation to Culture Undermines Unity of Understanding

Pluralism fractures truth and unity of understanding. In other words, it tears down the essential idea that the Bible is a revelation of truth from God that communicates absolutes and clarity. Instead, a pluralistic culture breaks down into small segments of knowing, for no one knows any universals. We are left with only fraternities living in isolation from one another without truth to connect them to a universal. All we know is our own ideas of private experience; no one can claim to speak for God. Pluralism marginalizes God; only the self, standing apart from truth, remains.

The loss of theology or doctrine means the loss of knowing God and his values. Our society has shifted from knowing God to knowing self as the vital focal point of faith. This creates a loss of conviction about transcendent things. Focus on self puts the highest priority on expediency and subjectivity. Preaching becomes centrally psychological, therapeutic, and sociological and results in unadulterated pragmatism. Secularism sets the standard for what is proper belief. This is capitulation of gigantic proportion by postconservatives. Evangelicalism is losing its soul because its convictions are on the outer edge of its (no longer biblical) belief systems. David Wells warns us about this problem:

> The stakes are high: the anti-theological mood that now grips the evangelical world is changing its internal configuration, its effectiveness, and its relation to the past. It is severing the link to historical, Protestant orthodoxy. It is emancipating contemporary evangelicals to form casual alliances at will with a multitude of substitutes for this orthodoxy.[69]

Scripture warns that there will come a time when believers will no longer tolerate "sound doctrine." Biblical Christianity is truth oriented. That is why exhortations warn us about protecting doctrine and living the Christian life based on doctrine:

> For the time will come when they will not endure sound doctrine, but according to their own desires, because they have itching ears, they will heap up for themselves teachers; and they will turn their ears away from the truth, and be turned aside to fables. (2 Timothy 4:3–4)

The Bible calls for faith based on doctrine or propositions:

> For fornicators, for sodomites, for kidnappers, for liars, for perjurers, and if there is any other thing that is contrary to *sound doctrine*. (1 Timothy 1:10, italics mine)

> If you instruct the brethren in these things, you will be a good minister of Jesus Christ, nourished in the words of faith and of the *good doctrine*

which you have carefully followed. But reject profane and old wives' fables, and exercise yourself toward godliness. (1 Timothy 4:6–7, italics mine)

Hold fast the pattern of *sound words* which you have heard from me, in faith and love which are in Christ Jesus. (2 Timothy 1:13, italics mine)

Holding fast the faithful word as he has been taught, that he may be able, by sound doctrine, both to exhort and convict those who contradict. (Titus 1:9, italics mine)

Beloved, while I was very diligent to write to you concerning our common salvation, I found it necessary to write to you exhorting you to contend earnestly for the *faith which was once for all delivered to the saints*. (Jude 3, italics mine)

Paul and Jude brooked no compromise in the face of a culture that was more pluralistic than ours is. Compromise always dilutes belief and conviction. They did not view Christianity as one perspective among many or as one possible interpretation of God; they viewed it as absolute truth.

## Loss of Theological Soul

Evangelicals are now uncritical of culture because they have lost their theological bearings and doctrinal soul. Living the Christian life is no longer the application of truth to experience. The new focus is to find success, to function in society, and to seek self-fulfillment. Pop psychology is the new remedy for evangelical wholeness. Contemporary practicality has displaced application of doctrinal principles to life. Seminaries accommodate their curriculum to this new demand for church ministry. They shift from a doctrinal focus to training seminary students for successful careers in ministry. Denominations care little for maintaining their doctrinal distinctives. They accept the reality that churches no longer want pastors who teach the Word of God but who can meet the psychological needs of their members.

Pastors who declare the mind of God to the minds of man are now obsolete in favor of pastors who orient to practical interests. Churches want pastors who are leaders and meet psychological needs. There is little call for pastors who preach the truth. This is nothing more than wide-ranging capitulation to culture.

Capitulation to culture occurred at the end of the nineteenth and at the beginning of the twentieth centuries. Liberals saw themselves as preserving the faith from modernity. Postevangelicals today see themselves as preserving evangelicalism from postmodernism. Both end with the same result—departure from the truth. Both have the same cause—doctrine falling into disrepute. To put it another way, loss of truth spells loss of the essence of Christianity. As Wells says, "It is this weakness, this loss of nerve that led Peter Berger to scoff that theologians today are so afraid of being pushed into the ditch by modernity that they have decided to fall into it of their own accord."[70]

Modern society decided that a person defines what to believe, rejecting external authority because authority resides within. This is the essence of the battle—doctrine versus inner self-consciousness. At the end of the nineteenth century, the liberal rallying cry was "life, not doctrine," and that is the rallying call of evangelicals today. Today's postevangelical thinking finds itself deeply rooted in this relativizing process. Private belief without doctrinal distinctive is acceptable to a culture of pluralism. This is why postconservative evangelicals despise doctrine and certainty. They love belief but deride doctrine.

## Secular Fundamentalism

Out of pluralism and the philosophy that the individual person is the authority comes the viewpoint that no authority has ultimate truth. All viewpoints about life are interpretations of reality. This philosophy itself became the unexamined and unchallenged belief system of pluralistic society. It became essential secular fundamentalism.

Secular fundamentalism defines the cultural sentiment of our day. Postevangelicals take their cue from this sentiment. The last thing they want is to lose face with culture, so they undermine their own convictions about truth. They do not want the world to see them as narrow minded or as those who challenge customary beliefs of society. They fear to stand apart from society, so they emasculate doctrine. Again, Wells explains:

> That this emasculation has taken place among the evangelicals is, on the face of it, most surprising. After all, they have steadfastly resisted until relatively recently every attempt to ease the difficulty implicit in believing in truth in the modern world. . . . They staunchly opposed the

Modernist effort to surrender doctrine in favor of "life," as if religious consciousness could be a substitute for biblical truth. And it is as doctrinal people that they have defined themselves through much of the 20th century. But this identity is now rapidly dissipating.[71]

Doctrine served evangelicals in maintaining the integrity of their convictions. Evangelicals used doctrine to establish standards for belief and ethics in the previous century. This affected how evangelicals functioned within society, and they held culture at arm's length to protect these values. Worldliness was a rejection of the biblical values society currently held, so evangelicals recognized that the standard for measuring values was the inerrant, inspired Bible that spoke authoritatively to these values. David Wells distinguishes between the values of fundamentalism and evangelicalism: "The great sin in Fundamentalism is to compromise; the great sin in evangelicalism is to be narrow."[72] This change in attitude brought evangelicals into the mainstream of religious acceptance in North America. Wells maintains the point that when this happened, their ability to distinguish themselves from the world diminished.

> For no sooner had the evangelicals begun to think like the status quo than their theological and moral distinctives began to evaporate like the morning midst. In entering the mainstream of American cultural life, they were brought face to face with the great shaping forces of modern life, and one of the immediate casualties was their sense of truth in both private and public life. Almost immediately, their capacity to think theologically about themselves and their world also disappeared.[73]

North Americans viewed evangelicals as having a certain kind of religious experience separate from their belief. Evangelicals came to terms with pluralism's lack of interest in truth and came to believe that the movement does not need a doctrinal view of life. Wells makes the further point that evangelicals believe they need only experience, not doctrine.

> Evangelicals today only have to believe that God can work dramatically within the narrow fissure of internal experience; they have lost interest (or perhaps they can no longer sustain interest) in what the doctrines of creation, common grace, and providence once meant for Christian believers, and even in those doctrines that articulate Christ's death

such as justification, redemption, propitiation, and reconciliation. It is enough for them simply to know that Christ somehow died for people. For both Liberals and evangelicals, the search for "essence" has been a tactical retreat.[74]

## Unwitting Contextualization of Truth

Postconservatives shape their theology and viewpoints from the prevailing demands of a psychology of conformity taken from a society that operates upon a presupposition of the self. Individualism has turned into a movement accountable only to the self, where all of life is psychologized in a shift from the objective to the subjective. No meaning exists beyond the self—a philosophy called solipsism—and objectivity is totally lost, with only private meaning remaining. This flies in the face of objective biblical viewpoint.

Postconservatives fail to recognize this shift from the objective view of truth to the subjective viewpoint, or perspective view of life, producing pervasive relativism that holds all ideas provisional. There are no objective grounds for coming to truth; thus there is no certainty, so life in postmodern North America becomes banal. We went through this once before with theological liberalism when that movement did not want to distinguish between belief and unbelief. Christianity, it held, was not about truth but about intuition and feeling, which has become the religion of "spirituality" of our day. Liberals traded in orthodox Christianity for a bowl of modernism's porridge. They got a spot at the table of acceptance in modern society, but they lost their message and eventually dissolved from within by the end of the twentieth century. Evangelicals today are adapting their theology for a place of approval and acceptance, but they do not realize how much truth they have sold for a new porridge of subjective spirituality, nor how conviction about truth is on the wane among the general evangelical population. This new kind of evangelicalism is about system and style, and has very little to do with truth. We live in a day of spirituality without doctrine or truth. There are very few theologically shaped movements among evangelicals today.

Cultural nihilism is the psychological and philosophical popularization of postmodernism, and it maintains that life is made up of private preferences and perceptions. The nihilistic world, devoid of meaning, is indifferent toward convictions beyond the self. Movement occurs without a destination, leaving mankind with fragments of meaning but no whole. Uncertainty pervades everything with this assumption. Values are little more than preference.

The Word of God views the self as totally depraved and incapable of coming to truth autonomously. People need the Holy Spirit to "convict" them of the objective "truth" of the Word of God. Postevangelicals fail to recognize the depravity of human perspective without objective truth. Their thinking precludes accountability to an outside source of authority.

The 1960s brought a sense of despair, and that generation turned to the subjective self in search of hope. People began to search for transcendence in the mysticism of Eastern religions and in drugs. Self-consciousness did not produce the results for which they had hoped. There was a loss of what is normative. External objectivity buckled under the weight of the presupposition of the self as ultimate authority. North American culture now determines good and evil by the prevailing viewpoint at a given time and place. The culture defines what is right simply by definition from the winds of opinion. There is little or no conviction because there is nothing outside of self.

Evangelicalism previously held that orientation to life came as a by-product of applying the principles of Scripture to experience. Now evangelicals accept the idea that orientation comes from self-actualization or self-fulfillment. Effectiveness of personal experience ratifies fulfillment. This is the viewpoint of autonomy, which sets itself apart from the Word of God. The issue for postmoderns is not whether there is any objectivity in the experience but simply whether it appeals to the person. Accommodation to culture always results in disillusionment down the road, for unbiblical Christianity is always an illusion. A postmodern view of Christianity will disappoint just as the liberal view did a century ago. Postconservatism no doubt will produce a robust following, but like all false teaching before it, it will end in despair. Just as liberalism ended in collapse, so will this form of evangelicalism. Liberalism based its belief system primarily on a form of experience, just as postevangelicalism has. Experience without truth is vacuous and will have the same ending. The therapeutic model of experience without truth will cut the heart out of evangelicalism because of its premise that the self is autonomous. It is therapy without theology, but biblical Christianity rests on truth.

Genuine Christianity includes experience, but not experience autonomous from the Word of God. In this view, experience is subject to the norms of the Word of God. This requires an understanding of the principles of the Word of God and of how to apply those principles to experience. However, many evangelicals do not take this direction; they head pell-mell toward the cliff of inane subjective Christianity.

Listen to Wells:

> Popular evangelical faith has developed a bias against theology (not to mention against the intellect), and what is more, it has elevated the bias to the level of a virtue, defending it as vigorously as democracy.
> In the presence of this bias, the leader is reduced to serving as a cautious pollster.[75]

There is great incredulity toward evangelical certainty, but if evangelicals do not have certainty, they have no message. Either evangelicals simply have a belief that they call their "story," or they have a message that is certain and sure. Christianity rests on an indubitable first principle from which we can deduce the universal, absolute truth of God's mind. The Bible is a deduction from God's fixed principles. The Word is not derived from, or logically posterior to, sense experience. It transcends our experience. The Bible offers apodictic knowledge, certain knowledge, albeit not exhaustive universal knowledge. Insofar as God has spoken, it is objectively true and certain.

## Pluralism Undermines Certainty

Christianity is fixed, absolute truth that does not adapt its message to culture, although it does adjust to culture in method. Cultural pluralism will not allow such exclusive truth, so some in the evangelical church adapt their message to the current condition. Postconservatism no longer defines itself doctrinally but rather stylistically, methodologically, and culturally. Doctrine is dying among evangelicals and is no longer the center of evangelical belief, but is cast to the outer periphery of evangelical practice. Although evangelicals today hold to basic evangelical beliefs, those beliefs are now at the margins of their commitments. They relegate doctrine to the remote borders of evangelical life. Doctrine no longer defines what it means to be an evangelical. Secularism pours into this vacuum of evangelical conviction the normative assumptions of exclusion of religion. Something other than doctrine becomes the center of evangelical life. The practical displaces doctrine. This will take the passion and heart out of the evangelical movement. Wells says, "The most obvious consequence of this unabashed desertion of the cognitive substance of faith is one that few have pondered, at least out loud. It is the disappearance of conviction."[76]

Postmodern evangelicals reject the ways of knowing from the Enlightenment but put priority on a system called deconstruction, a skeptical system that attempts to show inconsistences in postulates. Deconstruction accompanies postmodernism and seeks to take apart rational and objective ideas of modernism. By this, they deny objective truth and even the ability to know truth itself. However, the problem is that deconstructionism deconstructs itself!

Evangelical Daniel Taylor, in *The Myth of Certainty,* claims that evangelicals who assert certainty do so because they are insecure.[77] Taylor ultimately retreats to reliance on faith without factuality. Luke, on the other hand, appealed to evidence by "many infallible proofs" (Acts 1:3). Taylor is unaware of his dependence on the presupposition of philosophical pluralism.

## Pluralism's Correlation to Tolerance

Postevangelicals have changed the meaning of tolerance from the concept of charity toward people in a social sense to the acceptance of ideas in the philosophical sense, declaring most ideas equal in worth and validity. They hold not only to moral equivalence but to truth equivalence, and they view any criticism of others as narrow minded. The upshot of this distorted form of tolerance is reduced capacity to critique the most blatantly false religious beliefs. It leaves them vulnerable to pluralistic winds that blow nowhere, and with little conviction to convert those who embrace false doctrine. Religious pluralism elevates truth-equivalence above arriving at exclusive truth.

Postevangelicals portray evangelicals, with their intolerance to other ideas, as the quaint residue of a long-gone era. They see evangelicals as closed-minded and narrow bigots. D. A. Carson describes the new open-mindedness, which

> no longer means that you may or may not have strong views yet remain
> committed to listening honestly to countervailing arguments. Rather,

it means you are dogmatically committed to the view that all convictions [that hold] that any view whatsoever is wrong are improper and narrow-minded. In other words, open-mindedness has come to be identified not with the means of rational discourse, but with certain conclusions.[78]

Serious cracks in the evangelical worldview are beginning to emerge—cracks not of method but of message. This manifests itself in a social discourse that gives priority and protocol to unbiblical trends and snuggles up to the prevailing worldviews. But Christians must not inductively derive doctrine from social environments; rather, our doctrine is deductively obtained from the Word of God. Postevangelical postmoderns claim that a biblically deductive approach to worldview is a closed loop of bias toward the Word of God. This, to them, violates the principle of "provisionally coming to truth." They view propositions as telling people what to think and not subjecting oneself to checks and balances, and they regard those who assert truth as defensive in their mindset and lacking in intellectual integrity on both the individual and institutional level. The resulting deductive or propositional approach encourages intellectual dishonesty because it flounders in the compartmentalized thinking of a closed loop of truth.

## Personal View of Revelation

There is a tendency among postevangelicals to believe in personal revelation as over against propositional revelation. Bernard Ramm, Baptist theologian and apologist, switched from a propositional view of truth to a personal view of truth after studying with Karl Barth (neo-orthodox and existential theologian). To Ramm, it is God who is infallible, not the human document of the Bible. The Bible is merely a witness to revelation.

Stanley Grenz suggests a closer relationship between inspiration and illumination. He sees a tie between community and how the Bible was produced. God did not write Scripture through individual Bible authors such as Paul; rather, the Bible was produced by the church community along with Paul. According to Millard J. Erickson, Grenz makes "no distinction between the norm and source of theology; the terms are, in fact, used interchangeably. This, however, seems to confuse two types of authority; or two roles of authorities, of originating or supplying the content of a theology and of interpreting, evaluating, or judging such content."[79] Grenz believes the debate between liberals and fundamentalists in the early twentieth century hardened the issue of inerrancy of Scripture so that evangelicals became card-carrying inerrantists. His view is that evangelicals need to return to a more personal relationship to the God of the nineteenth century, an experiential piety.

## False Dichotomy: A Person and not a Proposition

The assertion that God is not a proposition but a person is a false dichotomy, for faith always rests on biblical content. How can someone trust in a God whom one knows nothing about? There can be no confidence in God's trustworthiness and fidelity without first knowing the content that he is credible, immutable, and faithful to his promises. Faith does not seek understanding without having understanding first. There is no rejoicing in his presence without knowing that his presence is worthy of joy. In other words, Christianity does not rest on experience. There is no heart belief without head belief. Emotions follow belief, they do not lead belief. Experience is not the ultimate presupposition of Christian belief, for Christianity is more than personal encounter; it is an engagement with God's truth about himself. It is no leap of faith into the dark, into propositionless content, but rather trust in God's propositional content about himself. There is no irrationalism in biblical belief. Biblical belief rests on the internal consistency of the Bible, the reliability of its historicity, and the validity of its truth claims. All belief systems rest on presuppositions, but not all presuppositions are equally probable.

The essence of neo-orthodoxy is that truth is not propositional but personal, and that we do not find truth in objective statements but in a personal encounter with God. Neo-orthodoxy was existential theology, and emergents mimic neo-orthodoxy. But propositions compel belief, and that is the emergent problem. Some ideas have to be true and others false. Emergents want to accommodate many ideas pluralistically, and propositions do not allow them to do it. Propositions do not lend themselves to synthesis but to certainty. But emergents preclude certainty by their acceptance of the presupposition of postmodernism. Their alternative is to turn to mystical experiences. It is too bad for them that we have to face right-brain issues in the Bible! Francis Schaeffer was correct;

the neo-orthodox of his day had to "escape from reason." The postconservative of our day places his faith in faith of whatever preferences he may hold, a faith that ends in mystical morass because it is alienated from the objective content of God's Word. Jesus apart from the Word of God is an alien Jesus. In the next chapter, we examine the nature of deductive, conclusive truth and how we can know it.

## Not Limiting Revelation to the Original Intent of the Text

Clark Pinnock buys into the view that revelation is not limited to the original intent of the text but that new revelation can arise out of an interaction between the text and the Spirit. He contends that God did not close the canon in the theological sense but that we can achieve a revelation beyond Scripture itself. The core of Christianity is the salvation story, not the safeguarding of the text and meaning of Scripture. The Christian community brings tradition ahead and can move revelation forward. We can add personal experiences to tradition and make it relevant to a person's life. Reason is the result of a faith search. The task of theology is not to establish propositions but to tell the salvation story, Pinnock maintains.

These postconservatives want to dislodge evangelicals from thinking propositionally about the Word of God. They desire to "deconstruct" the Bible into doctrinal mush without conviction about sure truths. They contend that those who believe doctrines such as the virgin birth are believing in a "fall-back position" of the truthfulness of the Word of God. They want to abandon this mentality because they do not believe we can dogmatically establish the truthfulness of statements of Scripture. They see the problem as the expectations we bring to the text (interpolation) and not interpretation itself, and they caution that we need to be wary of treating the text of the Bible as a privileged text and, instead, treat it with more "contingency." These postevangelical, postconservative postmoderns believe that we need to move away from doctrinal commitments to historical belief in Christianity, which in their viewpoint is to say very little, by the way. After all, what do we know about Jesus except through the Bible? Nevertheless, according to them, the evangelical is the one who lives in a glass house of bias. They view the evangelical notion of salvation as "myth" embodied in elaborate propositions.

Postevangelicals believe that evangelicals adopted the philosophy of modernism. Through this grid, evangelicals deciphered propositions that came from our cultural environment since the Age of Enlightenment. According to postevangelicals, evangelicals explain the world by naturalistic assumptions. For this reason, postconservatives need to "deconstruct" doctrines that rose out of doctrinal battles. They view the Bible as having little certainty and possessing errancy.

According to these people, we need to buy into the "narrative theology" of continuing interpretation that has few fixed conclusions. We must reinvent the Bible for our postmodern generation. We should take the didactic, doctrinal passages of Scripture with a grain of salt because the global, literary, and narrative passages appeal to postmoderns. Postconservatives tend to equate propositional statements of Scripture as "proof-texting." The worst error, they would say, is to believe what we have been told. We need to reject all those years of progress of doctrine where scholars worked long and hard to carefully conclude truth of Scripture. This is the only way to rediscover the truth of Scripture in a postmodern culture. We need to reject the propositional model because it is inflexible.

The postevangelical postmodern approach to Christianity is a house of cards that destabilizes essential tenets of evangelical faith. Postevangelicalism, finding its roots in current postmodern skepticism toward objective truth, has difficulty in coming to exclusive claims of Christ and Christianity. The horrible thought that Christianity is superior to other religions is foreboding to a pluralistic mindset. The assumption of both philosophical and religious pluralism preys on the postevangelicals' minds and controls their viewpoints.

## Minimizing Certainty by Hermeneutics

According to McLaren, the fact that Bible requires interpretation introduces huge doubt into the attempt to find certainty about what God said. Thus, interpretation creates a "problem" for certainty.[80] However, God clearly expects the Bible to be understood with perspicuity (1 Corinthians 2; 2 Peter 1).

Postmodern presumption is the assumption of pluralism. No other ideology has the right to pronounce itself right except pluralism. This is unadulterated presumption, for no claim can be true except the claim that pluralism is true. Those who hold any truth hold it arbitrarily. They construct it arbitrarily; consequently they must deconstruct it by the assumptions of pluralism.

Most people do not understand how they came to believe in pluralism, but it is a commonly held belief on the streets of North America and Europe. This culture precludes absolutes and final truth. It is a society without conviction. No wonder relativism is the norm of culture; we live in a culture of consensus. All so-called truth is subjective and individualistic. By absorbing and declaring it true, postevangelicals capitulate to culture. They are awash in radical subjectivism and antipathy toward certainty. This timid approach toward truth does not assert itself above other claims about reality. It tries to include as many people in the kingdom with as broad a swath as possible. Some go so far as to believe that other religions can save people eternally.

Unbelievers of the mid-twentieth century rejected Christianity because it was unbelievable, but today they reject it because it claims exclusive truth. True evangelicals hold to truth that stands in accord with the law of non-contradiction; that is, if Christianity is true, then other claims about God are false. This does not imply that religions of the world have no truth whatsoever. Judaism holds to one God and that is a truth. There is no religious parity if the Bible is true; otherwise, there could be no heresy. Warping of the Bible by postevangelicals creates a softening of conviction about what they believe, as we will see in the next chapter.

Adding to doctrinal aberrance, postconservatives have entered into the fallacy of accommodating truth to culture by imbibing postmodernism as an interpreting principle of Christianity. Deconstruction was originally a method of literary criticism. Today deconstructionists say we must deconstruct all assertions of belief. We cannot know objective reality and there is no transcendent meaning. The universe is closed to outside influence such as the Word of God, so all reality is subjective. Reality, such as it is, comes to us only through language.

The objective of postconservatives is not to find the original meaning of the author but the subjective interpretation of the reader. They deeply resent "totalizing" or coming to a universal truth, because they judge that holding to a universal creates power-lust and dominance over other groups.

The task of deconstruction is to expose contradictions and reveal the hidden meaning behind beliefs. Deconstruction tries to expose social or personal motivation behind those who claim to arrive at truth. We live in a day wherein postconservatives seek to "deconstruct" what evangelicals previously believed. They want to redesign, redefine, and reconstruct evangelical doctrine just as the liberals did before them. They move our belief-system from the objective Word of God into a mishmash of countervailing opinions, undermining the inerrancy of Scripture and the omniscience of God himself. This is a great danger to biblical Christianity, and few recognize this seismic shift right under our noses. Once this shift takes place, evangelical values and morality will take on very a different picture. Evangelicals have already caved in to unbiblical egalitarianism, but this is just the beginning of this evangelical disaster.

Postconservatives attempt to deconstruct the propositional approach to Christianity by evangelicals of the twentieth century. They assert that these evangelicals bought into assumptions of modernism that claim to come to conclusions about truth. They say there is arrogance and moral superiority in making exclusive claims of certainty.

Evangelicals of the twentieth century rejected the subjective experientialism of the late nineteenth and early twentieth centuries. The liberal position was a presupposition based on the self's ability to come to truth autonomously. Today's postconservatives follow closely on the heels of that view.

Postmodern philosophers take a "linguistic turn" when they declare that we cannot come to know the real world as such. The only way we can come to perspectives on truth is through our communities. We cannot know the essence of language because that would mean we could know something as it actually is. No, all we can know are languages being used in particular times and places. According to postmodern philosophy, our talk about reality shapes reality for us. There is no universal truth, objective truth, or meaning that corresponds to facts. All perspectives are embedded in the community's viewpoint. Even though evangelicals claim that Jesus is the exclusive way to God, there is no way to prove it.

Postconservatives claim to be evangelicals not because of propositions from God's Word but because their community shapes their thinking. This raises the question as to why their community is the right community. Objective reality is unknowable to them. Christianity is functional rather than propositional. For them, a doctrine is true because of what it does (it forms a way of life), not because of what it says, not because of a correspondence between the doctrine or proposition and reality. All this boils down to the presupposition that the self is the source and arbiter of truth. This approach starts with the self rather than with the deductive presupposition that God spoke in his Word. It all rests on the ineffable experience of the self as a particular linguistic member of a believing community. This new form of modernism rests on the self rather than the God who has spoken.

Deconstructionists view all interpretations of Scripture as subjective. We get the answer from the Bible that we ask of it. There is no objective answer in Scripture. Absolute and objective truth is a polemic people use with those who agree with them. Above all, they desire ambiguity and not clarity of position or certainty. This is postmodern interpretation (hermeneutics). It is a usurpation of the authority of both the Holy Spirit and the original human writer of Scripture. The postmodern brings meaning to the text. The reader then becomes the author of the meaning of the Bible.

Churches use this process (often unintentionally) in their small groups. Rather than teach a passage didactically, they dialogue by thesis, antithesis, and synthesis. The group comes to consensus about the meaning of the text. The new synthesis is the formulation for belief.

McLaren believes that although Protestants "transferred the fulcrum or center of authority from the church to the Bible . . . the Bible requires human interpretation, which was a problem." He sees the issue as knowing "nothing of the Bible without *my own involvement* via interpretation" (italics mine).[81] He thinks that appeal to principles of hermeneutics is an appeal to authority.[82] He characterizes evangelicals as afraid to ask whether authority rests in the Bible or the church, which is ridiculous; this, along with his other statements, makes me think that he is uninformed about evangelical scholarship or that he intentionally falsifies that scholarship.

Once again McLaren characterizes evangelicalism as something it is not. He says that conservative biblical interpretation justified dubious causes such as "slavery, male chauvinism, horrific treatment of aboriginal peoples, identifying the mentally ill as witches."[83] What evangelical scholarship holds this today? This is clear characterization and a straw man. The reason McLaren can do this is that he overlaps generalized Protestantism of centuries ago with evangelicals of today.[84]

Another characterization by him is that evangelicals are involved in "name-calling," as if the issue were not content but simple, shrill distortions of other positions. McLaren's lack of fairness is staggering. He does this under an organizational assumption of Christianity.[85]

Does the Bible put an end to further investigation or is it a platform for constant uncertainty? Every system ends its search in its first principle. If God has a final answer, then the search must stop somewhere; if there is no final answer, there is no basis to establish an objection. The dialectical process of McLaren never ends, so dialecticism can never decide. This is chaotic skepticism. This dialectic of change and continuity leans on a flawed method, for the Bible presents itself propositionally, logically. There is such a thing as real apostasy and heresy. There is no way to determine what is true from what is false apart from propositions of Scripture.

It is also the view of William James, a pragmatist philosopher, that knowledge is an instrumental process, not a conclusion; as well, personal will and interest are primary. For him, truth is only the expedient in our way of thinking. Ideas do not produce objects but prepare the way for them. This unadulterated pragmatism, a philosophy of pure experience, is devoid of conclusions about truth. Thinking must of necessity reject all transcendent truth and find experience organized by means of conjunctive relations that are a matter of direct experience as the things themselves. There is much of William James in McLaren.

Orthodoxy is more than process and pursuit of truth;[86] it is conclusion about truth. If everything is process, then everything is a possibility and not finality. The book of Romans specifically argues that God is absolutely righteous and requires human beings to be declared as absolutely righteous as he is righteous by faith alone in Christ alone. This belief requires conclusion. This is why McLaren does not like propositions—because there are conclusions from propositions. Jesus scorched the Pharisees with his words, "You are of your father the devil, and the desires of your father you want to do. He was a murderer from the beginning, and *does not stand in the truth, because there is no truth in him.* When he speaks a lie, he speaks from his own resources, for he is a liar and the father of it. But because *I tell the truth, you do not believe Me*" (John 8:44–45, italics mine). Jesus did this because they would not come to a correct conclusion about truth. The opposite is a lie of the devil. Jesus made a claim of mutually exclusive truth (cf. John 14:6; Acts 4:12—two other mutually exclusive claims for truth).

## Achilles' Heel—Accommodation to Prevailing Worldview

If anyone interprets Scripture through culture, it is the postevangelical postmoderns. They charge that evangelicals formulated doctrines from the philosophy and science of modernism; however, the truth is that most evangelicals stood apart from modernism as critics of the assumptions of modernism. They took the good of modernism, such as logic and true science, but rejected the methodology as an ultimate presupposition for finding truth. Yet the postevangelical postmoderns buy into postmodernism both as a method and as truth. This is their Achilles' heel, for they accommodate truth to the prevailing worldview.

Postevangelicals are so afraid that postmoderns might view Christianity as unreasonable from within the premise of postmodernism that they are willing to go AWOL from doctrinal truth. They reject the thought that most of the Bible is self-evident because they fear ridicule from postmodern thought. They want to run from the idea that Christianity is a struggle between truth and error because they must view truth from a collection of perspectives. Their idea is that the evangelical doctrinal viewpoint is leaky, as if interpretation of Scripture is without scholarship and rational care.

## Priority on Experience

Another fallacy among postevangelicals is their attempt to reduce Christianity to religious experience devoid of substantial truth. The other day I heard an evangelical pastor say that we need to reduce Christianity down to the "smallest orthodox box possible." He is afraid of orthodoxy because the more creedal we are, the less acceptable we are to people in postmodernism. The postevangelicals must open the loop of truth and reject the closed loop of evangelicalism.

The main issue in opening the "loop" is to reject the infallibility and inerrancy of Scripture. By doing this, they lose their identity with any sense of being evangelical.

Postevangelicals want evangelicals to buy into both a new way of looking at truth and a new way of coming to truth. These people no longer hold to an inerrant Bible based upon corresponding facts.[87] Neither do they any longer hold to absolute truth, but rather to truth in process that is provisionally believed.[88] Truth is in chaotic, constant revision. This results in aversion to conclusion and conviction. There is then nothing self-evident about the Bible. It is just a collection of incoherent miscellaneous texts.

Postevangelicals create their own gods of subjectivism and relativism from culture. They abandon objective, propositional truth—absolute truth. Truth to them is personal. Each person has personal truth, and they do not believe in universal truths. Truth is what one's group believes. They have lost a sense of certainty about their beliefs. R. Albert Mohler calls this a "promise of polymorphous perversity."[89] This results in cultural accommodation to the gods of this world.

Note David F. Wells's explanation of the change to a theology of experience beginning in the 1960s:

> It was these experiences that became the organizing centers in these new theologies, none of them making any pretension to having universal truth. They did not believe that there is such a thing. They were, therefore, expressions of our multiculturalism, and the intellectual currency in which they traded was pluralism.[90]

## Planting Seeds of One's Own Destruction

Postmodern evangelicals are planting seeds for their own destruction. Spirituality without propositions from the Word will produce Christian living without mooring. Everyone will do what is right in their own eyes by claiming, "I prefer to believe this truth." Truth, then, is not truth but personal preference. They believe what they prefer to believe.

How can evangelicals proclaim the gospel to people to whom the knowability of truth is not possible? This is a crisis of certainty in evangelism. The postevangelical postmodern believes that one can reach others only by the relative truth limited to oneself and others in one's community. One must abandon pursuit of universal truth that is true for all people in all time and in all places.

Postevangelicals use deconstructionism to strip texts of inherent meaning. Language is nothing but a social construct of personal perspective. Each interpreter is free to fashion meaning according to personal preference. This strips Scripture of authority and places the interpreter above the text. The interpreter does not get God's message but a personal message from the text.

The rejection of the knowability of God is a way to reject universal truth and norms. People do not like to "retain God in their knowledge" (Romans 1:28). Urge for sexual freedom and perversion correlates closely with rejection of truth (John 3:19; Romans 1). Rational arguments will not reach people who have a proclivity to reject truth. Only the convincing work of the Holy Spirit will penetrate their bias (1 Corinthians 2:4).

## Covert Claim of Rejecting Certainty

Postevangelicals who use postmodern methodology buy into pluralistic doctrine that denies others what they claim for themselves. Rejection of certainty covertly claims to know something (i.e., that you cannot know). This is an unadulterated assumption—a presupposition—about how to know. In other words, it is an act of faith. The contention that one cannot know something is an assertion incapable of proof. A more honest affirmation by the postevangelical would be that he does not believe that anyone can know truth and that he might be wrong in that belief.

Postevangelical rejection of certainty is a perversion of belief. Instead of buying into postmodernism, evangelicals would do much better to use the method of the apostle Paul in dealing with the question of truth, which we will discuss later (1 Corinthians 1:18–2:16).

## Neither Modernism nor Postmodernism

The question of certainty asks, How you can know that what you know is true? In turn, we could ask the postmodern, How can you be certain that you cannot be certain?

As modernism did not defeat Christianity, neither will postmodernism. A Christian who accepts a modernist or postmodern view of truth as the basic methodology for reaching postmoderns will undermine the truth of the Word and thus not effectively reach postmoderns. Christians cannot both accept and deny special revelation as theory laden.

Postmodernism is a wonderful opportunity for evangelism because it is self-vanquishing and challenges common sense. We will develop this more in the chapter "Reaching Those Without a Place to Stand."

Postmodernism is an indication of the bankruptcy of modernism. Postevangelicalism is an indication of the bankruptcy of present-day evangelicalism. Present-day postevangelicals are faddists who seek the novelty of cultural trends. By taking this approach, they must deny truth claims. Christian media types have great difficulty on television when the hosts asks them, "Is Jesus the only way to heaven?" and "Will Muslims or Jews not make it to heaven?" Their approach allows for no narrow gate of faith alone in Christ alone. Some of the proponents of postmodernism within "evangelicalism" are Thomas Oden, Stanley Grenz (deceased), James McClendon, Nancey Murphy, Clark Pinnock (deceased), and Robert Webber (deceased).

Postmodernism rests on the theory of probability and a posteriori approach to truth. It also rejects the correspondent view of truth. Evangelicals who abandon objective truth abandon authoritative truth. Modernism made mankind the end of mankind, whereas postmodernism seeks to dismantle the absolute nature of God. This affects everything an evangelical believes, especially revelation and certainty. Approximate knowledge of God produces a probable notion of truth. This is why postevangelicals want to renew evangelical theology.[91] Perpetual renewing or revisoning of Christianity weakens the authority of Scripture as factually true and its ability to reach all people of all time in all cultures. Post-conservatives negate propositions of Scripture for accommodation to custom. Their theology rests on the imagination.

## Individual Perspective

Radical postmoderns hold that we do all our knowing from a particular perspective and that each perspective is equally true. They do not find meaning objectively in the original intention of the writer or speaker but in the hearer's perspective of it. This might arise out of a worldview of sociology. Because we find competing ethnic and cultural perspectives in close proximity, we must reduce perspectives to the lowest common denominator for the purposes of harmony. Evangelical postmoderns want to address this issue, but in doing so they fail miserably. David Wells makes the point that individualized, private faith loses it power:

> As the nostrums of the therapeutic age supplant confession, and as preaching is psychologized, the meaning of Christian faith becomes privatized. At a single stroke, confession is eviscerated and reflection reduced mainly to thought about one's self.[92]

Wells's point is that truth adapted to culture does not transcend the individual. The modern pagan finds truth in private experience. The Christian view of truth requires us to believe in truth as absolute and not found essentially in experience, so truth transcends privatized experience. The Bible is not true simply for individuals or true for our time; it is true for all people universally and for all time.[93] The Bible stands in antithesis to the prevailing relativism of our culture. If something is true, then its opposite is false. No one can claim truth without antithesis.

Many postmoderns are afraid to assert a final or universal truth that stands in antithesis to prevailing ideas because they accept the idea that there is nothing but perspectives on truth—no one has final certainty about truth. This theory is blind to its own postmodern system for determining what is true. The idea that all theories are social constructions bites its own hand in that postmodernism is a social construction.[94] This is a vicious cycle of irrationality in its system of approaching reality. The theory by definition precludes mutually exclusive approaches to reality and thus presumes to know something about reality. All of this ties to the postmodern viewpoint on truth.

The perspective theory, when applied to morals, quickly breaks down. Does a pedophile have equivalent right to a preference to molest children as does the parent who wants to protect a child? Moral equivalence cannot stand the tests of society. In reading *A Generous Orthodoxy* by Brian McLaren, we find many politically left opinions about how we should view the world. Why should social justice be any kind of norm over any other norm if they are all perspectives? His view originates from the desire for autonomy. There are no absolutes because there is no absolute truth. Because postevangelicals have no absolutes, they cannot truly make the claim that "racism is evil." This is why certain postevangelicals wobble on issues like homosexuality.

Those who hold to truth orientation do not deny that interpreters of reality have their perspective. Culture and experience do influence our perspective or viewpoint, but it is possible to know some things truly, as we will see in later chapters.

## Sufficiency of Scripture

Bold confidence in the sufficiency of Scripture and competence of interpretation of Scripture will allow us to formulate principles for living the Christian life. This will preclude unhealthy skepticism toward Scripture.

The law of the Lord *is* perfect, converting the soul; The testimony of the Lord *is* sure, making wise the simple; The statutes of the Lord *are* right, rejoicing the heart; The commandment of the Lord *is* pure, enlightening the eyes; The fear of the Lord *is* clean, enduring forever; The judgments of the Lord *are* true *and* righteous altogether. More to be desired *are they* than gold, Yea, than much fine gold; Sweeter also than honey and the honeycomb. Moreover by them Your servant is warned, *And* in keeping them *there is* great reward. (Psalm 19:7–11)

God's communication of objective, propositional truth indicates his transcendent ability to communicate himself to people. If God cannot effectively communicate himself to man, then no one can have certainty of the truth of Jesus or of salvation but only an approximate understanding. If the Holy Spirit can communicate across time and culture, the Word will give conviction and certainty. Satan veils truth (2 Corinthians 4:4, 6). If we abandon the ability to know with certainty, then we are left to our own inventions and autonomy from God. Postevangelicals make a paradigm shift away from evangelicalism by accepting this view. There is little hope of the non-Christian coming to knowledge of truth autonomous from God's revelation.

Postevangelicals want to believe in the ancient creeds and Jesus. What is their basis for doing so? They criticize evangelicals for asserting justification by faith alone, but why should anyone believe in Jesus at all? What is the verification for that? All they have in the end is a preference for believing in Jesus. What they argue against is a degree of subjective confidence that Jesus is Lord, but why should anyone hold to that minimalist belief? There is no way to find Jesus except through extant statements in Scripture. There is little ground in postmodernism for passionate conviction, as over against the powerful propositions in extant, explicit statements of Scripture. If asked to suffer martyrdom, there is little conviction in subjective preference to do so because there is little certainty that one is right about what one believes. All the postconservative postmodern can do is live in a selected fraternity with little authority to speak outside the fraternity.

# Four

# RENOUNCING CERTAINTY

## *Rejecting Certainty*
## *via Philosophical Assumptions*

The philosophy of the twentieth century (Enlightenment) was an interpretive framework that presumed philosophy (rationalism) and science (empiricism) as the way to find truth. Twentieth-century thinkers accepted this approach to truth. This philosophy became embedded in North American society and became what we call modernism. Modernists viewed anyone who held contrary thinking to this presupposition as obscurant. Modernism produced postmodernism. Postmodernism became skeptical of modernism's promises of progress, seeing its hope for ultimate answers as red herrings and its idea of man's autonomy as a delusion. Postmoderns came to the view that modernist assumption could not fix the problems of mankind. Their conclusion was that modernism produced vacuous banality and, by the middle of the twentieth century, lost hope of solving problems in society. Another dimension is that postmoderns came to the place where they did not believe they could come to God through reason.

The essential presupposition of postconservative theology is postmodernism, whereas (despite current criticism) the presupposition of evangelicalism is not fundamental philosophical modernism. The evangelical view of modernity is not limited to accepting or rejecting its premises, for evangelicals use a broader perspective and see certain, universal (although not exhaustive) knowledge as that which God revealed in his concursive (written) and general revelation. Evangelicals rejected both modernism and the radical philosophical pluralism of postmodernism. Postconservatives argue that evangelicals are modernists, but that is a false charge; evangelicals were always skeptical of modernism.

All views of postmodernism believe that certainty ceased. Postmoderns have no ground for belief, no way to find certainty, for no authority exists outside the autonomous person. Postmodernism is a belief in self rather than in revelation. It is a belief of cynicism, a bitterness of disillusionment. Postconservatives pander to this cynicism and reject doctrinal certainty.

Pluralism holds that objective truth is inaccessible and that meaning resides not in reality but in the interpreter so that there is no normative truth for all people of all time. No one expects anyone to give a valid reason for a belief (1 Peter 3:15).

Although postconservative pluralism hesitates to give equal validity to all religions, it denies that any one religion has exclusive truth. Christianity is just a stubborn viewpoint, but it is good if it is subjectively and personally useful. All viewpoints are revisable, and so is the Bible. Postconservatives do not seek to close down Christianity but to reduce it to private viewpoint that has little bearing on culture as a whole but functions best in transforming a faith community. Authority lies in the function of the community, not in doctrines of the objective Word.

## Unending Uncertainty

Postconservatives such as Brian McLaren believe that the story is never over. He does not want to get to the place where "only we've got it right," and he has serious doubts about his own views:

> If I seem to show too little respect for your opinions or thought, be assured I have equal doubts about my own, and I don't mind if you think I'm wrong. I'm sure I am wrong about many things, although I'm not sure exactly which things I'm wrong about.[95]

Because McLaren believes that "clarity is sometimes overrated," he overtly sponsors murky obscurity.[96] He does not want to come to a conclusion about truth, for he functions on a dialectic that cannot make conclusions about truth; elsewhere he expresses antipathy toward propositional statements of Scripture. His dialectical postmodernism will not allow him to operate with propositions essentially but only with stories of personal perspective. He runs on a dialectic that cannot make conclusions about truth. The Word of God warns us about those who are "Always learning and never able to arrive at a knowledge of the truth" (2 Timothy 3: 7 ESV).

Even though McLaren rejects modernism, he is at heart a modernist because he operates on the assumption of dialectical and instrumental thought. He views religious viewpoints as "perpetually re-formable" and believes we need to "seek again and again the true path of our faith."[97]

Evangelicalism rests on the primary doctrines of the *solas*: *sola scriptura* (only Scripture), *sola Christus* (only Christ), *sola fides* (only faith), *sola gratia* (only grace), *soli Deo gloria* (only God's glory). McLaren believes that evangelicals must relinquish these *solas* for the sake of "community" among religions. Although he does not reject the *solas* outright, his dialectical method in reality washes them out.

Truth, for McLaren, is best understood "in a conversation, a dialectic (or trialectic), or dynamic tension."[98] That is why the *solas* are unnecessary in his view; they are reductionistic.[99] It is important for him to resist the "reductionist temptation to always choose only one thing over another," preferring instead to "learn to hold two or more things together when necessary."[100] As he points out, Anglicans do not hold to *sola scriptura;* rather, "Scripture is always in dialogue with tradition, reason, and experience. None of them [sic] *sola* can be the ultimate source of authority: that source is God alone, the only ultimate *sola*."[101] However, how does he know about this God other than through God's revelation? One cannot know about the specifics of God's revelation without the Word of God; general revelation is another matter.

This dialectical process causes constant uncertainty: thesis produces an antithesis, which leads to a synthesis, and that in turn becomes another thesis that has another antithesis, and on it goes. This is how McLaren can have "an element of liberalism" and "an element of evangelicalism" in his theology.[102] He claims that his generous orthodoxy is not "a simple merging, mixing, conflating, or reconciling of the two schools of thought, though. Rather it disagrees with both regarding 'the view of certainty and knowledge which liberals and evangelicals hold in common.'"[103] In other words, his essential consistency is in pluralistic postmodernism. Throughout *Generous Orthodoxy,* McLaren picks and chooses his preferences between varying viewpoints, using unadulterated subjectivism devoid of certainty.

"Dialogue" is a code word for "dialectic" among many postconservatives, who think that the worst thing that can happen among diverse peoples is for someone to hold to exclusive truth. This new kind of Christian must have an open mind to every viewpoint except to certainty. Certainty violates the code of universal interdependence. God, however, calls Christians to "separate" themselves from the world's system of thinking (2 Corinthians 6:14–18).

McLaren's dialectical process requires him to distort theology into something he would like to make it. It is difficult for him to accept didactic truth because his dialectical approach prohibits him from doing so. Because postconservatives are dialectical in their approach to truth, it is difficult for them to come to conclusion or certainty about truth. McLaren expresses his dialectical process in the nomenclature of "emergent." For him, emergence is like a tree with concentric rings that grows larger and larger yet embraces what has gone before. This integrative thinking is his presupposition for finding truth. To the contrary, the Bible is propositional and didactic in polar opposition to McLaren's dialectic. Because of his dialectical process, clarity for McLaren is "overrated."[104] Truth is always elusive for those who operate on antithesis—their fluidity goes on and on without certainty and without conclusion. This is why he can lump Protestants and Catholics together with a nice dose of Eastern mysticism.

To conclude that salvation is by Christ alone, by faith alone, by Scripture alone is somehow appalling to him, even though God set these truths in extant statements of Scripture. A "generous orthodoxy" cannot tolerate these singular truths.[105] McLaren assures his readers that emergent thinking does not reject the thinking that preceded it but enfolds or includes it. The idea is that community is a greater presupposition than a narrow-minded statement of the gospel. All this is distinction without a difference. Thus, the central thesis of *Generous Orthodoxy* rests on dialectical synthesis and false dialectics.

McLaren's dialectical thinking correlates with his literary criticism approach. Deconstruction (which states that the true meaning of a text is not necessarily the meaning that the author intended) is McLaren's tool of choice to decipher truth. Images and feelings replace words so that no one can come to any conclusion other than the conclusion of personal preference. This system has no universal truth; consequently, there is no certain good news.

McLaren admits that he is not a trained theologian. It is amazing that he has become the theological guru for many postmodern evangelicals, for his whole construct and methodology revolve around his deconstruction methodology and radical systems of interpreting literature. His bias from teaching English in secular university influences his view of Scripture and theology.

Dialectical thinking began before Socrates, but Immanuel Kant used this system of thinking to pose transcendent ideas beyond what humans might experience. He believed that certain contradictions in human thinking showed the limitations of finite person, and he did not believe that a person could have rational knowledge beyond sensory experience. A man could hold two mutually plausible alternatives at the same time. Religion was merely the practice of ethics, not belief in exclusive or certain truth.

The dialectical model asserts that the thesis (being) gives rise to its anti-thesis (non-being) which is reconciled in a synthesis (becoming). This synthesis forms a new thesis, which in turn forms a new antithesis, so the cycle continues. Although Hegel never used the term "dialectical" except once, and not in the sense of the current understanding of dialectical, new truths keep forming on this model, so there is no final truth. Dialectical thinkers deemed that contradictions were the heart of how humans should think, thus their method emphasizes contradictions to expose weakness in assumptions. They believed that we can see incompleteness of thinking by exposing these contradictions; for error is incompleteness of thought. Inadequacies of finite thought are apparent in this.

Dialectical philosophy is a philosophy of paradox: that is, the theory of posing opposites against each other to find truth that emerges from the tension. This philosophy believes that propositional truth is not enough to understand truth; rather, we need to hold truths in opposition to one another. Followers of this view do not hold that it is possible to come to a synthesis or the ability to come to faith by reason. Reconciliation of this tension comes in a subjective existential act and a leap of faith. This is the neo-orthodox position, which is where many postconservatives are heading today. We need to live in paradoxical tension of belief. The dialectical model leads to a faith that lives in paradoxes. If concludes that universal truth is not possible, that the only way to find purpose is by a non-rational leap of faith. How can a wholly transcendent God reveal himself? We can grasp truth by rising above the paradox and thereby defy rational explanation. This experiential crisis with paradox becomes a revelation of truth.

All of this rejects the *sola scriptura* of evangelicalism. Postmodern viewpoint steps out of reason and rationalism. Stepping out of rationalism is good as an essential approach to truth, but leaving reason is a problem because we then have no measurable method for distinguishing truth from error. The dialectical method might work as a sub-method for a reasoning process, but it undermines Christianity as the core reasoning process.

Dialectical reasoning changes the formula for deductive reasoning. Deductive reasoning bases its premises on agreed-upon truth and leads to knowable conclusions. Dialectical reasoning resonates with North Americans because they have culturally accepted the fallacious premise of dialectical process without examining its assumptions. They have an unexamined habit of reasoning this way; hence, it "feels" comfortable. This is why many fall into postconservatism or postevangelicalism.

The dialectic produces a philosophy of community in constant philosophical conflict. There is no end to the self-perpetuating struggle between ideas. Dialectical ideas in the end simply justify conflict of ideas. Here is a syllogism of dialectical thought:

Major premise: We can hold truth only tentatively.

Minor premise: All ideas are in conflict.

Conclusion: Therefore, we can never know final truth.

No one can call a duck a duck by the dialectical process. The dialectic presupposes a system that precludes deduction. These dialectical philosophers need a different logic from deduction because they view that only the whole is true. Every stage is partial and so partly untrue.

Aristotle gave his principles for deductive logic in the fourth century BC. His logic was about separating ideas in a deductive pattern. Dialectical philosophers change this into a dynamic movement toward the whole. Their thinking is essentially negative by its ability to show contradiction in any category. They thus challenge the logical law of non-contradiction, making it impossible to come to final conclusion about truth.

The Bible presents didactic or propositional truth that stands in stark contrast to the current system of antithesis. The didactic model and the dialectical model cannot both be true. This does not deny a legitimate dialectical process (i.e., dialogue) where people reach a common ground (not a middle ground) by eliminating false ideas together. True dialectical process is an interchange of ideas. Clarity of certain or final position is evident in propositional truth. Biblical Christianity does not have a message without it.

Carson's *Becoming Conversant with the Emerging Church* lays bare the problems of the emergent church movement. After establishing the fallacy of false antithesis between biblical revelation and experience, where people must choose between the false dichotomy of experience and truth, he concludes with a cutting censure of the emergent antithesis approach to Christianity:

> Damn all false antitheses to hell, for they generate false gods, they perpetuate idols, they twist and distort our souls, they launch the church into violent pendulum swings, whose oscillations succeed only in dividing brothers and sisters in Christ.
>
> The truth is that Jesus Christ is Lord of all—of the truth and of our experience. The Bible insists that we take every thought captive to make it obedient to Christ (2 Corinthians 10:5).
>
> If emerging church leaders wish to become a long-term prophetic voice that produces enduring fruit and does not drift off toward progressive sectarianism and even, in the worst instances, outright heresy, they must listen at least as carefully to criticisms of their movement as they transparently want others to listen to them. They need to spend more time in careful study of Scripture and theology than they are doing, even if that takes away some of the hours they have devoted to trying to understand the culture in which they find themselves. They need to take great pains not to distort history and theology alike, by not carica-

turing their opponents and not playing manipulative games. And above all, they need to embrace all the categories of the Scriptures, with the Scripture's balance and cohesion—including, as we saw in the previous chapter, what the Bible says about truth, human knowing, and related matters.[106]

## Discarding Certainty by Raw Pragmatism

In postevangelical postmodern thinking, ecumenism carries a higher value than extant statements of Scripture. It assumes that any aspect of ecclesiastical polarization is wrong and that modernism creates this polarization. Certitude is not important, for what these groups believe is not nearly as important as saving "the village which we call planet Earth."[107]

Postconservatives hold to the idea that if it works, it is right. Mission defines theology rather than theology defining mission. This undermines the nature of truth and revelation by the presupposition of instrumental or pragmatic method. Our culture rejects the idea that someone has the truth; it sees all viewpoints as merely personal perspectives and ultimately subjective. Truth then for them is private: "You have your belief and I have mine." To this generation, truth turns out to be purely pragmatic, coming from subjective, personal experience and the opinions of a given community: "If something works for me, it is right."

Our present culture (postmodernism) looks at truth as pragmatic (it is right because it works), as personal (it is how I view truth), as emerging from a community (it is our perspective), and as experiential (it is my experience). In the light of this view of truth, antipathy rises toward anyone holding to a view of mutually exclusive, objective, independent, absolute truth: Those "narrow-minded evangelicals" are the problem. How can you say that Jesus is the only way? What about Jews or Muslims? This culture scorns and ridicules those who hold to an answer because of its extremely skeptical attitude toward anyone who makes a truth claim. In the light of this prevailing viewpoint in culture, some evangelicals have developed an attitude of shame toward the gospel: It is embarrassing to believe that Jesus is the only way to heaven.

Postconservatives view absolute truth claims as anathema. The gospel for them is not informational but relational/missional. They would rather invite others to a relationship with people of the kingdom than present a certain and conclusive message. In their view, presenting the gospel as information or propositions only exasperates communication to the postmodern world. Their idea is to accommodate skepticism rather than confront it. The gospel might be true for me but not necessarily true for you. Above all, we cannot accept metanarratives (all-encompassing explanations) but we must accept narratives (finite, limited explanations of reality). Because Christians carry limited understanding about reality, they must dialogue with other religions and philosophies to attempt to understand reality. There is no certainty, only uncertainty, with these people.

William James, in *Will to Believe,* presents an idea much like the emergents'— that we are in the process of finding truth. The lure of the quest is of utmost importance, and all that remains are the variables of human opinion. All we can know for sure are the pragmatic, tentative, relative, fleeting, and mutually contradictory opinions of human beings. Postconservatives take up this thinking by replacing the "sure" Word of God with the shifting opinions of men (2 Peter 1:19). They locate authority in men rather than in God and his Word. Man's doctrine mutates; God's doctrine is eternal and certain. There is no variableness in God because he imparts an eternal, absolute view of truth. Finite man cannot find certainty in himself.

René Descartes's rationalism (modernism) doubted everything in order to erect a pyramid of certain knowledge. His system fell into the fallacy of trusting self as the source of truth—"I think, therefore, I am." Man became the measure of all things. No wonder philosophy capitulated to skepticism; rationalism failed to come to certain truth. To this belief in the sufficiency of human reason, Kant added the autonomy of the human will. Man became the franchise of truth and acted like the spider that weaves its web from its own body. No wonder the human being cannot find God by his own means. Autonomous man hems himself in by the variables of his presuppositions (narratives). The depraved viewpoint cannot find God by operation bootstraps. " And this is the judgment: the light has come into the world, and people loved the darkness rather than the light because their deeds were evil." (John 3:19 ESV)

Postmodernism also carries a pragmatic view of truth. Richard Rorty, a leading secular postmodern, follows John Dewey's instrumental view of truth and dialectical in method. By manipulating his thesis through language, he avoids logic and evidence. According to Douglas Groothuis, professor at Denver Seminary, this amounts to propaganda:

> What Rorty is trying to dignify, through his own jargon, is what historically has been called a "snow job" or a "con job." It is not an argument, because arguments seek to persuade on the basis of logic and evidence marshaled to the effect that something is true or false. Rorty speaks simply of manipulating language. This is propaganda, not argument. Nazis, communists, fascists and assorted racists have excelled in such redescriptions. Such "dialectic" may well "work," but that does not make it a proper intellectual procedure.[108]

Postmoderns self-contradict and refute their own beliefs. Their claim that beliefs are nothing more than social construction or social perspective on belief is itself a claim for truth. By asserting what it denies, postmodernism commits intellectual suicide. If there are no facts but only interpretations, then everything is a matter of relative perspective. There would be no way to arbitrate validity between perspectives. Groothuis clarifies confusion between perspective and truth: "Our perspectives only affect our sense of what is true; they do not determine truth." He shows the *reductum ad absurdum* of perspectivism: "Perspectivism reduces to a kind of collective autism: everyone has a perspective; no one has the truth; but perspectivism as an epistemology is supposedly true." Then he declares that this system devours itself: "The philosophical immolation continues."[109]

If everything is a matter of perspective or interpretation, then there are no facts upon which to base anything. Words create all reality; there is no reality other than language. Such a functional view when applied to the Bible, dislocates the essence of the more proper view of didactic truth.

There is truth to the idea that human beings have a proclivity to inject their desires and biases into interpretation, but this does not *ipso facto* preclude objective reason or careful logic by those who interpret the text with integrity. Without logic or reason, postevangelicals cannot make distinctions about their postmodern view of Christianity. They surrender the integrity of evangelical propositional truth. If we forfeit evangelical certainty of truth, then we will lose the exclusive claim of evangelicalism. Evangelicalism itself will be lost.

Postconservatives seek to submit propositional truth to something other than didactics. For them, unity becomes a universal truth to which all other "truth" must succumb. An illustration of this is the postconservatives' attempt to syncretize their beliefs with postliberals. The obstacle to that is the desire for some measure of truth; if postconservatives could minimize or reduce their doctrines to the least common denominator (a minimalist orthodoxy), then ecumenical unity could be the outcome (a recognition of pluralistic culture). This, according to them, would foster "the pursuit of truth"[110] (dialectical process) as over against conclusion of truth (didactic). To them, doctrine divides (indeed, it does). This is why Brian McLaren prefers the term "orthodox" as over against "conservative" or "evangelical." He claims that he is not a minimalist in orthodoxy because he upholds the Apostles' and Nicene Creeds, which is to beg the question.[111] He tries to maintain that "Scripture itself remains above creeds" and "new creeds are needed to give voice to the cry of faith today."[112]

Many evangelicals who, like McLaren, teach in secular universities (and secularly trained professors in evangelical schools, for that matter) have a highly pragmatic or instrumental view of truth derived from William James or John Dewey. The pragmatic view of truth holds that a belief is true only if it yields advantageous results; it is true because it works. This speculative claim assumes certain unsubstantiated theses. How do we know what is good or how do we evaluate what is true? By abandoning the correspondent truth, postmodern evangelicals appeal to Christian community. They have no certain word to those without Christ, who do not believe in the community's viewpoint. They flounder without any verifying method of coming to truth. Why should a Jehovah's Witness believe what the evangelical community has to say? Maybe the evangelical should believe the Jehovah's Witness community.

To support his own version of correct belief, McLaren titled his book *Generous Orthodoxy,* based on G. K. Chesterton's book *Orthodoxy.* But Chesterton himself assailed raw pragmatism. Douglas Groothuis quotes Chesterton, who held that one of the necessities for the human mind is "a belief in objective truth."[113] The pragmatist philosophy, according to Erickson, "makes nonsense of the human sense of actual fact."[114] Any view where truth depends on culture results in truth becoming subjective and relative. Truth must rest on factuality and correspond to reality. Note Groothuis's conclusion:

> Whenever postconservative evangelicals depart from the correspondent view of truth—which is both biblical and logical—and thus sink into the swamps of subjectivism, pragmatism, or constructivism, they should be lovingly but firmly resisted. Nothing less than the integrity of our Christian witness is at stake.[115]

An idea might work yet not be true. For the Christian, truth always transcends means.

## Incoherence of Tolerance

Many evangelicals today are in full-blown latitudinarianism and syncretism. Latitudinarianism holds a mentality of elasticity toward exclusive and certain truth. Syncretism is the attempt to combine different systems of philosophy and theology into one indistinct system. By bowing to these systems of thought, postconservatives lose their core message, not knowing what they believe for sure. This is another cycle of an old problem—infidelity to truth without unifying power.

The Church of England in the mid-seventeenth century tried to develop middle ground between religious truth and skepticism by advocating religious toleration; that ended in latitudinarianism. In other words, what they believed gave way to the least common denominator in order to encompass many beliefs. Postconservatives are latitudinarian when they want to affirm even Eastern religions. By professing to reject both absolutism and relativism, they find themselves caught in the dilemma of being either true to Scripture or true to latitudinarianism. Their answer processes through pluralism to something that lies "on the other side." A Christian should be a "welcome friend to other religions of the world, not a threat."[116] Obviously, Christians should not threaten other religions in the sense that the Crusaders did, but the Bible thoroughly attacks the idolatry of religion and its deception. The latitudinarianism of postconservatives runs counter to biblical revelation—to all of its exclusive claims. In biblical parlance, belief in other religions is idolatry. Latitudinarianism is just a mechanism for evading distinctive claims of Scripture.

Carson states that McLaren wants differences in religion to be "additive" so that he can learn from all religions. He wants to learn from Zen Buddhism because it teaches meditation, for example. Carson makes this statement about McLaren's "additive" view:

> But quite apart from the failure to address what we must do when the religions contradict one another, this merely additive approach carries a hidden set of problems. In this instance, meditation in Zen Buddhism is not conceived of as mere technique. It is integrally related to Zen's understanding of the divine, which is fundamentally alien to that of the Bible.[117]

Carson also makes the telling point that other religions of the world would find McLaren's approach insulting "because they hold that their own religious understandings are true and can be addressed respectively only by adjudicating truth claims."[118] Carson then lays a stinging indictment against McLaren's handling of truth claims:

> Regretfully, I cannot resist the conclusion that McLaren keeps ducking all the hard questions while claiming he has found a better way. I do not see how he has wrestled with the question of how abominable idolatry is to the God of the Bible. I have not found him coherent and convincing, precisely because he will not deal with the claims of truth.[119]

A fallacious current idea holds that no one individual belief is better than another, no matter how absurd, silly, immoral, or irrational it might be. This is a distorted view of tolerance. We used to understand tolerance to mean respect for other people and the positions they held, even though we disagreed. Tolerance gave opposing positions the right to disagree so that both parties differed civilly. The desire was not to suppress another viewpoint. Nevertheless, tolerance assumes disagreement; we can respect the person and his viewpoint and still engage him in public discourse. In other words, we might strongly disagree but respect the process.

Today secular postmoderns deem all viewpoints to be virtually equal in validity. Everything is permissible except the beliefs of those who claim certainty. Those who believe in objective and certain truth are the problem because the postmodern ultimate assumption of what is true is that there is no absolute truth, that relativism and subjectivism are paramount. Postconservatives want to identify closely with this position. Carson calls this "intellectually incoherent."[120] There is a huge distinction between catholicity or generosity of heart on the one hand, and tolerance of error or compromise of faith on the other. Catholicity of heart is the same as true tolerance. True tolerance comes with detection of error yet respects the person who holds that view but not the error itself. Postconservatives hold to an incoherent tolerance because they are intolerant of clarion claims of certain truth.

Postevangelicals want to reduce reality to perspectives of social groups. No group can claim certainty over other groups; postconservatives cannot tolerate an exclusive claim for certainty, and to do so would be intolerant and would be perceived to be intolerant. Christians should reduce their thinking to a personal or group story (narrative). Although they begrudgingly leave a place for truth, postevangelicals are uncomfortable with proclaiming it with authority. They reduce truth to its least common denominator, issuing an anemic Christianity. They cannot handle truth very well but cave in to secular postmodern culture. They have great difficulty in proclaiming truth the way Scripture proclaims truth (1 Corinthians 2:1–4).

If we cannot assert that other viewpoints are wrong, then we would bankrupt truth of God's revelation. If there were no place for truth claims, we would end in belief bankruptcy. Pluralism is a mechanism for imposing uniformity upon all beliefs. Postconservatives claim that Christianity is superior to other religions, yet they cannot assert a basis for that belief because of their reluctance to fix truth claims. Judgment is necessary even for them. They must assert the "truth" that we cannot know truth as certain. A deep-rooted myth among postevangelicals is that tolerance is neutral about truth. What passes for tolerance among them is not tolerance whatsoever, but rather cowardice that hides behind the myth of truth neutrality. They are even afraid to employ obvious extant statements of Scripture.

This tolerance is intolerant, but truth changes our approach to the nature of tolerance. We accept our medical doctor's conclusion when told that we have cancer and need surgery. Why do we not accept the advice of a psychic healer?

It is a matter of credentials and certification. There is a definite distinction between belief and truth. To believe sincerely in the psychic does not make the psychic's conclusions valid. This belief will not change facts that the surgeon found. The question is one of who is trustworthy. It is not narrow minded to believe in factual credibility.

Tolerance of behavior is a different matter. Society does not tolerate all behavior; it has certain limits. North American culture does not accept murder as a proper norm and generally views adultery as wrong. However, ironically, those who hold to exclusive an viewpoint are not tolerated, and postmoderns extend little tolerance toward those with the "bigoted, narrow-minded" idea that some ideas are heretical. In a 1987 address at Duke University, Ted Koppel, formerly of ABC's *Nightline*, established the need for drawing clear lines in the sand:

> We have actually convinced ourselves that slogans will save us. Shoot up if you must, but use a clean needle. Enjoy sex whenever and with whomever you wish; but wear a condom. No! The answer is no. Not because it isn't cool or smart or because you might end up in jail or dying in an AIDS ward, but no because it's wrong, because we have spent 5,000 years as a race of rational human beings, trying to drag ourselves out of the primeval slime by searching for truth and moral absolutes. In its purest form truth is not a polite tap on the shoulder. It is a howling reproach. What Moses brought down from Mt. Sinai were not the Ten Suggestions.[121]

Today even mission organizations try to negotiate away from truth by the syncretism of biblical truth with culture. Some evangelical missions attempt to fit Christianity into national religions such as Hinduism, Buddhism, or Islam to contextualize the gospel culturally with given countries. The World Council of Churches accepted religious beliefs such as Hinduism, Buddhism, and Christianity. This is an easy step for Eastern religions but a very difficult step for Christianity, if one believes the revelation of Scripture as exclusive truth.

Brian McLaren protests exclusivist claims of truth as elitism. He maintains that evangelicals say, "We're the only ones who have it right."[122] His idea of authenticity is to not make claims of certainty. He then asserts that we do not want to "lower our standards of authentic discipleship," but rather "raise our standards of Christ-like acceptance."[123] McLaren is employing pure exploitation; the issue is not about "discipleship" but about truth. He reasons by false dichotomy. This attempt at syncretism undermines the truthfulness of the Word of God. Jesus himself was very divisive when it came to truth. He even called religionists of his day children of the devil (John 8:44). Division over truth and the Word of God is a wonderful and glorious defense of God and his Word. This does not excuse slanting a perspective on truth without logical, rational, or biblical justification. No one could charge Jesus with supercilious hubris when he unapologetically claimed to be "the way, the life, and the truth" (John 14:6). There is a place for drawing a line in the sand biblically. Aristotle argued that mutually exclusive or contradictory statements cannot be true at the same time (logic of the law of non-contradiction).

## Catering to Uncertainty

The current emergent idea of the kingdom is that we can change the world by Christian socialism. This view of the kingdom equates to social justice, demotes the millennial kingdom to something irrelevant, and promotes a present kingdom concocted from eisegesis of Scripture. Emergent thinkers want to see youth correct injustices and poverty in the world with a method of evangelism that does not communicate the gospel. Bob DeWaay, a senior pastor in Minneapolis, Minnesota, says, "The Emergent Church movement is an association of individuals linked by one very important, key idea: that God is bringing history toward a glorious kingdom of God on earth without future judgment."[124]

Acceptance of inerrant Scripture is a problem to postconservatives; accordingly they do not make a stand on the inspired, inerrant, infallible, unadulterated Word of God. They compromise the Word of God in lieu of a utilitarian, pragmatic, functional approach. Brian McLaren equates divine authorship of Scripture with human authorship in a dual origin of authorship.[125] Nowhere in Scripture do we find the "dual origin" of truth that makes tradition and the Word of God equivalent.

The emergent church is missional; that is, it is a faith community that does not hold fast to a body of doctrines. It derives its belief from inside the community; this emphasizes belonging to a faith community as the priority rather than holding to a set of propositions or doctrines. The missional approach uses the incarnational idea that as Jesus walked among us to effect social change, so the church should do the same. People become Christians by association with the church rather than by the proclamation of the church. Emergent thinking is reluctant to proclaim the certainty of truth such as the objective gospel, believing it is better for non-Christians to absorb Christianity subjectively in order to see it "authentically." Christianity can by this "emerge" from the community.

Postmodern evangelicals also change other essential doctrines to adapt to a postmodern worldview. They question the nature of the Bible as the primary source of revelation by adding another source of authority; for them, Scripture came by "God's creation and the creation of dozens of people and communities and cultures who produced it."[126] The classical evangelical view holds that God spoke as the Holy Spirit moved authors of Scripture to write it down under his superintendence (2 Peter 1:20, 21). Thus, the Bible "alone" (*sola*) is God's ultimate authority; God's truth does not equate to the Bible plus tradition, the Bible plus community, or the Bible plus anything else. Radical emergent rejection of evangelical belief in the area of inspiration makes people the final arbiter of truth. This scheme flies in the face of the idea that "man shall not live by bread alone but by every word that proceeds from the mouth of God" (Matthew 4:4).

Because postmodern evangelicals can identify little with certainty, social justice is the true core of emergent belief. The norm for this conclusion is personal experience and the pragmatic view of truth, but knowing which experience or which practice has validity is impossible without absolute truth. Following the theological trail of liberals, the message for them is justice on earth.[127] However, the gospel is about eternal life, not temporal life or social justice.

Emergent twisting of the truth of the gospel into socialism and social justice is an attempt to change the gospel into a pluralistic message that accommodates everyone and quashes Jesus' claim to mutually exclusive truth (John 14:6). A panacean gospel of love is a selected or preferred gospel, a gospel of personal creation is a custom-designed gospel from culture. Like designer clothes, we now have a designer gospel situated for those who cannot tolerate a pure gospel. A mutated gospel requires a select gospel, a generalized gospel, a non-offensive gospel, a gospel from wolves in sheep's clothing. Postevangelicals do this to "suit" the "passions" of their hearers. "For the time is coming when people will not endure sound teaching, but having itching ears they will accumulate for themselves teachers to suit their own passions, and will turn away from listening to the truth and wander off into myths." (2 Timothy 4:3, 4 ESV)

Postconservatives cater to mutated forms of Christianity instead of the pure biblical message. They heed secular postmoderns' protests against the biblical gospel that says, "I cannot accept the idea that someone has to pay for my sin; that is offensive to me. I cannot believe in a God who sends people to hell." Some postmodern evangelicals worry about those who accept a God who sends people to hell and who sacrifices his Son to die for the sins of others.

Postmodern evangelicals adapt the gospel to the comfort zone of cultural preference by disregarding the God who confronts sinners to accept the finished work of Christ. Thus, these people carefully select what they preach; they talk about love and grace, and they neglect large sections of Scripture dealing with the whole counsel of God. They want a prissy and banal god who does not offend the sensitivities of postmodern thinking (unless, of course, it is something like egregious pedophilia). Their answer is to mutate the gospel, to accommodate it to the preferences of those who would play god and stand in judgment over the Bible.

People can formulate this hybrid gospel only by neglecting great sections of Scripture that deal with the nature of gospel certainty. They selectively take from Scripture only the portions dealing with God's mercy and love, and they neglect portions dealing with judgment and hell. They make Jesus into a sweet, sentimental, and caring social worker who deals with issues of justice. They reduce Jesus to the kind of person who does "nice" things for others, especially those who are the subject of injustice. By doing this, they ignore the idea that Jesus condemned the Pharisees in very caustic terms. He called them children of the devil because they did not have truth (John 8:44), hypocrites, blind guides, fools, whitened sepulchers, serpents, and a generation of vipers. That does not sound like a prissy Jesus to me, but this is what postconservatives would have us believe. Jesus even had the temerity to say that they could not escape the damnation of hell (Matthew 13). Postconservative ameliorators obviate Jesus' extant statements about hell (Matthew 10:28), and neglect his caustic judgment on religion (Matthew 23; John 8:44) and sin. They can do this only by neglecting great sections of Scripture, formulating a theology of their own making. Francis Schaeffer in *The Great Evangelical Disaster* made the point that this amounts to accommodation of truth to culture. This is accommodation of truth rather than accommodation of method.

David Wells warns against losing the evangelical message in the tactical maneuver to get the gospel a hearing. Evangelists who try to be contemporary to the point of changing the message ultimately lose the message:

> Inevitably, those enamored by its contemporaneity will find that with each new tactical repositioning they are drawn irresistibly into the vortex of what they think is merely contemporary but what, in actual fact, also has the power to contaminate their faith. What they should be doing is thinking strategically, not tactically. To do so is to begin to see how ancient this spirituality actually is and to understand that beneath many contemporary styles, tastes, and habits there are also encountered rival *worldviews*. When rival worldviews are in play, it is not adaptation that is called for but confrontation: confrontation not of a behavioral kind which is lack in love but of a cognitive kind which holds forth "the truth in love" (Ephesians 4:15). This is one of the greatest lessons learned from the early Church. Despite the few who wobbled, most of its leaders maintained with an admirable tenacity the alternative view of life which was rooted in the apostolic teaching. They did not allow love to blur truth or to substitute for it but sought to live by both truth and love.[128]

Above all, postconservatives do not want to be "judgmental," so they hide the exclusive gospel and the certain nature of the gospel from their listeners. They apply a "pick and choose" method to the Bible by masking what the Word of God has to say fully about a subject. They create doctrines of their own making by selecting Scripture portions that current culture prefers for pluralistic civility. Yet Jesus was very judgmental, so postconservatives carry a distorted view of judgment. The Bible never condemns judgment of facts but judgment of motive. To call an apple tree an apple tree because there are apples hanging from a tree is not judgmental. That simply judges or assesses the fact. To impugn motives without facts to document the assertion is judgmental, but Jesus based his judgment on patent fact.

Some evangelicals cater to pluralistic sensitivities to such a degree that they themselves are willing to be evangelized by other religions![129] This is an attempt to establish an inclusive model in evangelicalism as over against presenting an exclusive gospel model. Postconservatives deem that we must find what is true in other religions and then go back to Scripture to see if we interpret God's Word properly. We must go to Buddhists to be truly inclusive and see them as children of God, but the Bible calls them children of the devil. This radical redefinition of the gospel works against the true gospel. The true gospel is the conviction that there is no salvation apart from Jesus (Acts 4:12). This is an exclusivist message:

> *Enter by the narrow gate. For the gate is wide and the way is easy that leads to destruction, and those who enter by it are many. For the gate is narrow and the way is hard that leads to life, and those who find it are few.* (Matthew 7:13, 14 ESV)

> *Whoever believes in him is not condemned, but whoever does not believe is condemned already, because he has not believed in the name of the only Son of God.* (John 3:18 ESV)

> *Remember that you were at that time separated from Christ, alienated from the commonwealth of Israel and strangers to the covenants of promise, having no hope and without God in the world.* (Ephesians 1:12 ESV)

> *For there is one God, and there is one mediator between God and men, the man Christ Jesus, who gave himself as a ransom for all, which is the testimony given at the proper time.* (1 Timothy 1:5, 6 ESV)

> *Whoever has the Son has life; whoever does not have the Son of God does not have life.* (1 John 5:12 ESV)

> *And if anyone's name was not found written in the book of life, he was thrown into the lake of fire.* (Revelation 20:15 ESV)

Exclusive teaching was scandalous to the polytheism (pluralism) of the first century, just as it is to those who try to make Christianity relevant today by changing its exclusive message. Diversity is the shibboleth of the postmodern age. No one has the answer, so we have to learn from the whole spectrum and plurality of diversity. Every idea is "open" to dialogue. Relativism is necessary to openness and is the pivotal virtue upon which all else rests. Because diversity requires openness, it is a necessary condition for relativism. Multiplicity of viewpoint is incompatible with objective and certain truth, so no one can claim normative truth. This approach rests on the assumption that relativism is necessary to openness and that relativism is the only acceptable virtue to our times. Objective truth in Christianity does not fit this model. The relative assumption requires us to view competing truth claims uniformly. No one can know truth with certainty, so we must be open to all viewpoints, and Christianity cannot be exclusively true.

Postconservatives court evangelicals by manipulation. Many evangelicals are so vacuous about the Bible that they do not recognize the error of postmodern evangelicalism. Their thinking is that if a person shows passion about something, then it must be real. No doubt, passion is an indication of integrity, but there is more to discernment than passion. To hold to the single criterion that passion is the way to determine truth is to put evangelicals in great danger. Many cults display great passion for their followers, but their true interest is power lust. They use religious means to satisfy their hunger for power. False teachers fawn over people to get their attention (Galatians 4:15, 16; 2 Corinthians 11:13–15). The Galatians went from one extreme of wanting to give their eyes for Paul to the other extreme of treating him as an enemy, and all because he told them the truth (Galatians 4:15, 16).

 It is a precarious business to tell the truth, the whole truth, and nothing but the truth. Paul desired to be with the Galatians so that he could rebuke them with the proper tone. He wanted to adapt his voice to the true situation. It is always wise for leaders to understand the context in dealing with a problem situation. The Galatian relapse into legalism perplexed Paul, and he was at loss to find an adequate reason for their leaving the grace principle for legalism (Galatians 1:6–7). Good leadership does not rush into doctrinal error like a bull in a china shop but seeks to understand the context of the problem and adapt the tone to the situation. It is difficult to speak truth to those in error (4:16).

# PREFERENCE
# FOR PERSPECTIVE

## *Perspective from Self Precludes Certainty*

Our human capacity to come to certainty will never, on its own, allow us to find ultimate truth. The human perspective on certainty can be seen in literary quotes by famous personages: "Man is the measure of all things" (Protagoras); "In this world nothing is certain but death and taxes" (Benjamin Franklin); "Certainty generally is illusion" and "Certitude is not the test of certainty" (Oliver Wendell Holmes, Jr.); "The only certainty is that nothing is certain" (Pliny the Elder); "Doubt is not a pleasant condition, but certainty is an absurd one" (Voltaire).[130]

### Human Perspective versus Divine Viewpoint

Postconservatives want to believe a Christianity of uncertainty. McLaren, through the character Neo in *A New Kind of Christian,* argues that authority is dynamic as over against static, and that absolute authority is a modern invention. Neo creates a false antithesis between objectivity and omniscience.[131] Because Christians cannot have absolute objectivity (omniscience), they cannot adequately understand the Bible.

Jesus himself rebuked those who misinterpreted the Scripture (Matthew 5:17–48). McLaren in effect denies objectivity of absolute truth found in the inspiration of Scriptures. Certainty is "overrated" for him.[132] He is in a constant state of pursuit but never arrives at truth.[133] He is in "lifelong pursuit of expanding thinking and deepening, broadening opinions about God."[134] Because the Bible is unclear, multiple viewpoints hold virtually equal validity. He reduces all interpretation of Scripture to personal perspective. In other words, he reduces Bible doctrines to "opinion," and thus negates the authority of Scripture.

## Certainty ~ A Place to Stand

In a later book, McLaren declares that there are indeed areas where he can speak clearly: "In one of my previous books, I said that clarity is sometimes overrated and that intrigue is correspondingly undervalued. But here I want to say—clearly—that it is tragic for anyone, especially anyone affiliated with the religion named after Jesus, not to be clear about what Jesus' message actually was."[135]

Yet the message McLaren wants to be clear about is a social gospel. The secret message is a message about his peculiar view of the "kingdom." This kingdom message relates more to the social gospel of early twentieth-century liberalism. He avoids the extant, clear message of the saving gospel—belief in the death of Christ to pay for our sins. In doing this, he obscures patent clarity of Scripture. John MacArthur puts it pointedly: "By overturning the historical understanding of Scripture with a new, secret message of Jesus, McLaren has again under-mined the clarity of Scripture. Only a Bible that is impossibly ambiguous can fit McLaren's neo-gnostic model."[136]

McLaren claims that he does not hold to absolute relativism or assert that truth is a construct of language. However, he makes the point that, although absolutes exist, we cannot declare them unequivocally and with certainty. Incomplete knowledge of the transcendent God creates uncertainty. This is the essence of his generous orthodoxy. His view of orthodoxy has to do with humility directed toward certainty about truth. Because we cannot be certain about too much, we need to pull our punches about proclaiming certain truth. A generous orthodoxy cannot claim too much and it "walks with a limp."[137]

In the end, McLaren believes very little that has substance in Christianity because relativism prevails in his system. McLaren sees this as a benefit in reaching postmoderns, but in doing so he undermines the clarity, conviction, and certainty of Scriptures. Certainty stems from clarity. G. K. Chesterton makes a salient point about humility toward truth:

> But what we suffer from to-day is humility in the wrong place.
> Modesty has moved from the organ of ambition. Modesty has settled
> upon the organ of conviction; where it was never meant to be. A man
> was meant to be doubtful about himself, but undoubting about the truth;
> this has been exactly reversed. Nowadays the part of a man that a man

does assert is exactly the part he ought not to assert himself. The part he doubts is exactly the part he ought not to doubt — the Divine Reason.[138]

McLaren's viewpoint holds such subjectivity and relativism that certainty is not possible. No one is supposed to hold objective truth because tolerance trumps truth. It is a denial of the clarity and certainty of Scripture, and ultimately of the authority of Scripture. Sadly, it denies the exclusive and universal truth claim of Christianity.

The Bible calls this anti-exclusive attitude idolatry (Exodus 20:3–6). Christianity presents itself as exclusive—"No one comes to the Father except through me" (John 14:6), and "There is salvation in no one else, for there is no other name under heaven given among men by which we must be saved" (Acts 4:12). These verses violate the central thesis of postmodernism that no one has universal and exclusive truth. Postconservatives accommodate this truth to the alien philosophy of postmodernism.

## Man Reduced to Finite Perspective

Loss of certainty about God and about truth in general produced the belief that all beliefs are perspectives. This conclusion precludes the pursuit of ends and exists only for the means. A means-oriented belief is ultimately rigid pragmatism, an orientation that views all of life through this framework or grid. This pragmatic nihilism rejects ultimate truth and the idea of decisive certainty about truth. Everything disconnects because there is no certainty or ultimate end. People become lost in hedonistic, fragmented autonomous humanity. The postmodern self has lost substance and content.

Postmodern evangelicals now buy into this non-significant self. The core of the therapeutic evangelical self operates solely on surface and style. The surface is the substance for them. They have swung from truth that produces character to inane therapeutic personality. We find trust in self under this thesis. It is a fragmented self, devoid of universal certainty.

Postevangelicals are lost in a morass of syncretism along with their secular postmodern colleagues. That is why they cannot come to conclusions about certainty. They desperately seek to hold onto vestiges of Christianity without any basis except subjectivism. That is why they are irrationalists. Although

John R. Franke denies this in the preface to Brian McLaren's *A Generous Orthodoxy*, he claims "redescriptions and proposals concerning the understanding of rationality and knowledge."[139] He asserts that postmodernism produces a "more inherently self-critical view of knowledge than modernity."[140] This entirely overlooks the idea that evangelicals are not modernists as he supposes, but that they took the best from modernity without accepting modernism's essential presuppositions.

McLaren wants to deny nihilism and relativism, but he does not a have a means to do so. Orthodoxy to McLaren is something within the power of the individual, but no one can "own God" by asserting anything for sure. This is a premise of *A Generous Orthodoxy*. Various traditions reflect on God from varying viewpoints. None of them can claim exclusive truth. He wants all viewpoints to have some salutary advantage.

Ultimately, postconservatives are their own authority, so they must clear orthodoxy of any static absolutes. They do not rest their case on authority of Scripture. Orthodoxy for McLaren is opinion, not doctrine; it is "a way of seeing and seeking, a way of living, a way of thinking and loving and learning that helps what we believe become more true over time, more resonant with the infinite glory that is God."[141] His fatal flaw is that he views theology from what is important to his experience, not from extant statements of Scripture. However, the evangelical view is that Christians do not need to have absolute truth in themselves, but that they find it from God through the Scriptures.

By assuming postmodernism, McLaren embraces relativism at the cost of clarity about the Word of God, and eccentrically accommodates elements from all forms of Christianity. His glue of belief pivots around the Apostles' and Nicene Creeds. Yet, he denies propositional truth and affirms narrative "truth." But the question of authority remains: Are not the creeds based on the Bible itself? Brian McLaren does not distinguish reason from rationalism in modernism. Although he claims that he is not an irrationalist, his book is replete with subjectivism, experientialism, anti-reason, and anti-logic. Is not this irrationalism?

There is an embracing of irrationalism among evangelicals today in face of the fact that the biblical view of truth is objective and propositional. Whether people hold to the correspondent, coherent, pragmatic, or performative view of truth, they all believe that truth is propositional. Even the coherentists (whose view restricts truth of sentences to agreement with most other beliefs) understand that propositions must be logically consistent. The more biblical correspondent view of truth (which holds that the facts must agree with the statements) insists that propositions must agree with one another. The pragmatic view (the notion that meaning is determined by practical consequences) says that propositions become true when practiced, and the performative view of truth (which introduces emotivism in moral philosophy) claims that a proposition is true by assent to that proposition. Yet today many deny that truth is propositional, which results in the gibberish of mysticism. Mysticism does not require propositional truth but operates in the realm of subjectivism. No theological or doctrinal distinction is required here. What valid message from God is there in this? Zero. Mysticism has no content, so it is an irrational approach to Christianity. True biblical Christianity sets itself in antithesis to other religions.

## Perspective from Self Cannot Arrive at Certainty

Postconservatives prefer dialectical "personal knowledge"[142] as the way of practicing life instead of didactic propositions forming principles for living from the Word of God. This is unmodified experience again. It is something someone must "feel."[143] "If you ask, 'how do you know that?—the only answer can be, 'I don't know; I just know!'"[144] This is old liberal thinking from the nineteenth and early twentieth centuries. That which comes around goes around. Heresies do not seem to die. It also looks like neo-orthodoxy (that truth is not truth until you experience it). No, the only possible way we can know Jesus is through propositional statements from the apostles. Application of principles formed out of propositions and narrative literature from God's Word is God's method for living.

Stanley Grenz buys into the antithetical approach (dialectical) as well. He believes that either we know something exhaustively (omnisciently) or it is nothing more than a social construction. No one can assure us that this social construction of knowledge connects with reality; it is conditional and partial because we are finite. He wants to draw a dichotomy between knowing everything and knowing nothing. Evangelicals have never claimed to know everything, but this is the position Grenz wants to impose on the debate.

To suggest that evangelicals cannot escape their cultural understanding of what they believe is to make an assertion about what the Scriptures deny. The Bible asserts that we can be certain about what we know, as we will see in the next chapter. It is true that we are finite and our knowledge is therefore partial; however, this does not mean that we cannot know something truly. Obviously, we cannot know anything omnisciently even in eternity, because we will still be finite even then. We can know truly without knowing exhaustively with omniscient certainty. We can know absolutes so long as the absolutes are those from the Word and not our personal knowledge. Obviously, no belief system can capture God in a creed or doctrinal statement, but that is not the same as not knowing something truly, albeit not exhaustively.

Christians can know some things with certainty. Evangelicals know the difference between absolute objectivity (not possible except for God) and mediated objectivity, which allows us to know what is possible to know. Would God give us a Bible we could not understand? The nature of the Bible declares certainty of truth. The separation of biblical inspiration from biblical authority is an error of massive magnitude.

Note D. A. Carson's stinging critique of Grenz's neglect to interact with extensive literature in this regard: "Quite frankly, it is shocking that Grenz does not engage this very substantial literature. He has bought into simplistic antithesis, and he never questions it. This leads him to a merely faddish treatment of science."[145]

Carson also says Grenz cannot bring himself to truth because he is "hoodwinked by that one untenable antithesis."[146] Grenz must cast a blind eye to the myriad Scriptures that proclaim truth. This is because postmodernism "has snookered him."[147]

McLaren says, "[I am] a Christian because I have confidence in Jesus Christ—in all his dimensions. . . . I trust Jesus. I think Jesus is right because I believe God was in Jesus in an unprecedented way."[148] This is unadulterated subjectivism. On what basis does he have confidence in Jesus? His answer is, "Through Jesus I have entered into a real, experiential relationship with God as Father, and I have received God's Spirit in my life. I have experienced the love of God through Jesus."[149] He knows this because of experience, not because of objective truth. Later he says, "This is why, for starters, I am a Christian: the image of God conveyed by Jesus as the Son of God, and the image of the universe that resonates with this image of God best fits my deepest experience, best resonates with my deepest intuition, best inspires my deepest hope."[150] This is also pure subjectivity—God must measure up to human expectations.

Again, McLaren denies that John 14:6 (where Jesus says that he is the way, the truth, and the life and no one comes to the Father except through him) is an exclusive statement, but that is exactly what it is. His rationale for the man Jesus as an "inclusive" Jesus is that his life and message "resonated with acceptance."[151] That is bald falsity. It is amazing how he selectively excludes what he does not prefer about Jesus. The three paragraphs following this in McLaren's text of *A Generous Orthodoxy* are expressions of "sympathy" for this group or that. This is unadulterated, maudlin, mawkish sentimentalism. To him, tolerance rests on sympathy. Jesus had no sympathy for the moneychangers but lashed them with whips and threw them out like stray cats. At the heart of McLaren's thinking is an unbiblical view of love; postevangelical love is romantic, sentimental love. It is philosophy based on feelings. Feelings justify subjective love. This is a far cry from biblical love.

## Spirituality—Sublimating the Self for Certainty

The basis for the postconservative argument rests on the assumption that the self is the starting point for knowing. This is solipsism. The independence of the self and its individualism autonomous from truth outside of self is at the heart of postmodern presupposition. Psychological preference over objective truth is the issue. For postconservatives, there is little reality outside the self and its relationships. The right of the self stands at the center of reality, for self-discovery is the core of this philosophy, which resists doctrine or revealed truth from God. Absolutes and the norms or standards that flow from those absolutes are barriers to this belief system, as David Wells demonstrates clearly:

> This, then, is spirituality of those on the move, those who live in the interstices of the postmodern world, those who know its rhythms, its demands, and the punishments which it inflicts on any who are unwilling to shift as it shifts, those who will not change as it changes, those who look askance at expediency. This is spirituality, then, that is

contemporary as is contemporary society but, in other ways, as ancient as the world is ancient.[152]

Character according to the Bible is an ability to operate on principles derived from the Word of God regardless of what others think. That character involves giving to and living for others. Postmodernism changed that definition of character to acceptance of and accommodation to other beliefs to gain approval. This is at the heart of postconservative orientation. Note again Wells's assessment of postmodern eclectic spiritual ethos:

> With its individualism, its wholly privatized understanding, its therapeutic interest, its mystical bent, its experimental habits, its opposition to truth as something which mediates the nature of an unchanging spiritual realm, its anti-institutional bias, its tilt toward the East, its construction of reality, and its can-do spirit, it is something which is emerging from the very heart of the postmodern's world. This is, in fact, the postmodern soul. And its ancient forerunner was seen in gnosticism.[153]

Postmodernism emptied itself of certainty of truth and put in its place an ethos of subjective, ethereal spirituality. Postconservative postmoderns fell into this ethos when evangelicals vacated propositional truth. They also moved into a mode of therapeutic spirituality where they put great emphasis on the self, subjectivism, and a radical form of relevance. Evangelicals revisited the old experiential liberalism of the early part of the twentieth century. This therapeutic experiential subjectivism aligns closely with Eastern religions such as Buddhism and Hinduism. Postmodern decay of Christianity, with the arrival of many Eastern religions into North American, set the context for this ethos. With this trend beginning in the 1960s, and exploding in the twenty-first century, many non-Christians claim some form of spirituality. They prefer spirituality to organized religion and especially doctrine formulated by propositions.

Postevangelicals seized on this market but had to trim their doctrinal sails to do so. Because spirituality in culture was internal and private, postconservatives jettisoned objective doctrine that stands independent from the self. They avoided doctrine in favor of mystical experience. Many so-called evangelicals read horoscopes, believe in reincarnation, reject absolute truth as well as exclusive salvation, and believe that other religions contribute to genuine spirituality. They avoid universal truth claims by leaning on postmodern thought. Truth is the culprit because it divides. Spirituality that is personal and experiential can pick and choose what to believe without the messy process of discovering what is true or consistent with fact. It is a spirituality that relates to self rather than to God's objective propositions.

## Mysticism—Escape from Certainty

Because there is strong rejection of propositional revelation, the emergent church has entered into mysticism. There is a major paradigm shift from what God has said to what the individual subjectively feels.

Propositional teaching is a problem for postconservatives because it is objective, not subjective. Subjective mysticism is the postconservative answer to propositional truth and preaching. Mysticism attempts to connect to God directly by subjective experience rather than indirectly through objective Scripture. Postconservative mysticism contains "precious little expository prose" because postconservatives deem that only the mystic can enter the non-prose world. [154] They believe that to teach the Bible by addressing the mind is something mechanical. According to them, the Bible is a story that appeals to the emotions rather than to the mind, which in their view is modernism. The mystical better addresses the postmodern mind. McLaren sponsors the "hesychastic tradition, which discovers God in silence"[155]—part of Eastern Orthodox monastic practice. Mysticism does "not claim too much."[156]

Bob DeWaay says that rejection of Scripture as a way to get to truth produces "freestyle spirituality." He gets to the heart of mysticism with this statement:

> Emergent leaders have embraced mysticism—where truth is *experienced* rather than understood. By making truth an experience, the Emergent have liberated themselves from the "constraining" interpretations of flawed and narrow-minded Christian theologians. If words don't convey meaning but spiritual experiences do, language and thinking serve only as a springboard into mysticism.[157] (Italics in original.)

The issue of certainty is impacted by this thinking. If there is no absolute, universal truth, there is no certainty. A society that rejects the possibility of truth cannot find universal truth and certainty. The presuppositions of pluralism and relativism preclude the possibility of absolute truth. There is only private perspective and personal story: "You might be a Christian. I am glad, but I don't personally need it." This produces loneliness because people are lost in themselves and have no transcendent truth to believe. Spirituality of this sort restructures human nature into the self. Many churches today focus on spirituality without content, and experience without truth. They have vacated the mandate to build mature believers by understanding principles of biblical truth and encouraging believers to apply those principles to experience.

There is much spiritual superficiality today in evangelical churches. We have paid the price for abandoning doctrine. Much of so-called Christianity is hardly recognizable as Christian or biblical. Postconservative postmoderns do not know what they believe or even how to get to the place of certainty. All they have is experience without substance, which results in vacuous emptiness and uncertainty about what they believe.

Emergent churches are no longer distinctively certain about what they now believe and are ashamed of what they have believed. If they do not claim certainty for what they believe, they no longer differ from other perspectives, especially secular postmodern spiritualities. All roads do indeed look as though they lead to Rome with this theology. This emergent spirituality can no longer view Christianity as uniquely true or carrying privileged information from God. Emergent spirituality leaves the exclusive Word of God for an inclusive spirituality that would have been unimaginable to the mid-twentieth-century evangelical. Who would have imagined that some evangelicals would turn back to Gnosticism to find a mystical power in the subterranean self? Fallacious spirituality misses the point that God is transcendent and that we cannot find him in the self. God demands exclusive loyalty. We cannot find God's uniqueness in the god within.

This new spiritually is not formal in its Eastern religious orientation, but it does have a vague Eastern structure. The essence of this construction is personal consciousness. It is transformation by personal potential from the god lying deep within the self. This inner god stands in polar opposition to the transcendent God of the universe. The transcendent God reveals himself in extant terms written in the Word of God. His truth claims draw clear lines between the false and the true. Postmodern spirituality causes no division because it makes no claim to exclusive truth. Truth is for the individual, not applied to a crosscut population. The unifying principle in modern spirituality is to find connection to what the individual finds immanent within the self. True spirituality operates with doctrinal constraints and does not center in the self as a source for truth.

Early Gnosticism was pagan in its presupposition. The new spirituality of our day is not exactly parallel to the incipient Gnosticism of the New Testament, but Gnosticism does have its parallels to the spirituality of today. Ancient Gnosticism fermented in a time of immense uncertainty when philosophical structures of Rome were failing. Gnosticism became an escape or sublimation for lack of definite viewpoint. Loss of certainty in truth always causes dissonance. Dissonance is psychological disequilibrium, so people seek stability in self during times of discord. Hedonism is a result of finding self in self, losing truth, and failing to submit to the authority of that truth. The self as god does not submit to authority outside itself because the self is ultimate authority.

This radical subjectivism is difficult to challenge by those who are truth oriented because the prevailing culture runs counter to it. Radical subjective self in postmodernism "feels" more right than objective truth. This might be why *The Da Vinci Code* had such great appeal. Gnosticism is self-centered redemption. This self-knowledge operates in a revelatory way because self-knowledge is the object that offers insight into the self. It is knowledge (*gnosis*) of the divine through self. The more choices the self has, the less uncertainty there is. The greater the randomness and unpredictability we experience, the greater the uncertainty we experience. Because people deny objective truth, absolute truth, transcendent truth, they must turn to the solitary self, tossed like so much flotsam and jetsam upon an ocean of uncertainty. There is no polestar to give direction. Like pagans of old who did not believe in one God but in many gods, those who operate from the self-contained assumption do not have a unified field of knowledge and have no unified ethic. All ethics are relative to their individual gods. Today, as well, there is no ethic but the ethic of personal preference, the ethic of manifold individuals.

## Objectivity—the Core of Certainty

A biblical Christian, on the other hand, knows an absolutely righteous God who operates on unchanging absolutes. As a God of unconditional love and unaltered grace, he gives hundreds of promises and propositions of truth to those declared righteous as God is righteous. To be ignorant of these biblical truths is to miss much of what the Christian life is all about. The only way we can become cognizant of these things is by divine revelation of a body of truth known only by divine inspiration. Evangelicals today chuck these truths into the bin of irrelevance.

Christianity is not just our preference, something we like or want to experience. The idea that I prefer theism over atheism is a maudlin notion rather than a rational or logical idea. Because Christianity is true as over against false (the law of non-contradiction), I believe it. Why should anyone want to believe our preference as over against their preference if truth is not the mediator? The issue is not to make Christianity more likeable, pleasant, or nice. Rather, Christianity presents itself as true, and it is certain that it is true. If we choose the idea that Christianity is more likeable, we must take an entertainment approach, which ends in preference. If we accept that Christianity rests on truth, then we can appeal to truth. Christianity is a worldview, not something that turns us on. To appeal to preference is to rest belief on the falsity of shifting sands. To appeal to truth is to advocate for God. The true presupposition is God, not man; we need to keep in mind God's omniscient preference. This involves drawing the distinction of what God views as truth and what man believes is true. A human viewpoint of the world is limited in counterdistinction to God's omniscient view of the world.

Biblical Christian living always begins with God's revelation and not the self. Modern spirituality is essentially experiential. Its legitimacy comes through therapeutic outcome. People today find no one truth to order their lives; they must mix and match on a perpetual basis to come to the benefit of this process. David Wells quotes Friedrich Nietzsche's *Beyond Good and Evil,* which expresses this viewpoint well: "The noble type of man regards *himself* as a determiner of values; he does not require to be approved of; he passes the judgment: 'What is injurious to me is injurious in itself'; he knows that it is he himself only who confers honor on things; he is *creator of values.*"[158] The self as both the subject and object of the search is one form of Gnosticism. God gave both Colossians and 1 John as a critique against incipient Gnosticism. This Gnosticism denied the human body of Christ because Gnostics deemed that the body itself was evil.

> *By this you know the Spirit of God: every spirit that confesses that Jesus Christ has come in the flesh is from God, and every spirit that does not confess Jesus is not from God. This is the spirit of the antichrist, which you heard was coming and now is in the world already.* (1 John 4:2, 3 ESV)

Postconservative, postmodern spirituality tries to dislodge spirituality from doctrine and formulated belief. Postmodernists are suspicious of doctrinal faith, so they separate spirituality from truth. They abdicate doctrine for fear of the prevailing belief that perspective is all that can be true.

The very nature of Christianity is that it is deductive, doctrinal. We cannot take Christianity seriously by avoiding its teaching. At the very least, dodging doctrine undermines biblical Christianity. At bottom, it invites Christians to abandon biblical spirituality and truth. The belief of postconservatives is essentially different from a biblical Christianity. Their spirituality is a pursuit but, on the other hand, biblical spirituality is a find. The spirituality of pursuit is a spirituality of uncertainty, a spirituality of unbelief. Christian spirituality is a spirituality of experiencing revelation. Christianity is not an endless search for spirituality but a finding of God's objective truth about spirituality. Spirituality is not an extension of the self but a discovery of what God has to say. Postmodern spirituality marginalizes biblical faith.

Postmodern spirituality is essentially a psychological experience, but biblical spirituality relates to God's nature, standards, and sin. Postconservative spirituality is about anxiety, power, and personal pain; it is a therapeutic spirituality. Biblical spirituality turns on truth primarily and experience secondarily. Postconservative spirituality centers on emotion, but biblical spirituality centers on trust in extant promises from God. Postconservative spirituality distorts the concept of love into a shallow panacea neglecting other dimensions of God's Word. Banal love presents God as overwhelmingly immanent in relatedness, silencing his transcendent holiness. This spirituality is mainly about personal experience to the neglect of the great doctrines and truths of the Bible. We can see this clearly in worship choruses and other forms of evangelical music. Postconservative spirituality is mystical, ethereal, and not biblically and rationally concrete. Postconservative worship is about experiences and not about understanding God's attributes, such as his love expressed in sacrificing his Son and in providing reconciliation and redemption for us and satisfaction to himself.

Postconservatives quiet the concept of sin and domesticate sin to tensions within the self. Tolerance is a watchword imbibed from culture where postconservatives can accommodate their beliefs to the prevailing society. Accommodation of the Word of God to culture negates the essence of biblical Christianity. Under the guise of a distorted idea of love, radical emergents distort objective truth. This is not love but emotional, saccharine sentimentalism. Sentimentalism that flies in the face of objective statements of Scripture is not love but deception. Accommodation to culture in order to placate prevailing sentiments in society reduces Christianity to something maudlin.

Postconservative leaders know that most North Americans do not believe in moral absolutes or absolute truth. That is why they preach tolerance and are against those who hold absolutes, especially absolutes about truth. They base this on a new standard of tolerance not found in the Word of God. Tolerance is the new criterion that measures all methodology and communication in evangelicalism. This new form of relativism among evangelicals refuses to allow the transcendent Word of God to speak in certain terms, yet the Bible binds moral absolutes to absolute truth. Recasting of biblical viewpoint into psychological tolerance turns Christianity into something it is not. Postconservatives, left without a center, have nowhere to stand logically against the presuppositions of postmodernism. They no longer realize that they are moving off-center to the presumption of the vacuous self.

The Bible warns against subjective spirituality (1 Corinthians 12:2f). Many Corinthian Christians were Gentiles who worshiped in mystery religions and pagan cults. They were "carried away" to this system; that is, Satan carried them captive to idols by subjective and ecstatic means. This put them in a subjective, random place without principles to guide them, being "led astray to mute idols, however [they] were led." They permitted themselves to be led in a self-abandoned manner without the Word of God. Paul wanted them to "know" objective truth.

Ecstatic utterance does not point to spirituality. Evidently, some of the Corinthians thought that speaking in ecstatic utterance was the essence of spirituality. A test of spirituality is our view of Jesus. The particular false doctrine here might have been Gnosticism. One view of Gnosticism believed that the physical body was evil. Because Jesus had a physical body, he was evil and accursed. John wrote 1 John against this error. Other New Testament books warn of this error as well. Spirituality originates in the Holy Spirit's revelation of propositional truths, not in an ecstatic experience.

Christians need to beware of false, subjective spirituality. It is easy to haul our subjective, pre-Christian ideas of spirituality into our view of spirituality when we become Christians. One criterion that will save us is the unmistakable objective mark that Jesus is Lord. If we distort the person and work of Christ, we distort Christianity. Ignorance of extant, objective truth will put believers in a bad place spiritually. Any teaching that makes us (1) overly introspective navel-gazers of the self or (2) passively and subjectively open to any teaching will put us in a seriously negative danger spiritually. Objective truth always counters subjective influences of the ecstatic idols of our day.

Personal encounters and mystical experiences are not the experiences of those in the Bible. Illumination of the Spirit does not replace propositions in the Word but rather makes them clearer.

> *That which we have **seen and heard** we declare to you, that you also may have fellowship with us; and truly our fellowship **is** with the Father and with His Son Jesus Christ. (*1 John 1:3, bold italics mine)

> *If we say that we have fellowship with Him, and walk in darkness, we lie and do not practice **the truth**. But if we walk in the light as He is in the light, we have fellowship with one another, and the blood of Jesus Christ His Son cleanses us from all sin.* (1 John 1:3, 6–7, bold italics mine)

## Comprehending and Understanding God's Revelation

Postevangelicals place emphasis on story, mystery, and metaphor but reduce propositions of the Word of God to the outer edge of the periphery in their thinking. They reluctantly concede some propositions, but propositions stand as an embarrassment to their perspective viewpoint on truth. Their focus on the person of Christ to the negation of the Word of God is a serious mistake because all that we know of the person of Christ is in propositions of the Word of God. God gave believers "a sure and steadfast anchor of the soul" (Hebrews 6:19). Peter speaks of the "prophetic word" (the Bible) as "more sure" than the personal experience of seeing Jesus personally on the Mount of Transfiguration (2 Peter 1:19–21).

> *Therefore, brothers, be all the more diligent to make your calling and election* **sure**, *for if you practice these qualities you will never fall. For in this way there will be richly provided for you an entrance into the eternal kingdom of our Lord and Savior Jesus Christ.*
> (2 Peter 1:10, 11 ESV, bold italics mine)

Peter speaks of the need for diligence in making our calling and election "sure." Salvation is not unstable from God's viewpoint but from our viewpoint. The word "sure" is emphatic in the Greek sentence and means "firm, permanent." "Sure" was a legal term in the first century for a legal guarantee obtained by a lawyer from the seller. We gain stability from our summons and selection from God. The Christian stands on solid ground when he legally validates the confirmation of the "sale" of his salvation. God will make good on his promises, for he himself secures payment of our salvation. There is no "money back" guarantee, because God himself guarantees we will get the product of salvation. We obtain this assurance upon the naked, unsupported Word of God. "Therefore I intend always to remind you of these qualities, though you know them and are *established in the truth* that you have." (2 Peter 1:12 ESV, italics mine)

Verse 12 begins a new section dealing with the importance of the Word of God for the believer (1:12–21). We turn from the focus of the work of God in individual Christians to the Word of God as the instrument of nurture. Peter's purpose is to "remind" Asia Minor Christian that they live their lives by truth (1:12, 13, 15; 3:1). We cannot overstate the importance of God's Word for the

Christian. Harry Ironside, longtime pastor of Chicago's Moody Church, used to say, "If it's new, it's not true, and if it's true, it's not new." The novelty of post-conservatism should warn us about its lack of validity.

Peter wants us to be "established in the truth" that we have. "Established" means "to fix, make fast, to set, to put something firmly in a location." The idea is to be stable about knowing truth. The Lord called on Peter to stabilize his brethren (Luke 22:32); Paul wanted to visit Rome to establish them (Romans 1:11) and Timothy at Thessalonica (1 Thessalonians 3:2). It is the work of God to stabilize the saints (1 Thessalonians 3:13; 2 Thessalonians 2:17). We are to stabilize our own hearts (James 5:8). Peter established Asia Minor saints in the truth and set them solid in truth. Peter's purpose is to set cardinal truth of their faith in their thinking. A shock absorber on a car gives stability to the car. Likewise, if we cannot take the shocks of life, we will lack stability in life. All Christians need equilibrium. What gives us equilibrium in our lives? The "present truth," God's truth. Equilibrium is a state of balance produced by two or more forces. There needs to be a balance between what we believe and what God says in his Word.

Peter knew his days were numbered. He spoke of important components of Christianity because so little time on earth remained for him. We speak of the things that are of most importance to us at the point of death. God's purpose for the believer is that we remind ourselves constantly of the importance of God's Word. This is a daily challenge for every leader.

We gain stability by knowing: we first gain knowledge; then we gain stability. We cannot reverse this process, for stability does not precede knowledge. All Christians need equilibrium. What gives us equilibrium in our lives? Truth, God's truth.

"The present truth" or "the truth that we have" is the truth that is present within us through instruction from our pastor-teachers. This is not truth at present under consideration. Truth is reality lying at the basis of an appearance—the manifested, veritable essence of the matter (Romans 9:1; 2 Corinthians 11:10; Galatians 2:5). "Truth" here is the deposit of faith (Jude 3) and is something we can always possess and never lose.

Stability in this passage is not strong character or human security. The stabilizer is the Word of God. The means to effect confirmation in our souls is the Word of God. We cannot live the Christian life without the Bible. The Word of God is our chart, our compass, our bill of rights, and our only infallible rule of faith and practice.

*I think it right, as long as I am in this body . . .* (2 Peter 1:13a ESV).

The phrase "I think" is an accounting term. This word originally referred to "leading, to lead the way, to preside." Later it came to mean "to consider or to lead before the mind, account" (Philippians 2:3, 6, 25; 3:7, 8; 2 Thessalonians 3:15; 1 Timothy 1:12; 6:1; Hebrews 10:29; 11:11; James 1:2; 2 Peter 3:9). This word came to mean "to think in principles." "Think" then means to "lead" principles "out before the mind." Character forms from what we think about God's Word. "Right" means "fitting" here. Peter is thinking in terms of a right principle. It means to do the right thing. "It is fitting that I write to remind you because I am about to die." Peter developed a sense of responsibility to give Asia Minor Christians vital truth before he died.

*. . . to stir you up by way of reminder.* (2 Peter 1:13a ESV)

Here, Asia Minor Christians and all successive generations of Christians will have a lasting capacity to remember apostolic teaching. "Remind" means to recall information from memory, but without necessarily implying we have actually forgotten what we know. It carries the idea of "to recall, to think about again" (1 Thessalonians 2:9; Hebrews 13:7; 2 Peter 3:2). This entire book of 2 Peter reminds them of truths they can think about repeatedly. Here we are, more than 2,000 years after the writing of this book, and God still reminds us of "these things."

As one of the eight or nine writers of the New Testament, Peter wrote two of the twenty-seven books of the New Testament. Peter wants to guarantee his readers will "always" remember what he taught. That guarantee comes from the Holy Spirit who enables him to write Scripture (1 and 2 Peter). Our guarantee of remembering Peter's teaching comes from the written legacy of these two books. Thus, 1 and 2 Peter are permanent reminders of apostolic teaching. Our only accurate source of information about eternity comes from the Bible. We cannot know anything accurate about Christ's death apart from the Bible. The only way we can prepare for death and eternity is to accept forgiveness from God by Christ's death for our sins. We cannot over-emphasize the importance of the Bible for declaring doctrines about eternity.

Peter's expression "way of reminder" means "to remind with authority." When we communicate truth, we inculcate authoritative principles for life. Peter is in the course of explaining his approach to death; thus, he gives his perspective on death. Repetition of principles is a key to leadership.

> *Since I know that the putting off of my body will be soon, as our Lord Jesus Christ made clear to me. And I will make every effort so that after my departure you may be able at any time to recall these things.*
> (2 Peter 1:14, 15 ESV)

Peter repeats himself for emphasis. In spite of Peter's approaching death, he will leave a legacy that nothing can destroy—2 Peter itself. "At any time" refers to a series of occasions—on any occasion that we read 2 Peter, we will know apostolic teaching (the New Testament).

> *. . . to recall these things.* (2 Peter 1:15 ESV)

Asia Minor Christians and all successive generations of Christians will have a lasting capacity to remember apostolic teaching. Peter's goal is to establish autonomous Christians, not autonomous from God but autonomous from depending on any given leader. Here Peter uses a different word for memory. "Recall" means "to recall information from memory," but again without necessarily the implication that we have actually forgotten what we know. It carries the idea of "to recall, to think about again." The repetition of memory words shows the importance of not neglecting apostolic teaching.

Peter here leaves his last will and testament. The doctrines of 2 Peter go on as a legacy for all Christians after Peter's death. Truth does not rest in any great leader or pastor. Truth lasts forever (1 Peter 1:23). It is not the person but the message that is important. Leaders will come and go, but the Word of God abides forever. The great thing a pastor can do for a congregation is to teach them the Word (this is the point of the pastoral epistles, 1 and 2 Timothy and

Titus). Other pastoral functions pall into diminishing priority in light of the communication of God's Word. The pastor's real legacy is people who know the Word. No Christian should depend on some scintillating or pleasing personality. We must depend on the Word, for the Word lasts forever.

> *For we did not follow cleverly devised myths when we made known to you the power and coming of our Lord Jesus Christ, but we were eyewitnesses of his majesty.* (1 Peter 1:16 ESV)

Christians do not base their faith on clever stories as the false teachers did (whom Peter attacks in chapter 2). Rather, the Christian faith rests on the historicity of God's revelation. The Greek word for "follow" comes from two terms: "to follow" and "out." This intense term conveys the idea of conforming as a follower of myths in a dependent manner. It carries the idea of following someone personally to the end (2:2, 15). The implication is to comply with some authority. Thus Peter and his companions did not follow "fables." "Fables" are not the authority of the New Testament church. Christians follow their Lord and the Word.

A "cunningly devised fable" is a clever piece of special knowledge created shrewdly and skillfully. We get our English word "sophistication" from the Greek verb for "cunningly devised." We also get our English word "myth" from the Greek word for "fable" here. A fable is a legendary story about supernatural beings, events, or cultural heroes. A fable in this usage is a fabrication, a concocted tale to mislead subtly. These people have special knowledge involving capacity to produce cleverly contrived myths. Peter did not contrive his message. Christianity does not come from human invention.

The Greek tense of "devised" means these tales were formed in the past with the result continuing to the present, showing these were long-standing myths. Christianity is no myth. It is not a fairy story for children or folklore for adults. Christianity operates on fact, not fiction. It is no religious fairy tale. Neither is Christianity the work of someone's imagination that has no basis in fact.

The truth of the Christian faith closely binds with the historicity of the New Testament. Toward the end of the nineteenth century, under the influence of the Age of Reason (which assumed rationalism as the essential source for truth), a belief system arose to attack Christianity. Some of its methods claimed the

Bible was myth. These claims were based more on subjective theological presuppositions than on historical fact. The question of the historical fact of Scripture is of little importance to those who deny the truth of Christianity. It is of immense importance to those who believe in its credibility, for the truth of Jesus Christ can be known only from New Testament records. The influence of the New Testament records is tantamount to the influence of his character.

The heyday of liberal higher criticism has passed, but their critical method severely undermined the credibility of Scripture. Although many of their methods (such as the Wellhausen theory) are no longer accepted, advocates of liberalism face a dilemma because their attempt to make the Bible a book of myths does not square with the demands of objective evidence from archaeology and elsewhere.

The New Testament is the most trustworthy piece of writing that ever persevered from antiquity. There are greater resources for reconstructing its text than for any document of the classic age. Some papyri go back to the time of the writings of the apostles. By contrast, the dialogues of Plato, the works of the Greek dramatists, and the poems of Virgil have come down to us from very few copies. Some of their manuscripts are separated by as much as 1,400 years. The earliest manuscript for the *Gallic Wars* was 900 years after Caesar's time. The two oldest copies of Tacitus' work are dated eight and ten centuries after his original writings. The *Iliad* has only 643 manuscripts. Caesar's *Gallic Wars* has but ten good manuscripts. However, there are 5,366 Greek New Testament manuscripts plus 45,000 copies of New Testament texts in papyri, lexicons, dictionaries, and the church fathers' writings. In the New Testament, there are fewer than fifty variant readings of any importance. There is no case where an article of faith is left in question. The Bible is the most reliable historical document in the history of the world. It obviously is not myth!

God speaks through the Bible (Luke 1:70; Romans 1:1, 2; Hebrews 1:1, 2; 2:3, 4). Therefore, it is of highest importance that we recognize that the Bible we possess is true and reliable. Peter "makes known" two things about the Lord Jesus Christ: his power and his Second Coming. Peter uses the doctrine of the Second Coming as the basis for establishing true criteria for truth. Because the Second Coming did not happen during Peter's day, this makes Peter's point more dramatic. Peter, therefore, goes beyond his personal experience. Truth is more real to him than experience. If there is a conflict between experience and the Word, experience is wrong; the Word should be the deciding factor for determining truth. The Word of God is the only way to evaluate experience from God's viewpoint. Some people do not have the ability to evaluate experiences because they do not have principles of Scripture to measure their experiences. We all have a tendency to overestimate our experience and underestimate the principles of God's Word. We will never know whether we are right or wrong without objective criteria against which to measure our experiences. God gives us an absolute criterion in his Word.

How do we determine what six inches is? First, we must know what an inch is. You say, "Well, someone says it is 'this' long and someone else says it is 'that' long." Which person is right? If I say six inches is equivalent to three feet and am dogmatic that it is, how are you going to prove me wrong? I have made up my mind. Don't confuse me with the facts. How do you know that an inch is an inch? We must find a ruler, an established and commonly accepted standard (worldwide) for determining how long an inch is. In biblical parlance, our ruler is God's Word. God's Word is from eternity and operates on eternal and absolute norms.

After we decide to use the ruler, we have to know how to use it. We cannot measure an inch by the end of the ruler. We must turn it sideways and use it as designed. Many people distort the Bible by fallacies such as pretexting (taking a verse out of its context). These people have the right standard, but they do not know how to use it. The best way to understand the Bible is to examine it verse by verse in its historical, grammatical, cultural, and contextual meaning. If we do this, we will not scramble Scripture. Another distortion in understanding the Bible is the error of interpolation (imposing one's own view on a passage of Scripture).

The "but" in "but were eyewitnesses of his majesty" is a term of strong contrast. There is a contrast between some subjective observation and exposure to the facts. Peter, James, and John actually observed Jesus transfigured on the Mount of Olives. The Greek word "were" means to become something that you were not before. They were not eyewitnesses before the transfiguration, but the three observers of the transfiguration became eyewitnesses. They looked onward from the transfiguration of Jesus into his millennial glory. Peter, James, and John had a foretaste of the coming of Christ on the Mount of Transfiguration (Matthew 16:28–17:2).

An eyewitness is one who watches or observes as an overseer. These people personally saw an event and thus had first-hand knowledge and could attest to the occurrence of an event. This is the only occurrence of "eyewitness" in the New Testament. The Christian faith is credible because of historical facts, not stories. The Christian faith requires eyewitnesses who can corroborate those facts. Peter defends the doctrine of future things on the basis of the historicity of the Mount of Transfiguration. "Eyewitnesses" is a rebuke to pre-Gnostic adversaries at the time of writing 2 Peter. This was a technical term used in mystery sects to designate those initiated into a higher knowledge. Peter excluded false teachers as true eyewitnesses. Peter, James, and John personally witnessed Christ revealed in glory. Peter considered eyewitness experience as valid for corroboration of truth. Experience itself is not reliable to arbitrate truth in a final sense because interpretation of experience is subjective. Experience is valid as a corroborating element, for we can see truth confirmed in an incident.

"Majesty" is a state of greatness or importance. Jesus was prominent and important to Peter's thinking. "Majesty" in the Greek means far more than the English equivalent; it carries the idea of *magnificent* glory. "Majesty" can mean the manifestation of great or mighty power. Here "majesty" refers to the splendor and magnificence of Jesus' transfiguration of great grandeur and sublimity. Peter, James, and John witnessed Jesus' majestic appearance. Jesus is "His Majesty King Jesus." We can never use that term for Isaiah or John but only of the Lord Jesus. We never say, "His Majesty Peter" or "His Majesty Paul." We do say, "His Majesty King Jesus, king of the world to come and the sovereign king of the universe." Peter, James, and John at the Mount of Transfiguration (Mount Olivet) saw with their own eyes as the Lord was transfigured before them into a foretaste of his millennial glory. The experience on the mount then was a sneak preview of the Second Coming (Mark 8:34–9:13).

This was a bona fide experience of historical fact. What a thrill it would have been to be there! It was a great privilege for Peter, James, and John to see the coming millennial kingdom unveiled before their eyes. Thirty-two years later

Peter spoke of it in this second epistle. He now declares that the event has to do with Christ's coming again. The trio on the Mount said, in effect, "You can't fool us. This was no hallucination or optical illusion. This was real. We actually saw Jesus transfigured before our eyes." These three men objectified truth.

> *For when he received honor and glory from God the Father, and the voice was borne to him by the Majestic Glory, "This is my beloved Son, with whom I am well pleased." (2 Peter 1:17* ESV)

The "when" here is the Mount of Transfiguration experience on the Mount of Olives. Peter's desire is for his readers to see beyond the first coming of Christ to his Second Coming. He gives a running commentary on the Mount of Olives transfiguration experience. The transfiguration was a foretaste of Christ's coming.

Many evangelicals today, sadly, diminish the doctrine of the coming of Christ.

> *We ourselves heard this very voice borne from heaven, for we were with him on the holy mountain.* (2 Peter 1:18 ESV)

It is important to tie "hearing" in this verse with "eyewitnesses" of verse 16. Peter, James, and John both "heard" and "saw." People have every reason to receive the testimony of Scripture because the Bible is based on facts and true history. These three men actually and personally experienced the Mount of Transfiguration incident.

> *"For the Son of Man will come in the glory of His Father with His angels, and then He will reward each according to his works. Assuredly, I say to you, there are some standing here who shall not taste death till they see the Son of Man coming in His kingdom." Now after six days Jesus took Peter, James, and John his brother, led them up on a high mountain by themselves; and He was transfigured before them. His face shone like the sun, and His clothes became as white as the light.* (Matthew 16:27–17:2)

Peter now continues with an implication of his Mount of Transfiguration experience, but he draws an even more convincing documentation of truth than the transfiguration.

> *And we have something **more sure** [more sure than the personal experience on the Mount of Transfiguration], the prophetic word, to which*

*you will do well to pay attention as to a lamp shining in a dark place, until the day dawns and the morning star rises in your hearts.* (2 Peter 1:19 ESV, italics mine)

The Word of God is surer than the experiential, personal, apostolic witness of the account of the Mount of Transfiguration. Our faith primarily rests in what God says, not what we experience.

"Sure" means "firm, permanent," and is the same word as in verse 10. "Confirmed" also comes to mean "reliable, dependable, certain." The New Testament uses this Greek word (βέβαιος) and its cognates nineteen times. Secular Greek used it as a legal term for unassailable position or guarantee. These are people with a firm faith because what they believe in is altogether reliable. We can rely and depend upon the Scriptures because they are trustworthy. The apostles could trust God's Word more than their own senses. We can trust the empirical evidence of the trio seeing the transfiguration, but we can trust even more the message of the prophets: the Word of God. The issue here is certainty. We know Scriptures to be true by the apostolic authority; for that reason, they are certain (Hebrews 2:2). There has been a process of verification by the apostles and they confirmed the Bible to be true.

The "prophetic word" pertains to inspired utterances—prophetic (of the prophets). In other words, this is Old Testament Scripture. It is the prophetic word that is more sure than the experience on the Mount.

The phrase "do well to pay attention" has to do with seriousness toward Scripture. We are to search the Scripture so we can apply principle to experience. We want to mold and fashion our lives according to the Bible. "To pay attention" means literally "to turn one's mind to." It can mean "to hold to, to be in a continuous state of readiness to learn of any future danger, need, or error, and to respond appropriately." We need to pay attention to, to keep on the lookout for, to be alert for, to be on one's guard against neglecting God's Word for our souls.

The phrase "as a light shines" means "to give light." The Word is a bright light in the darkness of this world. It brings everything to light and makes it appear as it truly is. Light dispels darkness. When Jesus comes again, he will dispel the darkness of our world. The phrase "until the day dawns" means to "shine through." We get the English word "phosphorus" from the Greek term for "morning star." Literally, "morning star" means "light-bringer" or "light-bearer." The "morning star" bears and gives light. The eye gives light to the mind. The morning star is conspicuous and thus illumines our minds. Until Jesus comes again, darkness will prevail. "Rises" comes from two Greek words: "through" and "shine;" thus, "rises" means "to shine through," with special reference to the dawn. This is the breaking of daylight upon the darkness of the night. When Jesus comes, he will break into the darkness of this world. He will break through time and space; things will become clear when Jesus comes.

Truth is more reality than experience. Peter lived with Jesus for three years. Jesus rebuked, corrected, and commended Peter over that period. Yet Jesus became more real to Peter in knowing truth than through Peter's personal experience with him. That heads some of us off at the maudlin pass! Some say, "If I had lived when Jesus lived I would love Him better. I would not have done some of the dumb things spiritually that I have done." Malarkey! You would not be any different than you are right now. You have enough of the Word to love him thoroughly.

> *Knowing this first of all, that no prophecy of Scripture comes from someone's own interpretation.* (2 Peter 1:20 ESV)

This section of 2 Peter deals with Scripture itself. No book in the world is as valuable as the Bible. God's Word is indispensable because only it tells us the truth about God, Christ, sin, and eternity.

The phrase "knowing this first" points to priority. Invariably, what God asks us to know, we do not know. God wants us to know the subject of this verse "first." He desires that we know something about divine inspiration above everything else. When we interpret Scripture, we need to begin with the principle that God, not humans, inspired the Bible. This is paramount.

Peter's opponents denied the divine origin of Scripture. They claimed that their writings came from visions, signs, and dreams. These prophecies came from adversaries, from their own origin. But Peter says that the apostolic writings came from God, not a human author. "Prophecy" here is the message of a prophet. "Scripture" means "writing." Peter here refers to the Old Testament and the writings of the New Testament written to this point. "Scripture" is singular. The Word of God is one single unit. It does not contradict itself.

Some verses are difficult to understand. We must interpret these verses in light of other passages dealing with the same subject. In addition, we should interpret unclear passages of Scripture in the light of clear passages. If a passage is crystal clear, that portion of the Bible will help us interpret the unclear portions. God is the author of all of Scripture and he makes no mistakes. He used human authors to write his book, and they wrote in different times and different places; many lived centuries apart from one another, yet all sixty-six books fit together as one. The Bible is one in its teaching, and picking certain verses out of their context to establish a doctrine is a dangerous practice. We must understand each verse in the light of its context. Otherwise, we risk distorting the meaning of that passage and then operating on incorrect information. This is much like misleading advertising in that it misrepresents its product. Verse-by-verse Bible exposition saves us from this problem. By taking each verse successively and including all of its words, we can come to a true meaning of Scripture. This also presumes that we interpret the Bible in the time in which it was written, and to whom and on what occasion it was written. It is also of great advantage to know the original languages in which the Bible was written. This is the way to discover what God truly says. We must always be careful not to make the Bible say what we want it to mean.

> . . . *That no prophecy of Scripture comes from someone's own interpretation.* (2 Peter 1:20)

The word "private" means "one's own." A prophet cannot speak a personal message. Scripture does not come from the prophet because Scriptures did not come from human origin. Scripture is not the human author's "own thing." The Bible is reliable because of its source; Scripture is reliable because God is reliable.

The word "interpretation" literally means "unloosing, solving, explaining," but metaphorically it means "interpretation." The word can mean the conveying or uttering of a divine proclamation and therefore carries the idea of producing or bringing forth. Scripture does not come from the human author's explanation of things. It is not a concoction of the author's own thinking.

The word "is" means "to become something that it was not previously." This probably means that the prophets did not originate Scripture. The Holy Spirit, not human authors, originates Scripture, for he gives the Bible by revelation. This passage is not talking about the interpretation of the Bible but the origin of the Bible. God used human authors to write the Bible, but the Bible does not teach their human ideas. Human authors of Scripture did not put their own spin on Scriptures. The Bible is not man's ideas about God.

In the NKJV, First Peter 1:20 says, "Knowing this first, that no prophecy of Scripture is of any private interpretation." The word "any" means "no — not even one." Every single Scripture came from God and not human beings. No Scripture springs from the mind of the human author.

No single passage of Scripture stands by itself. We must understand it both in its context and also as a whole. We need to understand doctrine in light of all of Scripture's teaching. We call this "theology." In true handling of Scripture, we cannot take passages we do not like and ignore them, so we include the entire body of truth from God to form a proper theology. This will deliver us from error. Every passage of Scripture has one interpretation but many applications. If we give the idea that an application is an interpretation, we misrepresent what God says.

Our senses deceive us at times: I thought I saw Sue, but it was a look-a-like. I thought I heard a burglar, but it was a mouse. I could have sworn that there was someone in the kitchen, so I came downstairs with my baseball bat. Our senses can fool us, but the Word of God does not fool us if we interpret it in its context.

No single church possesses the exclusive right to interpret the Bible. If a single church had this right, then individuals would not have responsibility to understand Scripture. If we blindly accept what a given church teaches, then we place ourselves at risk.

Each of us must take responsibility to understand the Word for ourselves. As Christians we all have the Scripture and the Holy Spirit to help us understand the Bible for ourselves. The issue is not what your church or pastor teaches, but what the Word teaches. What does the Bible itself teach?

*For no prophecy was ever produced by the will of man, but men spoke from God as they were carried along by the Holy Spirit.* (2 Peter 1:21 ESV)

Note that this verse begins with a word of explanation: "for." The previous verse explained that Scriptures did not come from a human source but a divine source. Scripture does not originate with human authors. The Bible originates with God. The human authors received God's ideas. Scripture comes by divine inspiration. Revelation comes from God to man. Religion is human ideas about God. That is why religion does not have the answer.

If the Bible did not come by human will, how did it come? By people who "spoke from God." Approximately thirty different men wrote the thirty-nine books of the Old Testament. About eight men wrote the twenty-seven books of the New Testament.

These men were not automatons or robots. They used their own personalities and vocabularies to write Scripture. The Holy Spirit, however, guarded them from error as they wrote Scripture. He superintended each word they wrote. Therefore, the authors of Scripture made no mistakes. We have the Bible exactly as God intended for us to have it. We can place our confidence in Scripture. The "men of God" are Old and New Testament authors such as Moses, Isaiah, Jeremiah, John, and Paul. God picked certain men to communicate the Bible.

In the phrase "but men spoke from God," "but" implies strong contrast. In contrast to human beings originating Scripture, the Holy Spirit superintended the writing of Scripture.

The Holy Spirit "carried along" these men. The book of Acts uses "carried" for wind carrying a ship (27:15, 17). The Holy Spirit so guided the human authors that they wrote without error. That is why Scripture is certain. Therefore, we can trust Scripture because it is the very words of God. The Holy Spirit upheld, or bore, the writers as they wrote Scripture. The writers of Scripture wrote better than they knew. That is why the Bible is not full of fables. The Holy Spirit governed the human author in the process of writing Scripture (2 Peter 3:16). The human author was aware of the content that he wrote, but the Holy Spirit "carried" him. The Holy Spirit so supernaturally superintended Scripture writers that without circumventing their intelligence, personal literary style, or personality, he enabled them to record Scripture with perfect accuracy.

We have a trustworthy Bible because the Holy Spirit superintended the writing of Scripture. The Bible is the unabridged revelation of the thoughts of an omniscient God. God put into writing everything that we need to know about him. Scripture is the only inspired book on earth. Other books might be profound and insightful, but God did not inspire those writings. Only the Bible is inspired because the Holy Spirit wrote Scripture.

If 2 Peter 1:20, 21 means anything, it means that we can comprehend and understand God's message to us in his revelation. We can know reality to the degree that God has revealed himself. We cannot know everything about all things. Finiteness will never be infinite, even in eternity. God is accessible through the text he gave. The Word of God is active and powerful beyond finite capacity (Hebrews 4:12). This goes far beyond the nebulous meaning of a community, with its limited perspective on the world. Peter argues for a sure and certain word from God.

*Six*

# LET YOUR YEA BE YEA
## *Correlation between Truth and Certainty*

### Antagonism toward Objective, Propositional Truth

Until postmodernism, most people assumed certain truth to exist. With post-modernism, truth is what you make it to be. There is now no transcendent truth other than what is found in the individual or in communities. Contradiction between viewpoints is inevitable. Augustine said, "All truth is God's truth," but postconservatives say, "Everyone's perspective in consensus is God's perspective." Above all, they contend, we must jettison certainty about truth. Some even discard a final criterion for truth. However, the pursuit of relevance as an ultimate assumption will catapult evangelicals into irrelevance. True relevance comes from the eternal God who speaks with utter relevance to human needs in his Word. Postconservatives sacrifice truth on the altar of unity. To them, we must be accepting at all costs, even at the cost of truth. There is a similarity between postmodernism and existentialism, for existentialism denies absolute truth. The difference is that postmoderns can create truth as a perspective on reality, rather than seeing truth as reality itself. Truth is communal, so they construct perspectives socially, but this socially erected truth is subject to change. This makes truth, or rather perspectives on truth, highly subjective.

Brian McLaren in *A New Kind of Christian* says through Neo that even Scripture is neither authoritative (in a "modern" sense) nor a foundation for faith.[159] McLaren claims in other places that Scripture should have a supreme place in the church, not because it is objectively true but because of its status in the Christian community.

Postconservatives demonstrate a proclivity to value doubt and distrust certainty. Postmodernism developed distrust in commitments to belief systems because of allegiances to radical ideologies of the twentieth century such as Nazism, fascism, and communism. They draw careless parallels to Christianity in this regard. Their only certainty is the self-contradictory proclamation that there is no certainty! This is their indubitable and self-evident presupposition. Jean-Francois Lyotard, professor of philosophy at the University of Paris, was the foremost defender of secular postmodernism. To him, it was impossible to make a universal truth claim. He believed that all claims of truth are limited and insular and come from different communities of meaning. Paul-Michel Foucault, another secular postmodern, claimed that a writer "died" upon writing, and those who read his text must deconstruct it as if the author were dead. All meaning must be deconstructed; thus, morals are relative to the individual. The thinking of these men led to a crisis in theology. George Lindbeck and Hans Frei of the New Yale School tried to grapple with postmodernism in relation to theology. They shifted Christian theology from propositional truth based on revelation to self-conscious, local, and particular claims embedded in cultural and language. All this was an attempt to remove the offensive truth claims of biblical revelation. Following postmodern theology, postmodern evangelical Stanley Grenz bought into theological postmodernism. Bernard Ramm, as well, in his book *After Fundamentalism*, shifts the basis of evangelicalism from a creed-based viewpoint to spirituality-based distinctiveness. He wants to move from propositions to practical orientation in theological viewpoint. Grenz wishes to move evangelicals from orientation to propositions of Scripture to spirituality.

This swing from propositions to spirituality is at the heart of an evangelical crisis. It is a move from doctrine to subjective spirituality. Theology for the postconservative becomes a practical discipline oriented to the Christian community. Truth claims are implicit in community belief; thus, truth resides inherent in the community, so the role of Scripture in theology is "ultimately unnecessary."[160] Grenz simply assumes the authority of the Bible because it is the universally acknowledged book of Christians; however, the issue is "community faith." According to him, the community must simply assume the Bible but not defend it. He shifts study of doctrine of the Word to internal discussion within theological systems. This view is similar to the New Yale

School of thinkers including Lindbeck.[161] Abandonment of universal truth to a community "is a massive concession fatal to any evangelical theology," according to Mohler:

> It is precisely at the doctrine of Scripture that Grenz's proposal is most dangerous—and yet most attractive to those seeking a retreat into a "postmodern" evangelicalism. By arguing that evangelicals should simply "assume" the authority of the Bible because we can establish an "integral relation" between theology and the Christian community, and by asserting that the Bible is the church's "universally acknowledged book," Grenz offers evangelicals a convenient way out of the pattern of debates and controversies over the inerrancy and inspiration of Scripture. Nevertheless, Scripture has been displaced as the foundation of Christian theology, and it must stand beside communal Christian experience. At root, Grenz's argument is more anthropological and phenomenological than theological.
>
> Though he directs evangelicals toward a renewed appreciation for narrative with the Christian community, he has effectively forfeited the historic Christian claim to the universal truthfulness of the church's meta-narrative, drawn from Scripture.[162]

Many evangelicals now affirm errors in biblical autographs. In 1979 Jack Rogers and Donald McKim of Fuller Theological Seminary wrote the book *The Authority and Interpretation of the Bible,* which propagated a functional, or coherentist, view of Scripture rather than a correspondent view of Scripture. The objective of the book was to separate the purpose of Scripture from its material content. John Woodbridge, Richard Gaffin, and Richard Muller decisively smashed the credibility of that book, but Rogers and McKim had done their damage to the evangelical world.

Most postconservatives are antagonistic to objective, propositional truth. They adapt their view of truth to postmodernism, becoming antagonistic toward objective knowledge of God. There is no one-to-one correlation between language and reality. All we can know is how truth appears in the perspectives of a community as postconservatives use their own given language to understand what is out there. All they can know in philosophy of social convention is what coincides with their community's social convention; thus, they cannot know propositions of objective truth. Doctrine for them is the product of human expression on the stories of the Bible. They have no universal, objective criterion to distinguish truth from error, yet the Word of God challenges us to identify heresy (Deuteronomy 13:1–5; 18:20–22).

For Grenz and Franke, the Bible is not the revelation of God but a means, or channel, of his revelation. It is the reflection of the Hebrew community and the early church. They displace the intent of the original authors of Scripture with how the current community of believers views the passage. However, the true approach is that the reader does not determine the meaning of Scripture, for if meaning of the text comes from the reader, this would result in chaotic interpretation of Scripture.

## Discarding Certainty of Truth by Assimilation and Accommodation

By decisively amending truth to suit postmodernism, postconservatives reject objective truth, final truth, absolute truth, or certain truth. In doing so, they incorporate postmodern presuppositions about what is true. They do this through emergent thinking and obliging culture. Douglas Groothuis argues against this attempt to reach postmoderns by accommodation of truth:

> Some Christians are hailing postmodernism as the trend that will make the church interesting and exciting to postmoderns. We are told that Christians must shift their emphasis from objective truth to communal experience, from rational arguments to subjective appeal, from doctrinal orthodoxy to "relevant" practices. I have reasoned throughout this book that this move is nothing less than fatal to Christian integrity and biblical witness.[163]

David Wells, in his 1993 book *No Place for Truth,* says evangelicals are so caught up in culture that "popular sentiment is allowed to define what truth is."[164] If that was true then, it is even truer now. Wells also makes this alarming statement:

> That this emasculation has taken place among the evangelicals is, on the face of it, most surprising. After all, they have steadfastly resisted

until relatively recently every attempt to ease the difficulty implicit in believing in truth in the modern world. They have refused to come to peace with doctrinal change as have Catholics after Newman's time. They staunchly opposed the Modernist effort to surrender doctrine in favor of "life," as if religious consciousness could be a substitute for biblical truth. And it is as doctrinal people that they have defined themselves through much of the twentieth century. But this identity is now rapidly dissipating.[165]

Again, Wells spells out pluralism's impact on truth:

And so evangelicals have also come to terms psychologically with our society's structural pluralism and its lack of interest in matters of truth. Good works are seldom offensive in the modern world; it is a belief in truth that is troublesome.[166]

Accommodation is another attempt to contextualize truth to culture. Just as Hilton hotels accommodate their guests, so postconservatives accommodate prevailing cultural conditions by adapting truth. This buys into the world system and undermines Christianity by accommodating viewpoints, perspectives, or cultures. The line of demarcation between Christianity and other viewpoints is the unique revelation of God in Christ through his Word. Hindus and Buddhists need to be converted, not accommodated.

All these attempts at accommodation result in negation of truth, the uniqueness of Christ, and Christianity. No doubt there is a necessity for each culture to express theology in each cultural context, but there is great danger in syncretism and adaptation of truth itself to placate culture. Postevangelicals do more than contextualize Christianity; they compromise its truth and distinctiveness. In an attempt to reconcile disparate and opposing beliefs, they meld various beliefs into one great glob.

Many other cultures have gone the route of syncretism. Greek paganism incorporated Hellenistic culture. Following Alexander the Great, the Greeks synchronized Persian, Anatolian, and Egyptian elements with an overall Hellenic formula. The Egyptian god Amun developed into Zeus after Alexander went to the desert to seek Amun's oracle at Siwa. Rome identified with Greek deities. Serapis, Isis, and Mithras are syncretic deities. The Greek Dionysus was imported to Rome as Bacchus.

Syncretism is an inevitable consequence of internationalism. Attempts to fuse differing systems of belief are due to an overarching craving for oneness in culture. When two religious systems fuse, they form a new philosophy or religion, and the old belief becomes passé. However, strict adherence to biblical identity maintains purity of belief. Syncretism is a flagrant compromise of truth it is truth co-opted by culture. It holds an ambivalent attitude toward truth.

## Discarding Certainty by Denying Finality of Truth

Evangelical postmodernism does not believe in finality of truth, so it rejects certainty about truth. Postconservative spirituality rests essentially on experientialism devoid of substantive objective truth. Because postmodern evangelicalism operates in the domain of spirituality, it will lead evangelicals more quickly down the path of doctrinal decline. Loss of confidence in the Word of God will deeply unravel convictions and standards among evangelicals. Already it is difficult to distinguish moral standards between Christians and non-Christians.

Postconservatism represents a paradigm shift away from classic evangelical doctrines such as the doctrine of Scripture, the doctrine of God, and the extent of salvation. These postevangelicals move from an inerrant Scripture to an errant Scripture that communicates theological truths in general but fumbles the facts in particular. In lieu of human freedom (open theism), they shift from an absolute God who knows all things at all times, both potential and actual, to a more finite god who does not have the capacity of foreknowledge. They extend those included in the category of "saved" far beyond what evangelicals have normally defined as saved. According to postconservatives, salvation is by Christ's work—but God might save some without believing in Christ.

Because postconservatism moves away from the rational and logical based on factual observation, it now operates on experience and mysticism. It is no longer possible to hold to objective propositions (doctrine) about truth. There is no absolute truth, for all beliefs are relative to the individual perspective. The gospel in propositional form (people are sinners; Jesus paid for their sin by his substitutionary death; we must trust in Jesus' death for eternal life) is arrogant and dogmatic. Postconservatives want to present a moderate gospel that accommodates culture. In doing so, they change the message of the gospel. They believe if we offer the gospel in the form of a present social kingdom, that would be acceptable to a postmodern generation.

Postevangelicals rob the gospel and the Word of God of its power. Stanley Grenz is typical of those who do this. D. A. Carson says that Grenz's writings, representative of the theology of the emergent church, are so committed to postmodernism that he is "utterly unable to detect any weakness in postmodern epistemology, and therefore all his prescriptions for the future assume the essential rightness of postmodernism."[167] Carson speaks to the danger of selling out to postmodernism: Grenz constructs "a form of Christianity that is so deeply indebted to a reigning epistemology that he sells something of its birthright."[168]

## Sliding down the Slope from Sound Doctrine

Metanarratives are out, and narratives are in. This blatant rejection of systematic theology or doctrine is at the heart of postconservative postmodernism. Postmodernism cannot accept any universal truth because it is at heart nihilistic.

What postmoderns cannot see is that rejection of metanarrative is itself a metanarrative! Postconservatives hold to the postmodern view that truth does not consist essentially in objective reality but in social constructions; therefore they have no way to get beyond cultural conditioning because they accept a premise that will not allow them to do so. Presuming this view, endless plasticity of interpretations cannot be true, because postmodernism is a claim of truth itself. Christianity is more than a preference or individual choice. It is not essentially something to use, but something to believe and practice. If we do not believe in something for sure, then we have tentative Christianity, devoid of certainty. Why should Christians commit to high-level Christian living if we are not sure of Christianity's credibility or truthfulness? All that remains is an opinion, passion, or feeling instead of confidence in certain and objective Scripture. There is a big difference between confident objective knowledge of Scripture and spiritual preference.

Brian McLaren claims that the Bible itself "contains precious little expository prose."[169] However, the epistles exude prose; even the so-called "personal letters" pulsate with prose. He claims that Paul uses poetry in Romans 11, Philippians 2, and Colossians 1, but these passages comprise prose with very little poetry.

McLaren claims that Paul comes out looking like a lawyer patterned after lawyers of the Reformation such as Luther and Calvin, but Paul uses legal terms himself such as the forensic term "to justify (*dikaiow*), to cause to be righteous, to declare righteous." McLaren qualifies his attack on propositional truth by saying this mystical/poetic approach can be "pushed too far."[170] Evidently, he accepts a certain level of propositional truth but does not define its extent. He states that he has never taken a "single for-credit seminary class," but now he is not "embarrassed by" his "lack of proper credentials anymore because his literature training helped him to be sensitized to drama and conflict, to syntax and semantics and semiotics, to text and context, to prose and poetry."[171] This helped him to see "how a generous orthodoxy must be mystical and poetic."[172] In other words, literary criticism governs his approach to Christianity; it is his grid for understanding Christianity. He has built his own system of theology based on precarious principles resident in postmodernism. He never questions his dialectical approach to truth, which is the essential approach of *A Generous Orthodoxy*.

In attempting to explain the doctrine of inspiration, McLaren portrays the evangelical view of inspiration as "dictation": "Often we have treated the Bible as if God dictated it, with no organic participation at all."[173] No evangelical scholar I know holds this viewpoint today, so this is blatant mischaracterization. He makes the outlandish statement that "it may be worth noting that many Christians have an understanding (dictation theory) of their sacred text that is more Islamic than truly Christian."[174] This shows McLaren's stark lack of theological training. No credible evangelical theologian would make such a statement. On top of this, it is extremely pejorative, and it characterizes evangelicalism out of unadulterated theological ignorance. Maybe he should have gone to seminary after all!

McLaren characterizes evangelicalism as believing that Christ would come within twenty-five years of the 1960s. Is this generous? No, because it does not represent evangelicalism; it is instead rank mischaracterization of evangelicalism. He also characterizes the evangelical view of the Word as a "rule book" that made the Bible "objectively clear, with no subjective ambiguity."[175] But evangelicals view the Bible as a book of principles for life. Evangelicals also do not believe that the Bible is without ambiguity or mystery.

Repeatedly, McLaren presumes doctrine in his attempt to negate doctrine. In his chapter "Why I am Catholic," he says that we need to bring "blessing to our needy world" and to "become part of God's solution." [176] But what is the basis for blessing and how does he know "God's solution?" He cannot know it without a premise of doctrine. He charges "reformers" with "inflated self-image."[177] Self-image is not the problem; conviction about extant statements of Scripture concerning the condition for salvation is the issue. In other words, if evangelicals hold to conviction, they have an "inflated self-image" and an elitist attitude.[178] McLaren mistakes certainty for inflated pride because certainty violates the postmodern perception of things. Again, McLaren claims certain ends for the church, but how does he know this—by tradition or revelation? If by revelation, then he is certain about something. This is a flat contradiction. What he rejects in others, he holds for himself. He says that there is a "special pride that comes from being part of the exclusive, the elite, the prime."[179] Is there not pride in making this statement? Again, another contradiction. To him, a generous orthodoxy "refrains from judging. It just rejoices where good seed grows."[180] The Bible, in counterdistinction, does differentiate between error and truth, and quite extensively, as do all the prophets and books of the Bible that attack false doctrine.

While claiming that doctrine or truth does matter, McLaren links orthodoxy with a participatory process in finding truth. He wants to differentiate orthodoxy (Apostles' and Nicene Creeds) from doctrinal distinctives. By this, it appears that anything that is not in those two creeds is open for debate. That would preclude faith alone through grace alone as God's way of salvation—doctrines McLaren puts out on the margin.[181] What is important to him is "orthopraxy" without doctrinal distinctives. [182] On the other hand, the entire construct of New Testament epistles bases belief on doctrinal understanding of a point in order to apply it to experience. From a biblical viewpoint, there is no orthopraxy without orthodoxy (doctrine).

McLaren does not want to see other religious adherents as "enemies," but this is exactly how God sees them—as reprobates (Romans 1:28) and heretics

(2 Peter 2). In his chapter "The Seven Jesuses I have Known," McLaren picks and chooses bits and pieces from various theologies. This takes place in the name of sympathy![183] What is the basis of this sympathy? It is preference for subjectivism and pragmatism. This is an attempt at definition without distinction because it is devoid of truth and syncretistic to the core:

> Why not celebrate them all? Already, many people are using terms like post-Protestant, post-denominational, post-liberal, and postconservative to express a desire to move beyond the polarization and sectarianism that have too often characterized Christians of the past.[184]

McLaren blends open theism, N. T. Wright's new perspective on Paul's doctrine of justification, and inclusivism, with minimum focus on biblical truth. Formations for his conclusions come from his experiences, dreams, expectations, and predilections, but not from propositions of the Word. He represents his experiences as biblical but does not root them in the Word. Postconservatism seriously compromises the truth of biblical Christianity.

## Perspectivism Produces Cynicism

Postmoderns reject absolute, objective truth. They deem that reality is in the mind of the beholder and that everyone views reality through one's own culture. Logic is not as important as experience or mysticism. Cynicism pervades postmodernism, so we can take nothing at face value. The only valid value is the value we create. We must deconstruct all viewpoints and constantly reconstruct them. Postevangelicals now claim that we cannot directly know the truth of Scripture without contaminating its original meaning. Therefore, the best hope for understanding God's revelation is through a consensual community of Christians who check with fallible understandings of the individual. In this view, we are to hold multiple meanings or at least "modestly" dialogue with other viewpoints. By constant dialogue with others who disagree with us, we come closer to understanding the Bible.

Postmodern evangelicals emphasize narrative theology as over against propositional theology; they prefer community interpretation as over against individual interpretation, positive dialogue with other traditions, and the delimitation of the individual interpreter as the source for understanding Scripture. The idea that God can communicate formal truth with clarity in his Word is a menacing idea to them. In other words, they diminish the perspicuity of Scripture.

Obviously, there are enigmatic portions of Scripture that demand humility in interpretation. It is one thing to take a probability approach to enigmatic passages, but it is another to take this tack with all Scripture. Not to draw lines on anything is to end in polyvalence, relativism, and subjectivism. Rejection of our ability to know truth with certainty undermines Christianity at its heart and results in theological compromise. If postmodern evangelicals were consistent, they would adopt nihilism as a formal construct. If our understanding of truth is only approximate and probable, then our perception of God and his principles for life can only be probable. We weaken God's propositional revelation in favor of open interaction with traditions, and we supplant the authority of Scripture (*sola scriptura*) and the lucidity of God's Word (perspicuity) with a theology of human imagination.

## Correspondent View of Truth

Postconservatives confuse reason and rationalism. Rationalism came out of the Enlightenment's naturalistic assumption about reality. Reason and logic did not originate in the Enlightenment, for Aristotle had something to do with logic! Christians cannot communicate God's Word without logic and reason, and in using logic and reason they do not have to resort to rationalism. Postconservatives who reach past reason into irrationalism go beyond Christianity itself. Christianity revolves around truth and not privatized spirituality. Christianity is essentially about God and not the self, for it relates to God-revealed propositions.

Christ accepted the truth of the Old Testament wholly. He referred to the Old Testament with the saying "It is written," implying its concursive authority. Jesus relied on propositional statements to convey his ideas. Scripture (what is written) imposed a necessity on Jesus (Luke 24:25–27). Jesus rebuked the Pharisees for not believing what the Scriptures said about him (John 5:45–47). Jesus insisted on belief in every word of the Old Testament (Matthew 5:18). He was adamant that his disciples accept the truth of his words if they were to love him. We cannot separate personal illumination from propositional revelation.

Both Paul (2 Timothy 3:16) and Peter (2 Peter 1:20–21) held to God as the author of Scripture. If the Bible is the record of God's writing, then it carries his truth. God always identified his Word with the written record in the canon and as an adequate vehicle to communicate his ideas.

The logic of non-contradiction is true because it corresponds to all of reality. A is not non-A. That is true in all places at all times. God never contradicts himself, for he knows all things exhaustively and truly. Everything he says in his Word matches reality. His truth is exclusive property not common to all assertions. Postconservatives want to locate authority in community as a source for doctrine. To place the community's tradition and culture alongside Scripture as final authority flies in the face of *sola scriptura* and would disallow the Bible's exclusive critique of the community. The correspondent view of truth holds that a statement must correspond to reality (i.e., be factual). Facts establish truth or falsity. The Bible consistently portrays itself in this way, but postconservatives want to deny that the Bible presents itself as objectively real. They believe that because the authors of Scripture present their ideas in ambiguous ways, the reader cannot understand the original intent. They, therefore, have the need to "deconstruct" the meaning of Scripture to their personal encounter with the text because no objective truth exists independent of the reader, which leads to relativism and skepticism within the evangelical camp. These people are hostile to those who hold absolutes. What is worse, they are skeptical of the exclusive truth claims of the Word of God itself in a compromise of staggering implications. By setting up a false antithesis, postconservatives claim that evangelicals hold to bombproof certainty. What evangelicals actually hold to is real, or true, knowledge that corresponds to facts.

Grenz and Franke want to differentiate doctrine from Scripture. Doctrines to them are second-order assertions within a community that regulate how a community thinks about itself and God. Because their view is that doctrines do not make actual assertions about God, all they have left is dialectical antithesis and not didactic thesis. Is God's Word revelation or is it communal thinking? Provisional perspective on truth leads to distrust in confident proclamation of truth. Postmodernism rejects any claim to universality, so when this pluralistic assumption goes without challenge, we are left without objective truth and possess little ground to our claim for truth.

To Grenz, doctrines are second-order beliefs, not first-order propositions. This destroys objective truth in doctrine because it precludes doctrine from the process. All that is left is the community's culture and language. This reduces doctrine to cultural perspectives, and would fail to speak anything for certain, including the gospel itself. Postmoderns allow for mutually pluralistic contradictory beliefs because there are no first-order beliefs. There is no overarching standard for determining truth from error in differing communities. This elevation of tradition of communities to the level of Scripture is a major defection from evangelical faith. Although Grenz identified Scripture as the most important of sources, placing tradition and culture in the same category as Scripture preempts the principle of *sola scriptura.*

Grenz does not want to identify the Bible with revelation. He wants the community to encounter the Bible as an act, and this becomes revelation, which is very similar to the older neo-orthodoxy (also dialectical). This viewpoint looks at revelation as personal, but we cannot know a person without propositions from the Bible. Revelation exposes the person by proposition.

Postconservatives who hold this view of truth have no way to universally verify what they believe. By rejecting objective and factual truth, they cannot come to certainty; they cannot claim with certainty that Christianity is true. The Bible, on the other hand, presents a unified view of truth and falsity. By not starting with the Word of God, postconservatives wallow in subjectivism, with no ability to discern truth from error. All that remains is subjective mysticism arising out of subjective illumination. Apostasy was rampant in both the Old and New Testaments, so how can a modern Christian community decipher whether its beliefs are true or not?

> But I fear, lest somehow, as the serpent deceived Eve by his crafti-ness, so your minds may be corrupted from the simplicity that is in Christ. For if he who comes preaches another Jesus whom we have not preached, or if you receive a different spirit which you have not received, or a different gospel which you have not accepted—you may well put up with it! For I consider that I am not at all inferior to the most eminent apostles. (2 Corinthians 11:3–5)

Grenz and Franke set up a false distinction between propositional and personal revelation. What is important, they contend, is not the text of Scripture but the Spirit's use of Scripture for appropriation for the contemporary church. This puts the Spirit's present speaking outside the text of the canon and twists the Bible into something other than its original intension. Conversely, we can know nothing about the person of Christ without written revelation of Christ. God is more than talk about a community. True authority does not reside in the readers of Scripture but in what the Holy Spirit revealed to the original writers. Scripture's use of Scripture is very different from how Grenz and Franke use it. By accepting a postmodern approach to truth, these people diverge from evangelicalism by denying that people can know truth in an objective, universal way. All of this presupposes an autonomous, sovereign, finite self, with each person having a provisional perspective on the world. It amounts to interpolation of Scripture.

If truth is only personal and not propositional, then there is no adequate way to explain the passages where truth means propositional correspondence. Of the approximately one hundred passages where the New Testament uses the word "truth," only one passage undisputedly uses it for a person (John 14:6). Some passages relate truth to being in a person or not being in a person (John 1:14, 17; 8:44; 1 John 2:4), but these passages involve true or false propositions. The normal usage of "truth" in the New Testament is in the propositional sense. We can know truth (Romans 2:20). Any Scripture that uses truth in reference to a person is understood as meaning a person who speaks truth or whose word we can trust (Revelation 3:14; 21:5).

Even passages understood in a practical or personal sense still require the correspondence view of truth. An action must correspond to God's expectations in order to be true. We cannot explain passages where the Bible uses truth propositionally in a strictly personal sense, a sense that is not factually correct. We need to get our view of truth about the Bible from the Word of God. That God reveals himself as a person does not preclude the fact that he reveals himself through propositional truths about himself (1 Corinthians 2:9–12, 16). Some of God's plans for humans are not discoverable by man. Only God can know fully what is in the mind of God.

## Propositions

A proposition is an assertion about what is true or false. It is whatever we can deny, assert, presuppose, maintain, or imply. Propositions are the building blocks of logic and communication. A proposition is simply the meaning of a declarative sentence. It is the content of a sentence. The content, or facts, of a sentence makes it true. Truth is a quality of proposition that conforms to God's assertions. False propositions do not conform to data. God's statements in Scripture are true to reality.

Truth is more than encounter or something personal. If it were possible to commit to a person without propositions, then it would hypothetically be possible to commit to an evil person as well as a good person. Truth is exclusively propositional, for it is a property of propositions. Truth is not an encounter, an event, emotions, or something personal. To view truth as those things abandons truth for personal relationships. The Word of God overwhelmingly uses the term "belief" and its various cognates hundreds of times with an object. That is, belief in the gospel is belief in the object of Christ's death for forgiveness. The Bible uses the idea of "commit" and its cognates very little, and mostly with the commission of sins. Substitution of commitment to a person instead of a proposition has led many astray. This is an anti-reason or anti-doctrine approach to reality.

The Bible is a propositional disclosure of God's fixed truth, so it presents itself in propositional form. Listen to what Carl Henry has to say about propositions:

> We mean by propositional revelation that God supernaturally communicated his revelation to chosen spokesmen in the express form of cognitive truths, and that the inspired prophetic-apostolic proclamation reliably articulates these truths in sentences that are not internally contradictory.[185]

We cannot know God's personal presence without propositions. Those who say that we can know God's personal presence without propositions confuse ontology with epistemology. God is ontologically different from humans, but we can know this only propositionally. Biblically, there is no such thing as a personal encounter other than in propositional form. We cannot contrast personal revelation with disclosure of information, for on what basis would we distinguish personal revelation from satanic suggestion? It is only through propositional revelation that we can know God. God is the source of all revealed truth, but there are more propositions about him than he revealed in Scripture. However, if we adopt a non-propositional approach to truth, why should one person's preference for God be any better than the next person's preference? If God cannot communicate himself properly and shows himself only personally, then we cannot know truth with certainty. If God's truth is propositionally clear, then we can know how truth differs from falsehood.

We cannot establish a non-propositional thesis simply because the Bible reveals God's personhood. Paul addresses general revelation to the "mind" and understanding (Romans 1:19–20, 32). God intends that the Bible reach reason and conscience. Special revelation presents propositional content of general revelation. God told Old Testament prophets to protect propositional revelation (Deuteronomy 18:18–20). This is how we can distinguish truth from error. The Bible warns against the person who presents a personal perspective as over against God's propositions (Ezekiel 13:3). The Holy Spirit revealed the "things we speak" (1 Corinthians 2:10–13) so that truth stood revealed at one point in the past (aorist indicative). The New Testament regularly uses terms of revelation for disclosure of propositional truths (Revelation 22:6–7). Although the Bible communicates itself in many literary genres, such as parable and poetry, all genres have conception adequacy. All biblical literature is revelation.

Postconservatives openly favor certain types of passages, such as those about the incarnation, narrative passages, and parables, because they want to ignore propositions. Their underlying motivation is to preclude passages that set forth propositional truth and present ideas in their most non-offensive, bland way. They want to blunt the distinctiveness of God's Word and make it adaptable to cultural mores so that it makes for more diversity and the greatest acceptance by the greatest number. Postconservatives are a threat to revelation as doctrine. Evangelicalism historically has rooted its beliefs in objective truth, cultural or theological trends notwithstanding.

## Truth Corresponds to God

The correspondent view of truth has been the long-held view of most evangelicals until recently. Correspondence holds that a statement is true if it corresponds to the facts or reality. The statement that my house is in Saint Cloud, Florida, is either factually true or false. That is the law of the excluded middle—either my house is in Saint Cloud or it is not. There is no other, or middle, option. The law of non-contradiction says that A cannot be non-A in the same way and in the same respect at the same time. My house cannot be in Saint Cloud and not in Saint Cloud in the same respect and on the same day. This is not a matter of preference or taste; it is a matter of fact.

Truth is not arbitrary in God, for it is not a product of his will but a matter of his knowledge in complete self-coherence; truth is constitutional with God. Truth is what corresponds with God; it is propositional expression revealed by God. Truth and fact are synonymous. Truth is more than what corresponds to reality, because truth resides essentially in God. Only God knows fully who he is and what he willed. If this assumption is true, then human thinking must correspond with the propositions God revealed. Truth is subject and predicate (information, concepts). Propositions are the only means by which thinking minds can process information. Non-propositional thinking is inherently contradictory. People like Grenz and McLaren must use propositions to attack propositions. Propositions correctly correspond to states of affairs. Truth is interlocking propositions in one corresponding system.

God as a God of truth means that he is eternally self-consistent. He never contradicts his nature; he is eternally correspondent to fact, so his knowledge is perfect, exhaustive, and absolute. Truth is not a product of his will but the essence and constitution of his being. That is why he cannot lie (Hebrews 6:18). Truth is what corresponds to God's mind, and he is ultimate reality. Because only God knows truth exhaustively, he alone can declare truth with certainty. Mankind can know ultimate truth only if we know truth that corresponds to God. We can know ultimate, universal truth only deductively, not inductively, because only God can reveal God. God's deductive truth contains eternally directed propositions.

Instead of propositions, postconservatives use "conversation" to come to theological meaning. "Conversation" never presupposes that ideas in the Bible are true from exegesis. Truth and falsity are not an issue to postconservatives. Ideas are always open to synthesis. They think of propositional truth as a "freeze-dried, shrink-wrapped, or fossilized" approach to thinking.[186] This is a false characterization of traditional hermeneutics. Evangelicals have never asserted that they have the final answer to all things. However, they assert that they can know some things from Scripture. McLaren does not see the Bible as the final source for coming to truth. He runs pell-mell to a plethora of other sources for finding truth. By abandoning exegesis and exposition, postconservatives entered into a free-fall from meaning. Escape from Scripture has devastating consequences: radical emergents can receive truth from pantheists as well as theists; they come to God as they see fit; the self is the basic source for meaning. The Bible writers never shared this idea about not finding certainty about meaning.

## Distinguishing Orthodoxy from Heterodoxy

Paul commanded Titus to speak with authority and certainty in order to silence false teachers (Titus 1:9–16). This is not the same as a militant, pugnacious, ugly approach to confrontation. Postconservatives cannot contradict falsehoods in any sense. They cannot affirm truth because they reduce truth to include feelings. If authority is relative to the culture's idea of authority, then there is no authority for anyone. Postconservatives float with the flotsam and jetsam of culture on an ocean of relativity without a shore. If they protest that this is not true, then they must appeal to propositional truth to assert their viewpoint. No, they wish to rest on subjective authority and the consensus of the group.

The Bible warns everywhere against false prophets and teachers. False teachers teach doctrines that do not correspond to truth, so writers of Scripture warn their readers of those who distort and misrepresent truth. (All the major and minor prophets of the Old Testament, John 8:44, Jude, 2 Peter, and, in fact, all of the second books of the New Testament such as 2 Corinthians and 2 Thessalonians, warn against apostasy.) The evidence for this is overwhelming in Scripture.

The Bible clearly distinguishes truth from untruth propositionally. Propositions are the only way to distinguish truth from error. Attacking error presumes knowing truth. It is one thing to be narrow-mindedly intolerant by not dealing with others with integrity and honesty; it is another to deny implicitly what one believes by snuffing any contradiction of falsity. The Bible proclaims false religions as idolatry and as purveyors of error.

Paul warns leaders to guard their flocks against error (Acts 20:24–31). Paul declares the "whole counsel of God" but warns that doctrinal "wolves" will come, not sparing the flock, speaking twisted things, and drawing disciples after themselves. Scripture constantly warns against not straying from propositional doctrines of the Word.

> *But God be thanked that though you were slaves of sin, yet you obeyed from the heart that form of **doctrine** to which you were delivered.*
> (Romans 6:17, bold italics mine)

*Hold fast the pattern of **sound words** which you have heard from me, in faith and love which are in Christ Jesus. That good thing which was committed to you, keep by the Holy Spirit who dwells in us.*
(2 Timothy 1:13–14, bold italics mine)

The word for false teaching (ἑτεροδιδασκαλέω, literally "against teaching") occurs in 1 Timothy 1:3; 6:3 for those who disseminate false (ἑτερο, "another of a different kind, heretical") doctrine. The idea is to teach error.

*As I urged you when I went into Macedonia—remain in Ephesus that you may charge some that they teach **no other doctrine.***
(1 Timothy 1:3, bold italics mine)

*If anyone teaches otherwise and does not consent to wholesome **words,** even **the words** of our Lord Jesus Christ, and to the **doctrine** which accords with godliness, he is proud, knowing nothing, but is obsessed with disputes and arguments over words.* (1 Timothy 6:3, 4, bold italics mine)

## Didactic Role of Pastor-Teacher

The primary purpose of the church is for believers, not non-Christians. The emergent church has lost sight of this. Evangelism is one thing; building believers in the faith is another. It is impossible to build believers without solid didactic teaching from God's Word. How can Christianity maintain its distinctiveness without teaching truth? We cannot play to the fringe element and hope to maintain strong believers. Jesus did not try to play to the Pharisees or Sadducees. He made distinction and difference. He viewed heresy as a reality. David Wells explains how postconservatives have turned theology on its head:

In an extraordinary fashion, then, the theological wheel has turned full circle. Evangelicals, no less than Liberals before them whom they have always berated, have now abandoned doctrine in favor of "life." . . . For evangelicals today, this life is also an "essence" detached from a cognitive structure, a detachment made necessary by the external modern world in which it no longer has a viable place, and it really does not require a theological view of life.[187]

The Bible calls the pastor of the local church "pastor-teacher" and applies both functions to the same office (Ephesians 4:11). This role communicates revealed truth deductively and propositionally to the congregation. The Holy Spirit illumines truth to the mind of the expositor (1 Corinthians 2:10–14). If God illumines the Word to individual believers, why is there a need for pastors? God bestows upon certain men the gift called pastor-teacher (a single gift, not divisible). God assigns this gifted person to a local church. Many people in local churches do not have this gift. It is the responsibility of the listener to check out the trustworthiness of what they hear from the pastor-teacher (Acts 17:10–12).

Thus, the epistemology of Scripture is that we can know truth through the illumination of the Holy Spirit. This illumination does not teach anything beyond what God already revealed in Scripture. Illumination does not constitute additional revelation but is an application of Scripture already in existence. The Holy Spirit illumines what is in the text of Scripture. This is not additional normative revelation but rather application of principles of Scripture to experience. As a fallible human being, the pastor-teacher is not absolute, and so believers must constantly measure what the pastor-teacher says against the Word of God. The Berean example of checking is the biblical standard. Scripture is the normative tool for verification.

> *Now we have received, not the spirit of the world, but the Spirit who is from God, that we might know the things that have been freely given to us by God. These things we also speak, not in words which man's wisdom teaches but which the Holy Spirit teaches, comparing spiritual things with spiritual. But the natural man does not receive the things of the Spirit of God, for they are foolishness to him; nor can he know them, because they are spiritually discerned. But he who is spiritual judges all things, yet he himself is rightly judged by no one. For "who has known the mind of the LORD that he may instruct Him?" But we have the mind of Christ.* (1 Corinthians 1:12–16)

> *Be diligent to present yourself approved to God, a worker who does not need to be ashamed, rightly dividing the word of truth.* (2 Timothy 2:15)

Thus, the pastor's role is to teach the Bible; the congregation's role is to hear the Bible but check what the pastor says against the Bible. The pastor-teacher does not monopolize divine truth or hold a special monopoly on knowing truth. Any believer can verify claims presented by the pastor-teacher (Hebrews 13:7, 17).

The pastor-teacher's interpretation is not identical with illumination. The Holy Spirit enables the believer to discern, receive truth, welcome it, and apply it to experience. This does not imply that a pastor-teacher has a totally comprehensive and completely accurate interpretation of the Word of God.

The pastor is the communicator of biblical truth, and the Holy Spirit illumines truth to the believer (John 14:26; 16:13–15; 1 Corinthians 2:10–14). This truth is not new revelation but understanding of existing revelation. A pastor's interpretation is not infallible, for the Spirit's help in interpretation is not something beyond validation or verification. The Spirit's work in illumination first means that the Holy Spirit helps the believer understand the passage, but, more than that, illumination is not complete until the believer appropriates truth to experience.

In 2 Timothy 3:1 Paul challenges Timothy to "know" something so as to keep it in mind. Timothy is to remember that "in the last days perilous [hard or difficult] times will come [set in]." Then in verses 2 to 7 he describes characteristics of the ungodly people living in these times, concluding with the words "always learning and never able to come to the knowledge of the truth." "Never able" indicates finality in their fruitless endeavor to find the truth.

Paul then gives an illustration of two men who rejected (set themselves against) the authority of Moses' message:

> *Now as Jannes and Jambres resisted Moses, so do these also resist the truth: men of corrupt minds, disapproved concerning the faith; but they will progress no further, for their folly will be manifest to all, as theirs also was.* (2 Timothy 3:8, 9)

As Jannes and Jambres rejected doctrinal teaching, so people in Paul's day also rejected the truth. They had a "reprobate" (*adokimos*) mind, a mind that rejected truth after a test. Timothy, however, "carefully followed [Paul's] doctrine" (3:10). The word "follow" means to follow after as a standard or rule. Timothy conformed himself to the rule of Paul's apostolic teaching. Timothy was loyal to truth.

Paul establishes the realism that people will constantly allow themselves to be deceived:

> *Yes, and all who desire to live godly in Christ Jesus will suffer persecution. But evil men and impostors will grow worse and worse, deceiving and being deceived.* (2 Timothy 3:12, 13)

Then Paul challenges Timothy to maintain doctrinal integrity:

> *But you must continue in the things which you have learned and been assured of, knowing from whom you have learned them.* (3:14)

Beginning in 3:14, Paul appeals for doctrinal soundness. Paul challenges Timothy to "continue" in what he taught his son in the faith, that is, to be loyal to Paul's teaching. Timothy had become "assured" of what Paul taught. Timothy had to learn Scripture before he became "assured" of God's Word. The phrase "been assured of" (ἐπιστώθης) means "firmly believed" (aorist—at one point). Timothy could trust the authority of the Holy Spirit's revelation and inspiration through Paul.

> *And that from childhood you have known the Holy Scriptures, which are able to make you wise for salvation through faith which is in Christ Jesus.* (3:15)

The "Holy Scriptures" refers to the Old Testament. "Scriptures" means "that which has been written, writing, or document." The Scriptures do not save, they only point to salvation.

Paul then proceeds to describe the nature of written Scripture:

> *All Scripture is given by inspiration of God, and is profitable for doctrine, for reproof, for correction, for instruction in righteousness, that the man of God may be complete, thoroughly equipped for every good work.* (3:16, 17)

"Doctrine" refers to didactic content. The term "doctrine" occurs fifteen times in the three pastoral books (1 & 2 Timothy; Titus). Doctrine means "instruction, teaching." Scripture instructs by content or propositional truth (Romans 15:4).

God gave "all" (literally "every"), not "most," inscripturated writings by inspiration. God inspired each passage as a unit. Every part of these writings God views to be inspired. "Inspired" is literally "God breathed." God (not humans) breathed into writings, so every written Scripture is God breathed. This is not referring to the process of God's inspiring men (1 Corinthians 2:9–16) but to the fact of inspiration itself; God did not breathe into the writers of Scripture but into Scripture itself.

Inspired Scripture is profitable for "teaching" (doctrine); that is, teaching factual material. Scripture is also valuable for "reproof" (conviction). The Bible convicts of sin and brings "correction"; that is, restoration to an upright state. The Word of God also gives "instruction" (*paideia*), which is training resulting in cultivation of mind and morals, chastening. The idea is not punitive but corrective. God's revealed Scripture brings maturity to the believer, that he "may be complete." To be "thoroughly equipped for every good work" carries the idea of being fitted out for service.

Paul continues with the same approach about objective revelation of propositional truth with a serious warning in chapter 4:

> *I charge you therefore before God and the Lord Jesus Christ, who will judge the living and the dead at His appearing and His kingdom. Preach the word! Be ready in season and out of season. Convince, rebuke, exhort, with all longsuffering and teaching.* (2 Timothy 4:1, 2)

There are five aorist imperatives in this verse, making these commandments urgent. His final charge to the young pastor Timothy was that he "preach the word." There will come a time when people will not "endure sound doctrine." This is why Paul charged Timothy before the presence of God and the Lord Jesus Christ. Jesus will judge people who responsibly handle God's Word and those who do not.

The word "preach" is a sharp command in the Greek. The idea is to preach as a public proclamation. Timothy was to be an official herald of King Jesus. In doing this, he was to preach the "Word." The "Word" is the whole body of revealed truth. Timothy cannot herald his own message, for God gave him a message to proclaim. He is to do this in a state of constant readiness ("instant"). He is to do it "in season" (an opportune season) and "out of season" (an inopportune season). He does this in favorable and unfavorable seasons. There is no season to stop preaching. There is no dialogue in this command.

Paul challenges Timothy to "rebuke" (or reprove) his listeners so that they will be convicted of sin. Timothy is to rebuke in a sharp, severe sense. He is also to "exhort." He is to do all these commands with a sense of "longsuffering and teaching." The word "longsuffering" carries the idea of having patience with people, dealing with the manner of handling those aberrant in doctrine. There is skill involved with this, for a good preacher does not hastily pounce on people. The second element in correcting people is to do it with doctrine (literally, "with teaching content" or "instruction"). Didactic instruction in association with "longsuffering" is necessary to preach the Word properly.

People have a proclivity toward experience over doctrine, so Paul warns Timothy about this problem in 2 Timothy:

> *For the time will come when they will not endure sound doctrine, but according to their own desires, because they have itching ears, they will heap up for themselves teachers.* (2 Timothy 4:3)

The "for" gives the reason for verse 2; there is coming a time when people will not tolerate sound doctrine. There will come a time when "they will not endure sound doctrine;" the word "endure" means "to hold upright or firm" and carries the idea of accepting. There will be a time when people will not accept doctrine as valid. The reason for this is that they have "itching ears." "Itching ears" occurs only here in the New Testament and probably refers to the speculative teaching of chapter 1 (verses 3 through 7). These people have an insatiable curiosity for teachers that suit their liking. Not only will they listen to false teaching, but they will "heap up" false teachers for themselves. They handpick these false teachers to suit their preferences.

Congregations will not hold firmly to sound doctrine. The word "sound" means "healthy;" they cannot tolerate solid or healthy teaching. They will fall for the inane and experiential over doctrine. The definite article preceding the word "doctrine" speaks of the system of doctrine or teaching. It is important to be systematic in doctrine. Systematic theology is important after all!

The problem of not enduring sound doctrine is a problem of ego lust. People want their perspective on life to the exclusion of God's viewpoint on life. Their "itching ears" love to hear what they want to hear from their own perspective.

The word "heap" denotes "accumulating in piles." They will listen to anybody anywhere if it meets their perspective on life. They want to pile up teachers who give them what they want to hear, not the unadulterated Word of God.

The word "itch" means "to scratch, to tickle, to make to itch." These people take gratification in listening to some novel perspective (Acts 17:21). This is the orientation of postconservative postmodernism—relativism and uncertainty. They "turn their ears away [avert their ears] from the truth" (2 Timothy 4:4). They do not want their ears to be open to truth, so they will not meet the truth. The effect of this is that they will "turn away" (they do the turning) from the truth and "be turned" (someone else turns them) to "fables" (fiction as opposed to fact).

The second word for "turn" means "to twist out." The medical use of this term meant "to wrench out of its proper place," such as a limb twisted out of joint; the Greek used this term for a dislocated arm. When people avert their ears from listening to the truth, they open themselves to dislocated satanic influence. They put themselves out of adjustment to the Word of God, incapacitating their ability to think biblically. The Bible nails postconservatism at its uncertain core.

> *And they will turn their ears away from the truth, and be turned aside to fables.* (2 Timothy 4:4)

The result of not enduring sound doctrine is that these people turn away from the truth and wander into myths. To "turn away" carries the idea of deliberately refusing to open themselves to the truth. The word translated "myths" occurs four times in the New Testament and refers to doctrine that is not true.

## Exclusive Truth

Paul challenges Timothy to charge those in Ephesus to teach exclusive truth or doctrine from the Bible

> *As I urged you when I went into Macedonia—remain in Ephesus that you may charge some that they teach **no other doctrine.***
> (1 Timothy 1:3, bold italics mine)

The Greek for "teach no other doctrine" means that, first, doctrine is important for the Christian way of life and, second, there are teachings that violate correct doctrine. There is a standard against which we can measure truth to distinguish it from non-truth. There is such a thing as heresy or untrue doctrine and these doctrines are "destructive":

> *But there were also false prophets among the people, even as there will be false teachers among you, who will secretly bring in destructive heresies, even denying the Lord who bought them, and bring on themselves swift destruction.* (2 Peter 2:1)

Paul in Galatians 1:6–8 shows how seriously he views issues of heresy within the church:

> *I marvel that you are turning away so soon from Him who called you in the grace of Christ, to a different gospel, which is not another [of the same kind]; but there are some who trouble you and want to pervert the gospel of Christ. But even if we, or an angel from heaven, preach any other gospel to you than what we have preached to you, let him be accursed.* (Galatians 1:6–8)

The introduction to the book of Galatians covers the first ten verses. The occasion of the epistle (reason for the letter) runs from verse 6 through verse 10. This section carries a denunciation of the Galatian believers for leaving the true gospel for a false gospel, and this is conspicuous by the lack of any expression of gratitude toward the Galatian readers anywhere in the book, something that is normal in introductions. Doctrinal deviation deserves no thanks.

"I marvel": Paul moves abruptly into the problem at the church in Galatia. What a transition from praising the glory of God in the previous verse to this statement of shock about the Galatians' defection from the gospel of grace! "Marvel" means "to wonder." Paul is astonished and surprised that the Galatians would abandon the gospel of grace. Paul says in effect, "I am shocked that you are so unstable that you would move away from the gospel of grace so quickly." This beginning of the body of the epistle makes it very clear that Galatian Christians deserved severe rebuke. Very few evangelicals today express shock about anything, even defection from the gospel. Jesus marveled at this issue as well: "And He marveled because of their unbelief. Then He went about the villages in a circuit, teaching" (Mark 6:6). His "teaching" corrected unbelief.

The phrase "that you are turning away" carries the idea of changing places, putting in another place, removing a person or thing from one place to another, transposing. This is a military term used for deserting from the army. By changing from the gospel of grace to the gospel of works, the Galatians deserted the true gospel and capitulated to another gospel.

The present tense indicates that the defection of the Galatians from the gospel of grace was not yet complete at the writing of Galatians. They were still in the process of transposing the true gospel into another gospel; they were transposing the gospel from grace to legalism. By altering the gospel itself, they were deserting, or turning apostate from, the true gospel. This changes the nature of the gospel into a works gospel. People today change the gospel into something significantly different from God's original design through carelessness with doctrine.

The word "soon" in "so soon" means "quickly." The Galatians moved away from the true gospel in a very brief interval between the time that Paul gave them the gospel and the time when the legalizers came to Galatia. It took only a brief time for them to abandon their earlier convictions. They were rash in embracing false doctrine and moving into legalism. They failed to give due study to doctrine about the issue. False teachers can easily seduce ignorant and, therefore, unstable Christians. Instability in the truth of the gospel makes one vulnerable to false doctrine. There is such a thing as a true gospel and a false gospel. Our culture, holding to the absolute belief in tolerance, cannot, ironically, tolerate truth. If someone claims to have the true gospel, that person sounds like a bigot, or at least very narrow-minded. The gospel is as narrow as the multiplication table. Two times two equals four, without exception. We cannot have two gospels. It is incomprehensible that evangelicals today would hold to distortion of the gospel. This cancer threatens the essence of Christianity. Issues of heaven and hell are at stake.

The phrase "from Him" indicates the Galatians deserted God himself. When we defect from the truth of the gospel of grace, we desert from more than a doctrine; we desert God himself. God is the one "who called you." God called the Galatians in the sphere of the grace of Christ, but they deserted their call in grace for works salvation. Paul says that they are not true to their calling. Their apostasy was from God and his grace, not simply from Paul.

The prepositional phrase "in the grace of Christ" indicates the sphere of the Galatian defection from the truth. God called them to a gospel that rested upon the finished work of Christ on the cross (Galatians 1:4). Christ suffered all that needs to be suffered on the cross. Because he did the suffering, we do not need to suffer for sins. He took my hell that I might have his heaven. This is grace. It is a gospel of salvation by what Jesus did, not by what we do. There are no strings attached to this salvation, for it is free because Jesus did all the work. He bore all of our sins in his own body on the cross.

God called us in the sphere of grace, but the Galatians did not clearly understand the truth of salvation by grace through faith. Grace is the means of our call; that is, God effectually summons us to salvation only as procured by Christ on the cross. God freely bestows this gift. It comes from the unadulterated generosity of God with no strings attached. Christians are the objects of God's eternal favor. To revert to law is to miss this truth completely. God saves and sustains us by the finished work of Christ on the cross. Some Galatians believed that they came to Christ by grace but that works sustained their salvation, which also makes salvation dependent upon works.

There is such a thing as heresy. Note the phrase "to a different gospel." There are two Greek words for "another." One means another of the same kind and the other means another of a different kind. The latter idea is our word "different" here. We get the English terms "heretic" and "heterodoxy" from the Greek word. The gospel they were buying into was different in its very nature from the gospel of grace; their new gospel was different in essence. The hazard is high here because the very essence of the gospel is at stake.

> *For if he who comes preaches another Jesus whom we have not preached, or if you receive a different spirit which you have not received, or a different gospel which you have not accepted—you may well put up with it* [a facetious remark]! (2 Corinthians 11:4)

Counterfeiters try to make the fake look as much like the real thing as possible. A gospel with a touch of works seems reasonable to some folk, but God views this gospel as a "heretical" gospel. This is not an orthodox idea but a heterodox idea and the polar opposite of orthodoxy. A gospel of justification or sanctification by works is heterodoxy.

The test of the true gospel is the test of grace. We are under obligation to protect the purity of the gospel of grace. When we defect from the gospel of grace, we defect from God himself. If we lose sight of the Word of God, we can become turncoats to the true gospel very quickly. This is a deadly issue because we cannot live the Christian life properly without a true understanding of the gospel. Doctrine affects how we live as Christians. We need to restore our capacity for shock at distortions of the gospel.

The next phrase—"which is not another; but there are some who trouble you and want to pervert the gospel of Christ"—shows a heterodox gospel. This word "another" refers to "another of the same kind." If people change the essence of the gospel, it becomes no gospel at all. It is not another gospel of the same kind as Paul preached, but a perversion of the true gospel. When they modify the gospel, it is not the gospel at all.

Legalists came to "trouble" the Galatians with their false doctrine—"but there are some who trouble you" (Acts 15:24; Galatians 1:7; 5:10). Legalism always unsettles the soul and throws the church into confusion (Galatians 5:10–12). "Trouble" carries the idea of "shaking back and forth." A legalistic gospel makes trouble that shakes belief.

The Holy Spirit through Paul then makes an alarming statement—"and want to pervert the gospel of Christ." The idea behind the word "pervert" is to transform something into an opposite character. The Judaizers transformed the gospel into something diametrically opposite to its true character; thus, they perverted the gospel. They turned it around into the very opposite of its original design. They altered its message from a doctrine of grace to a doctrine of works. A distorted gospel is more dangerous than no gospel at all.

The gospel is Christ's gospel, not Paul's gospel. When people distort the gospel, they violate Christ. There is no alternative to the gospel of Christ, which is exclusive of any other gospel. A gospel that finds the completed work of Christ on the cross as insufficient to pay the penalty for sin is a false gospel. Salvation is always by grace through faith apart from works.

We live in a day of such theological latitude that we distort the gospel into something other than the New Testament gospel and no one blinks an eye.

Some say, "We must be tolerant of people who don't believe the same as we do." Fakers stand in affiliation with true believers as long as they are "sincere." Christianity is not fifty percent faith and fifty percent works. No, the true gospel excludes work as a way of salvation or sanctification.

> *Of how much worse punishment, do you suppose, will he be thought worthy who has trampled the Son of God underfoot, counted the blood of the covenant by which he was sanctified a common thing, and insulted the Spirit of grace?* (Hebrews 10:29)

Christians today need to deal with those who distort the true gospel. Tolerance means that we judge no one, but truth demands that we judge those who pervert the gospel. Salvation by works is not good news. It is bad news because then salvation would depend on us, not Christ.

Paul makes the point further in Galatians. Just in case some might think his team is an exception, he includes his gospel team in this hypothesis: "But even if we, or an angel from heaven, preach any other gospel to you." Paul draws the unlikely hypothesis that if even his gospel team or an angel from heaven were to preach a different gospel than the gospel of grace, God should curse them along with anyone else who distorts the gospel. It makes no difference who preaches the gospel: the gospel must be the unadulterated gospel of grace. This is not a question of who preaches but what is preached.

Paul now moves to the severity of how he views those who would distort the gospel of grace. If anyone preaches a gospel other than grace, "let him be accursed." If anyone preaches not only a markedly different gospel, but also any gospel other than what Paul preaches, then they should undergo a curse. The Galatians probably assumed that the gospel of the legalizers was not very different from the gospel of grace.

The translators take the Greek word *anathema* and carry it over as it sounds into the English. The metaphorical idea of "accursed" means "something devoted to destruction, a curse." People who preach a different gospel than the gospel of grace stand under God's judgment. We deal in a very serious matter when we distort the gospel. The tone of the Word of God is very different from the postconservative tone; in fact, it is the polar opposite.

Postconservatives try to make it appear that if you castigate false teaching, you are not Christian in attitude. If that is true, then Paul is not Christian in his approach in Galatians. The prophets' writings of the Old Testament and many statements in the New Testament would not be Christian under that thesis. Clearly, Paul declares that the Galatians violated a core principle in Christianity. He speaks plainly when it comes to people who defect from the gospel of grace. True unity revolves around faithfulness to the truth of the gospel. Few call a spade a spade when it comes to false doctrine. Many hate a gospel that claims that people are poor lost sinners, that they are helpless and hopeless without Jesus' death for them on the cross.

Paul refers to a warning in a previous visit about gospel counterfeits: *"As we have said before, so now I say again, if anyone preaches any other gospel to you than what you have received, let him be accursed"* (Galatians 1:9).

The phrase "said before" refers to Paul's previous warning about gospel counterfeits that hurt his team's visit to Galatia. This attack on false teachers was no temper tantrum. He calmly and deliberately reiterates his point—"so now I say again." Paul says in effect, "I told you before and now I am telling you again." He did not and would not change his mind on this crucial doctrine.

How different the biblical message is from the postconservative message! Postconservatives cannot "endure sound doctrine." They are like the people of Isaiah's day who wanted "smooth" ideas and "illusions":

> *And now, go, write it before them on a tablet and inscribe it in a book, that it may be for the time to come as a witness forever. For they are a rebellious people, lying children, children unwilling to hear the instruction of the Lord; who say to the seers, "Do not see," and to the prophets, "Do not prophesy to us what is right; speak to us smooth things, prophesy illusions, leave the way, turn aside from the path, let us hear no more about the Holy One of Israel." Therefore thus says the Holy One of Israel, "Because you despise this word and trust in oppression and perverseness and rely on them, therefore this iniquity shall be to you like a breach in a high wall, bulging out, and about to collapse, whose breaking comes suddenly, in an instant; and its breaking is like that of a potter's vessel that is smashed so ruthlessly that among its*

*fragments not a shard is found with which to take fire from the hearth, or to dip up water out of the cistern."* (Isaiah 30:8–14 ESV)

# Seven

# IS THERE CERTAINTY ANYWHERE?

*Relationship of Propositions to Certainty*

To proclaim every point of doctrine open to question weakens Christian conviction. This will cause great numbers of believers to waver in their faith, "carried about with every wind of doctrine" (Ephesians 4:14). For them, without a clear word from God, most beliefs will stay relative and tentative. God's way to convey clarity and certainty is through the teaching of his Word.

## Propositions Inaccessible from Self

God's propositions seem inaccessible to the person who wants to start from self because to do that one requires total knowledge. The Christian omniscient God gives accurate knowledge from the universal perspective. Biblical faith rests on the premise that revelation comes from an infallible and infinite source. Bible truth is not contingent because the law of non-contradiction can test it.

We live in a day of relentless attacks on propositional truth and even propositional revelation. This arises from a hermeneutic of uncritical suspicion. Uncritical absorption of postmodern thought has led postconservatives into a self-defeating strategy. The biblical worldview is a word-based belief. The Word of God stands at the center of evangelicalism. Any rejection of God's Word will lead to evangelicalism's destruction. God gave his Word with a normal range of meaning for all to understand. Any attempt to deny this is an attempt to silence the voice of God. Silencing God is the nub behind postconservative deconstruction of the Bible. They attempt to kill off the author, and by doing this they minimize God's message to man. Their message is similar to Satan's message—"Did God say?" If Christianity is rooted in what God said, then minimizing the propositions of what he said is to minimize Christianity itself. Treating the Bible in a marginal sense is a seismic shift in understanding Christianity. It is also an assault on scriptural perspicuity. We understand God mainly by the words he speaks. Note what the *Review and Expositor* has to say in this regard:

> Philosophers speak of several types of knowing, including 1) propositional knowledge (the cognitive awareness that something is);
> 2) non-propositional knowledge (the experiential awareness of something); and 3) functional knowledge (the analytical awareness of how to do something). Concerning the first two types, postmodernists reject the primacy of propositional knowing in favor of non-propositional. They argue that it is impossible to make definitively "knowledgeable" pronouncements because each person determines "truth" by how he or she perceives and expresses it. Truth, then, no longer necessarily corresponds to the world "out there." Thus, propositions are not the exclusive, or even dominant, proof of our knowing; instead, they now have "second-order importance."[188]

Christians can and should know God by what he revealed (Isaiah 14:24; Matthew 13:11; Mark 1:14, 15; John 7:17; 8:32; 14:17; 17:3, 7; 1 John 2:21). God presents his truth as firm. Luke wanted Theophilus to "have certainty (*asphaleia*) concerning the things" Luke taught him (Luke 1:4). In Acts, Theophilus needed to look at the "proofs" (*tekmeria*) through which Jesus showed himself alive after his death (Acts 1:3).

The evangelical church is moving away from doctrine, truth, and certainty. In the name of making Christianity "relevant," evangelicals change the method of presenting the message by denuding the message itself. They change the message because the current generation does not like the message. Biblical doctrine must take a back seat to a newly concocted current communication so that it does not offend the listener.

Pastor Doug Pagitt of Solomon's Porch church does not extract truth from the Bible to apply to lives, but "puts words around people's experiences to allow them to find deeper connection in their lives. . . . So our sermons are not lessons that precisely define belief so much as they are stories that welcome our hopes and ideas and participation."[189] He is more about dialogue than doctrine. His premise rests in the presupposition of self-authority rather than the transcendent Word of God.

Postconservatives negate understanding the Bible by propositions because they think there is no distinction between facts and assumption. One opinion is good as another, so it is not possible to know definitely what God says. They emphasize experience over propositional truth, the community over the individual, religious experience over logical propositions of Scripture, and the spiritual over application of principles of Scripture to experience. In other words, there is no ultimate authority. Authority rests in the faith community operating dialectically. This is pure relativity coming from a consensus view of authority. This dual authority combines the text of Scripture with culture in a way that results in no authority. It rejects truth as self-evidencing and indubitable. In this, postconservatives' highest value appears to be investigation and dialogue.

## Rejection of Referential Theory of Language

Postconservatives reject the referential theory of language, that is, that language refers to something objectively real in the thinking of the communicator. A true view of language is that it has more than private meanings for each hearer, that it transmits meaning independent of the hearer. This is how the Bible uses language. The Word of God presumes that God's message carries perspicuity. Perspicuity assumes clarity, contextualization, and capacity to defend its meaning:

> *If anyone teaches a different doctrine and does not agree with the sound words of our Lord Jesus Christ and the teaching that accords with godliness, he is puffed up with conceit and understands nothing. He has an unhealthy craving for controversy and for quarrels about words, which produce envy, dissension, slander, evil suspicions. . . . O Timothy, guard the deposit entrusted to you. Avoid the irreverent babble and contradictions of what is falsely called "knowledge."* (1 Timothy 6:3, 4, 20)

Because postconservatives reject the perspicuity of Scripture, they want to "deconstruct" Scripture by "encounter" with the language of the text. They reject objective meaning in the Bible because it has little meaning beyond subjective experience. This will produce a generation of skeptics unsure of much in the Bible. The only truth they can find is the perspective within a specific community, but not truth that is true for all people, all cultures, and all time.

Postconservative skepticism succumbed to relativism because they think that no truth can be normative. Belief is true only "for them." They disallow exclusive claims for truth because holding to exclusive claims is arrogant; they believe holding to universal truth is a power grab over other viewpoints. They are hostile to the idea that Christianity is true as over against other religions; they want a "new kind of Christian" who is uncertain about what to believe. This is a grave compromise of Christianity in order to suit prevailing viewpoints in culture. This attempt to remove categorical doctrinal truths from its base produces arbitrary uncertainty or opinion. It is lethal to biblical Christianity.

## Doctrine as Rule of Discourse

Doctrines, to postconservatives, are nothing more than rules of discourse for the believing communities because doctrines are not intended to say anything true. From a conservative point of view, it is accurate that doctrines do not save us, but the reality to which they refer saves us (rule of discourse). The belief that Christ's death satisfies a holy God saves us—that is the reference beyond the text. The doctrine does not save us *per se*, but the idea that lies within the doctrine does deliver us. If we worshiped the text, that would be bibliolatry. However, we cannot know truth behind doctrine without doctrine.

Stanley Grenz's writings avoid crediting the Bible as proclaiming anything authoritative or true. The Bible is nothing more than a primary communication partner. D. A. Carson puts Grenz's doctrine of Scripture outside evangelicalism:

> Grenz's reformulation of the doctrine of Scripture is so domesticated by postmodern relativism that it stands well and truly outside the evangelical camp (whether "evangelical" is here understood theologically or socially/historically).[190]

Grenz wants sound doctrine to play a crucial role in the Christian life but to him "sound" does not mean "true"; rather, he is promoting the belief-mosaic of a particular Christian community because he sees any doctrine is interpreted. If all doctrine is interpreted doctrine, then why should he believe the Bible is the Word of God or that Jesus is the Son of God? Why should the discourse of the believing community assert any truth at all? Grenz cannot hold to truth if all human knowledge is nothing but a social construct. Paul preached nothing but "Christ crucified," not the ramblings of a Christian church in community. In his books, Grenz opposes defining evangelicalism based on doctrine. He wants to "revision" evangelicalism into resting on experience rather than doctrine, which was the essential method of old liberalism. Christianity must be "sensed" rather than believed as a set of propositions or doctrinal formulation. Although he acknowledges that evangelical faith ties to the content of divine revelation objectively disclosed, he claims that there is something beyond revelation in a non-cognitive sense—the social or community dimension of theological discourse. The role of community in coming to doctrinal conclusion is important to him, for we get personal identity from social structure. Study of theology is not essentially study of biblical revelation but rather a "second-order" study of what the community already believes.

Grenz does not equate the Bible with revelation, for to him revelation is not the same as propositional truth. Revelation is an event in the community whereby the community can become a continual source of revelation. Truth that the community discovers does not directly correspond to truth but to a community understanding of it. Truth is a social construct, so what one community believes might be different from what another community believes. There are three sources of theology for Grenz: Scripture (the primary standard), tradition, and culture. According to him, we must move beyond a one-to-one correspondence between the words of the Bible and the very word of God.[191] We cannot equate the Word of God with Scripture.[192] Grenz rejects a propositional view of Scripture in lieu of a functional view that rests on experience rather than doctrine.

It is true that there is no authentic experience without experiencing the impact of God's words on our lives; however, experience is the result, not the cause, of engaging God's Word in our lives. Otherwise, experience would lead to relativism, and we would lose the unique distinctiveness of Christianity. All that is left in that case is emotion without content. If we make human experience the basis of Christianity, we revert to the liberalism of the early twentieth century. Friedrich D. Schleiermacher was the most influential theologian of the nineteenth century and the father of liberal Protestant theology, and his theology of religious experience is a good example of experience over factual truth.

## Instrumental View of Scripture

Brian McLaren's view of Scripture comes from pursuit of mission.[193] This is an instrumental view of Scripture. He claims that evangelicals use the Bible as a "weapon to threaten others, as a tool to intimidate others and prove them wrong."[194] This is exactly what the Bible does do; much of the Bible has to do with sorting error from truth. He makes the purpose of the Bible a panacea of instrumentalism: If it works, it is right. But one purpose of the Bible is to "correct" false doctrine because "there will be a time when they will not endure *sound doctrine*" and will turn away from the truth (2 Timothy 4:2–3, italics mine). This practical purpose of preserving sound doctrine is not the least among many purposes of Scripture.

McLaren's postmodern friends view the Bible as a barbaric book.[195] His answer to them is to use the Bible "as narrative."[196] This is consistent with his postmodernism. The Bible to him is a "story" that does not tell what should happen, does not make universals for all people of all time, but gives "what was necessary to survive in the world at that point. . . . God has to work with [people] as they are in their individual and cultural moral development."[197] This is ethical pragmatism at its core. He assumes that God is non-violent, whereas Scripture clearly declares that God is justly violent. He wants to read the Bible as a "timely" document, not a "timeless document."[198] All through this discussion, McLaren's paradigms are paradigms of the left politically (not all of which is anti-biblical). This viewpoint is a "whole new way of approaching the biblical," which is a redefinition of orthodoxy.[199]

Postconservatives like to attack past Princeton theologians as building their case for Christianity on rationalism. Critics of these Princeton theologians try to portray them as cataloguing a storehouse of facts. Yet the Princeton greats did not present their ideas this way, for they viewed Scripture as not accessible by natural reason. Their position was that we cannot discover the meaning of Scripture by natural or empirical investigation, for Scripture rests on what God wants it to be. In other words, they held that although humans possess finite, knowledge, yet it is nevertheless true knowledge. As empiricism is the foundation for empirical science, so revelation is the cognitive foundation for doctrine. Princeton theologians refused to bifurcate Scripture's formal nature from its material content.[200] There is a distinction between an absolute and an absolute understanding of the absolute.

The postconservative view subverts the Bible as "living and operative" in the life of the believer (Hebrews 4:12). By starting with human limitation, postmodern evangelicals confine Scripture to the realm of finite perspective, limiting the believer to approximations of the Bible. Each person wallows in personal strategies.

## Truth Propositional, not Personal

Truth is a property consisting only of propositions, so truth is not personal. Those who hold truth as personal put personal relationship and commitment in the place of propositional belief and undercut the gospel in the process.

Postconservatives want us to believe that Christianity is essentially narrative-shaped experience rather than belief based on propositional revelation and objective truth. They view holding to conviction about truth as hubris and bigotry. They fear truth that stands in counterdistinction to falsehood. They dismiss certainty as Enlightenment thinking and accordingly pander to privatized perspectives, and they are reluctant to assert finality of truth. They have the same problem as their secular cousins—they try to make the claim that there are no truth claims but only perspectives on truth.

Some emergent church thinkers place propositions in antithesis to the person of Christ. They minimize the propositions of Scripture in lieu of focus on the personal aspects of Christianity. This is a false dichotomy. This should not be an either/or but a both/and issue. We learn of the person of Christ through the propositions of Scripture. Faith is more than the preference to believe in Christ, for faith in the New Testament requires an object of truth in which to believe. Faith always correlates to the veracity of what we believe. The appeal to narrative as the essence of what Christians believe greatly twists the perception of biblical content. McLaren himself cannot keep from making propositional claims of how we understand the Bible and he cannot dodge truth issues in spite of himself. [201] He cannot sustain his attempts to domesticate the gospel. Carson makes an indictment against McLaren when he says, "And quite frankly, on this issue, as on so many others, McLaren has given us very little evidence that he is fairly described as a 'biblical' Christian."[202]

Stanley Grenz's writings seek to "revision" evangelical theology from resting on the premise of the inspiration of Scripture to something else. First, he wants to move evangelicalism from primarily resting on a theological system to spirituality with an emphasis on the experience of the new birth. Second, he wants to change the hub of theology from doctrinal teaching to the beliefs of the Christian community. Third, he expands the sources of theology from the Bible to church tradition and culture.

Grenz does not hold that knowledge of God is objective. For him, no one can approach truth in a neutral manner because one needs the community to check belief. Knowledge is relative to the community. We form our identity through sharing our stories with our community. On the other hand, he does not want to move Christianity into the irrational, but he has no basis for not doing that.

Theology, for Grenz, must preserve its dimension of mystery and move beyond propositions because we constitute our beliefs socially and linguistically. Experience and interpretation jointly interrelate. Personal encounter is at the core of the Christian experience. Propositions both express and facilitate experience by narrating religious transformation. Truth is reality, but evangelical postmodernism is anti-realist. Postmoderns do not rest truth on what is there but on the community. John Franke and Stanley Grenz question a realistic knowledge of God in Scripture. They reject logical knowledge and assert that we can know no propositional truth about reality in itself. All that we can know is the phenomena that appear to the community. This is social convention, and social convention binds these postconservative, so-called evangelicals to a socially constructed reality. Their ideas are relative to the community and are true for them. Propositions, to them, are not essential and have no universal criteria for distinguishing truth from error. They cannot factually verify truth claims. They cannot even affirm that biblical propositions assert truth about reality. They are culture-bound to the community.

Grenz and Franke cannot establish a one-to-one correspondence between revelation and the Bible. The Bible, according to them, reflects an ongoing conversation with the Hebrews and the early church. The Bible is not revelation but what the Holy Spirit is currently doing through the community. They, in fact, displace the original intention of the authors of Scripture with the pragmatic involvement of the current community.

## Anti-reason

Anti-reason is prevalent in Eastern religion, Roman and Orthodox Catholicism, liberal Christianity, and now in evangelicalism. To these people, somehow the heart takes precedence over the head. This idea, the prattle of much evangelical conversation today, is foreign to Scripture. This is a deviation toward an ecstatic viewpoint. What is important to these people is unity above truth. A nebulous view of love takes precedence over biblical love. It is not a unity of truth but a unity of emotion or subjectivism. A proposition to them is simply "opinion." All language is metaphorical. However, the Bible never teaches that truth is anything other than verbal declaration, or propositions received by comprehension. It never says that truth is an encounter, emotion, or experience. There are truths about persons, but those truths are always propositional. It is something that one person can relate to another and can be understood by others. This is the point of John 20:30–31 (ESV): "Now Jesus did many other signs in the presence of the disciples, which are not written in this book; but these are written so that you may believe that Jesus is the Christ, the Son of God, and that by believing you may have life in his name."

Doctrine to them is "second-order assertions" within a community. In their view, these second-order doctrines regulate how a community thinks about itself and God; doctrines do not make actual assertions about God. All they have left is antithesis and not thesis. Is God's Word revelation or is it communal thinking?

Grenz and Franke set up a false distinction between propositional and personal revelation. However, we can know nothing about the person of Christ without written revelation of Christ. God is more than talk about a community. What is important to these men is not the text of Scripture but the Spirit's use of Scripture for the contemporary church. This puts the Spirit's present speaking outside the text of the canon and converts the Bible into something other than its original purpose. True authority does not reside in the readers of Scripture but in what the Holy Spirit revealed to the original writers. Scripture's use of Scripture is very different from how Grenz and Franke use it. By their acceptance of the postmodern approach to truth, they divert from evangelicalism and deny that one must believe that Jesus is the Christ, the Son of God, and that by believing one might receive life in his name.

John wanted his hearers to "believe" three propositions that result in eternal life. The object of belief is always a proposition. It is impossible to believe something that is not propositional. Only propositions can be true or false. We can communicate meaning only by propositions. This is consistent with figurative uses of the word "true." "True worshipers" are true worshipers properly and literally.

Those who reject the correspondent view of truth rely on the correspondent view of truth to reject it. If a person says, "I cannot say anything in English," using English to do so is stating a contradiction.

Jesus made the statement, "I am the truth" (John 14:6), but Jesus is not a proposition. Jesus used the term "truth" figuratively, and all figures have a literal idea behind them. The literal idea is that he is the essence of truth, not the source of truth. We find God's very thoughts in him. "Truth" in this passage is a figurative use of the idea of truth understood only by a propositional use of the word. To believe in Jesus is to believe his words: "For if you believed Moses, you would believe Me; for he wrote about Me. But if you do not believe his writings, how will you believe My words?" (John 5:46, 47).

The idea that the Bible transcends language is a fallacy of a mystical approach to the Bible. To people who make this claim, God is not verbal; encounter with God is all-important to them. In other words, experience is at the heart of this belief system.

It is true that the Bible genre is more than propositions but, on the other hand, it consists of numerous propositions. The word "believe" has as its object propositional truth. We cannot believe until we know what to believe objectively. The object of belief is the Word of God revealed in Scripture that Jesus came from eternally existing as the Son of God to die in his humanity for the sin of mankind (2 Timothy 1:12). The Greek word "to believe" requires an object. Biblically speaking, there is no value in belief itself, but only in the object of belief.

## Negating Propositions

Brian McLaren wants to leave the "prose" of didactic writing and adopt a "mystical/poetic" approach to theology, saying, "Reduced speech leads to reduced lives."[203] He gives his definition of "prose" through theologian Walter Brueggemann: "By prose I refer to a world that is organized in settled formulae, so that even pastoral prayers and love letters sound like memos."[204] McLaren sets forth here another of his numerous false dichotomies by stating that wonder, awe, and worship cannot be attained by prose, as if prose and experience are polar opposites. According to him, writing needs to go beyond mere rationality by imagination and vision.[205] Does this mean that we need to go beyond rationality to irrationality?

McLaren says mysticism and poetry remind us of the limitations of language when talking about God. This, according to him, is a "rebuke to arrogant intellectualizing" for modern Christians; systematic theologies are "conceptual cathedrals of proposition and argument."[206] McLaren explains the purpose of systematic theology thus: "At the heart of the theological project in the late modern world was the assumption that one could and should reduce all revealed truth into propositions and organize those propositions into an outline that exhaustively contains and serves as the best vehicle for truth."[207] He quotes philosophically existential, dialectical, and neo-orthodox theologian Karl Barth in support of this thinking. However, no evangelical theologian that I know believes that evangelical theology "exhaustively contains . . . truth." This is another of McLaren's many straw men. All that is in the Bible is true as to its written factuality, but not all truth is in the Bible. No evangelical theologian believes that terms such as "omnipresent" or "omniscient" convey all there is to know about the expansiveness of God. These words are anthropathic and anthropomorphic delimiting vocabulary terms of humanity. Evangelicals have never put God in a box confined to their delimited understanding.

## Importance of Doctrine

Doctrine is the way God builds the edification structure of the believer. It gives perspicacity about God's method of building the believer (2 Timothy 3:15). The more we inculcate divine viewpoint, the more we adopt God's attitudes about life. How can we love God without something to love about God? We need content for that. We cannot apply what we do not know. Doctrine gives direction for "every good work" (2 Timothy 3:16–17). Doctrine also provides discernment about issues of life and allows us to distinguish truth from error

(John 7:17; 1 Thessalonians 5:21; 2 Timothy 4:3, 4). We cannot know the true from the false gospel without it. Sound doctrine convicts those who contradict truth (Titus 1:9). It sends a code blue alarm about the direction of certain leaders in evangelicalism today.

Faith is a conviction of truth found in a proposition. When a person says, "I believe this statement," that is affirmation of conviction about the statement's truth. If any doubt remains, then the person cannot claim to believe the statement. There is a close connection between faith and doctrine.

Romans 10:17 says, "So then faith comes by hearing, and hearing by the word of God." Faith comes "by hearing" a report. In the preceding verse Paul quoted a verse from Isaiah 53:1: "Who has believed our report?" There were definite statements of fact that Isaiah wanted his hearers to believe, which make up the gospel. He wanted them to believe these statements as true. This acceptance is faith of conviction. Conviction is not the entire dimension of faith, but it is a critical dimension of it.

Trust in a person without propositions to believe about that person is credulity. Admiration or reverence of a person can rest on emotion; if it does, then that trust is vacuous. Credulity is different from trust in that credulity lacks the thing trusted about the person; therefore, we cannot identify credulity with trust, for it is shallow and without content. There can be no true love, admiration, or reverence of a person without content. If these elements exist, then there is factual reason for them to be there.

To believe is to have a strong conviction about the truthfulness of a proposition. This is far more than to suppose or presume, as in the English word. Belief is the opposite of doubt. Trust is different from either knowing or credulity. It is not enough to know, for we must believe in what we know. The emotional element in believing is derivative from the essence of trust in a proposition, "for with the heart one believes" (Romans 10:10). If faith represents acceptance of statements from the Bible as true, then a conviction of the truth of propositions of the Bible and an attitude of trust reposing in a statement will carry an emotional element. Therefore, faith is not simply a matter of intellectual or mental assent. We can distinguish this attitudinal dimension from both knowledge and credulity. Knowledge sees, but faith trusts what it sees. Trust then is the distinctive mark of faith. In the case of the benefit of the cross, the believer wholeheartedly accepts the promise of forgiveness. Grace always rejoices the heart.

The word "faith" can designate something other than personal faith—something objective. The Bible refers to this in the Greek as "the faith" rather than simply "faith." "The faith" is the content of divine revelation as a unit (Ephesians 4:5; 1 Timothy 4:1, 6; 6:20–21; Titus 1:13; 2:2). Paul instructed Titus to rebuke the Cretans "sharply, that they may be sound in the faith." This passage warns against false teachers (vv. 10–12, 14). Sound faith refers to doctrinal soundness in antithesis to falsity.

## Relation of Propositions to Truth

The Bible sets forth universal truth. It is plain to anyone anywhere (Romans 1:19–20). Morality is not relative to each community or perspective. This view does not claim omniscience but simply that some knowledge is real.

The propositional view of truth holds that statements of Scripture must correspond to both verification and falsification. We can show a statement to be false if it does not correspond to objective reality. Subjectivism of necessity is shallow, for truth is more than personal and cultural values, a function of individual preferences. Objective truth does not depend on culture but transcends culture. Truth always corresponds to reality.

Hundreds of passages clearly assign truth to propositions within a correspondent view of truth (Isaiah 45:19). As well, hundreds of Scriptures differentiate explicit biblical propositions from falsehoods. The Bible warns against false teachers and prophets who do not hold to biblical propositions. Scripture clearly presents itself as objective reality that exists independent of subjective belief.

The Bible uses "truth" in two ways: (1) a quality of propositions that confirm affirmations in Scripture by coherence to data (false propositions contradict the data), and (2) a quality of persons who faithfully appropriate what they believe to experience. Jesus is an example of the latter.

All propositions in the Bible are inerrant in the original writings. These propositions are true to reality, and we can trust them for our lives. Assertions contrary to propositions in Scripture are false. Belief in the propositions of Scripture as real makes these propositions active in the life of the believer. This is far more than doctrinal assent. Far from obstructing the spiritual life, they are the basis of *modus vivendi* for Christian daily dynamics.

Truth is embedded in propositions only. We can call nothing true without the attribution of a predicate to a subject. This does not preclude speaking figuratively of a person being a true athlete. This is simply a derivative use. To say the Bible is true literally is not the same as saying that the Bible is true figuratively. Figures of speech in the Bible are not true literally. Jesus is not a door hanging on hinges! However, the literal idea behind Jesus as a door is that he is the access to heaven, so there is a literal idea behind the figurative. The Bible nowhere declares that there are inexpressible truths. No doubt, there are truths that God has not revealed and are in that sense inexplicable. Yet, if God chooses to reveal truth in logical, grammatical form, then it is not equivocal. We cannot apply the term "truth" to something unreasonable. God is capable of expressing the truth he asserts; hence he revealed biblical information in grammatical, propositional, and logical form.

The burden of proof rests on those who deny propositional structure of truth. Where is the evidence for "non-propositional truth?" Diminishing propositions detracts from the inherent authority of the Bible and makes it subjective. If we make the Word of God conditional on the ratification of human beings, then it becomes a conditional authority. It would be like saying that a traffic law is conditional upon a person's response to it. Obscuring the objective relevance of the Word of God distorts its final authority to the believer and equivocates content of Scripture.

Truth is a character of propositions that correctly corresponds to a state of affairs. These propositions are one coherent, interlocking system that comes from God. Truth is an infinite whole because God is an infinite whole. There is no truth outside God; consequently, all his truth is self-authenticating. The objective truth that Abraham Lincoln lived in history is equivalent to the truth that pedophilia is sin from a revelation viewpoint. We cannot divorce one from the other in a scheme of truth that covers all reality for all time. The error of pedophilia would have no meaning without this consistent interlocking system of truth.

All that is in the Bible is true as to its record, but not all truth is in the Bible. Two plus two is four; that is truth, but it is not in the Bible. The Bible does give us an understanding of a universal, unified system of absolute truth. The presupposition of an inerrant Bible is that we cannot reason from the viewpoint of autonomous humanity because humans are finite and cannot come to universal truth. All facts ultimately relate to God and take on meaning because of their relation to God. All reality is theistic reality. Rolland D. McCune, professor of systematic theology at Detroit Baptist Seminary, makes this argument in a poignant manner:

> The new evangelical thinking, on the other hand, posits Christ and His revelation as facts among other facts, a truth-option among other options, although perhaps the best option and the facts with the fewest difficulties. The Scriptures present Him as the truth and the only option if man would ever know truth. In order to avoid the charge of circular reasoning, the new evangelical methodology speaks of a body of facts as if it were something independent, free-from-God, and objective to both God and man, and objective to all mankind with one another. This is unbiblical, as we have seen, as well as self-destructive. The new evangelical apologist knows that no fact or truth is free-from-God, he knows that God planned, made, upholds, and directs the movement of the entire universe; in other words, he knows from theology who God is and His all-pervasive relations with the universe. He should also know that in apologetics when he appeals to a stockpile of supposedly generic facts, he is actually appealing to God-created facts to prove or verify the existence of God and His revelation-claims; i.e., he too is reasoning in a circle. This methodology is confusing, self-defeating, and utterly futile.[208]

Postevangelicals want to deny or minimize propositional truth, yet the Bible views truth as propositional and only propositional. Truth is an attribute only of propositions. This stands in stark contrast to the idea that truth is an encounter, an event, or an experience. Postevangelicals try to replace propositions with "commitment" to a person, and they want to substitute "personal relationship" for "belief." This flies in the face of the fact that the Bible uses "belief" and its cognates hundreds of times for belief in propositions of the Word (scores of times in the gospel of John alone). By substituting commitment to a person, postevangelicals abandon norm for belief. What is this nebulous entity entitled a "person" about? Belief in a person without propositions about the person is mysticism. We have no person without propositions about the person. This same prattle tries to make a distinction between head and heart belief—not that head belief is without heart; we cannot have heart belief without head belief.

Truth is conformity to fact. We know the Bible has a correspondent view of truth because the Word of God represents itself as true to fact or reality; it corresponds to assertions or promises.

A proposition is what a declarative sentence asserts, or means. A proposition is a bearer of truth. Although the Bible does not explicitly set forth a technical view of truth, it consistently matches the correspondent view of truth in usage. Non-Christians can assess its truthfulness because it functions within the realm of measurable truth. If the Bible were eccentric or unique in its approach to truth, no one could measure its truthfulness. Any truth claim could establish its own view of truth and make itself excused from evaluation.

Both Hebrew and Greek words for truth carry the idea of conformity to fact. God is a God who is true to truth (Psalm 31:5). His Word is truth (John 17:17). Jesus was "full of grace and truth" (John 1:17) and was truth itself (John 14:6).

The Bible uses "believe" or "belief" as the method for embracing propositions of Scripture. Even when the New Testament uses "believe" with a person as its object, it means belief in the word spoken by or about the person. The New Testament does not use the word "commitment" very often, but when it does, it rarely refers to salvation, if at all.

## Relationship of Propositional Truth to Belief

There is clear relationship between propositions and belief. The object of belief is always a proposition. Christ is not a proposition, but we can know him only propositionally. When he says, "I am the truth" (John 14:6), that means he is the basis of truth. That is a figurative idea. However, he is not beyond truth, otherwise that would be mysticism. Belief in Jesus involves believing his words: "For if you believed Moses, you would believe Me; for he wrote about Me. But if you do not believe his writings, how will you believe My words?" (John 4:46, 47).

Belief in Moses is belief in his spoken propositions and not belief as an encounter, for God "desires all men to be saved and to come to the *knowledge of the truth*" (1 Timothy 2:4, italics mine).

A belief does not depend on our mind believing it, for the truth of a proposition is independent from the mind. The statement "Henry Ford was one of the first mass manufactures of automobiles" is true whether I believe it or not. It does not depend on the quality of my belief. Statements need facts to be true, not the reverse.

Logical principles depend on their correspondence to facts as much as statements about empirical facts do. Principles must match truth outside their statements of truth. The logic of the law of non-contradiction is always true in any condition or circumstance. To be true, scientific fact cannot contradict itself. God's Word cannot contradict itself, if it is true. God cannot logically contradict himself; otherwise, he would be inconsistent with what he claims to be—an absolute and perfect God.

Propositional truth is the object of faith and stands in conflict with existential perspectives on truth. A. Duane Litfin, former president of Wheaton Colleges, makes this point well:

> Such a view of objective propositional truth is in serious conflict with modern existential views of truth. Hence it is not surprising that critics seek to dissociate it from Paul and attribute it to second-century followers. Yet to do so requires an unwarranted a priori assumption about the apostle's view of truth. A more objective assessment is that there is nothing in the theology of the Pastorals which requires a late date or which cannot be explained by the fact that these epistles represent Paul's last instructions to his two faithful representatives, Timothy and Titus.[209]

Postevangelicals convolute the Word by maintaining that we cannot establish truth by anything outside the mind. Language, mind, culture, and community (not objective factuality) shape belief, according to them. Truth is contingent upon language and culture and does not correspond to reality. We cannot know anything outside our language because language is self-enclosed and self-referential. Their implication that language cannot point objectively to propositions outside itself is their fundamental fallacy. This fallacy confuses the relativity of terms with the ability of language to represent objective truth. It is like saying we have different names for the earth, so we cannot identify the objective reality of the earth.

Another fallacy of postevangelicals is that they hold to the coherent view of truth. This view does not rest on correspondence of facts but on logical consistency. Truth simply coheres to various statements. This view would allow for two philosophies that cohere logically within themselves to both be true. Yet, one or both of these belief systems might not correspond to reality. The correspondent view of truth includes coherence of truth but demands objectivity and factuality as well.

To postmoderns, belief is a manifestation of sociology and psychology. This sociology of belief does not make judgments, because there are no overarching norms that judge other systems of belief.

## Christianity Not Transcendent over Propositions

Propositions are not "opinions" to be transcended by "love" or "unity." Many postconservatives want to present Christianity as indefinable, or something that transcends propositions. This is not the same point that we cannot put God in a box or that there are great dimensions that we do not know about God. That is obvious, but we can know some things about God expressed by propositions in his Word. This trend of presenting the idea that something can transcend propositions is more in keeping with Eastern orthodoxy or Eastern religions than with the propositions of the New Testament.

Jesus and writers of the New Testament spoke in the language of absolute authoritative certainty. "Thus says the Lord" appears over four hundred times in the Old Testament. Jesus used Scripture to rebuke Satan four times in the temptation. He used the Word to rebuke the Pharisees (Matthew 15:3–4). He claimed that the smallest letter of the Bible would not pass away until its fulfillment (5:17–20). I guess Jesus was closed-minded, arrogant, and mean-spirited, according to postconservatives! The Bible never leaves the believer with uncertainty about truth.

The upshot of the assertion that Christianity is without propositional truth creates an authority that is essentially relative and perilously unstable. It rests authority in the subjective experience of the individual, making the individual the authority. A consensus of a faith community that rests on dialectical assumption is untrustworthy. This quest for non-foundational authority (a binary authority that tries to combine the text of Scripture with the context of culture) is an oxymoron because it attempts to rest its case on the non-dubitable dubitable! Postconservatives do admit that there is no such thing as secured knowledge. All they have in the final analysis is pure subjectivism. They cannot define truth as a correct state of affairs or what corresponds to the mind of God.

Dialectical thought has made inroads into the so-called evangelical camp. According to them, personal encounters with God are possible, but the Bible is not God's Word; it is simply the early church's fallible testimony. The postconservative view is that the Bible is an irresolvable dialectic of irresolvable paradoxes and contradictions. They want to separate God's revelation from the propositions of God's Word; the Bible is not revelation but the channel of revelation.

Those who believe in dialectical thesis assert that those who propose correspondent truth presuppose their own assertions. They believe this to be a vicious cycle proving its own premises. However, they have to rely on the correspondent view of truth to make this case!

## Christianity Known Primarily by Propositions

What we know of Christianity comes primarily from propositional truth revealed by God in the sixty-six books we name the Bible. Propositional revelation is the starting point or axiom of Christianity. All viewpoints begin somewhere, whether feeling, culture, science, philosophy, or even postmodernism. Non-Christians choose non-Christian axioms. Science or philosophy cannot prove God because those fields of study cannot sense God by human faculty or inferences from sensation. Both the axiom and method are wrong in human systems because they rest on induction. Christianity rests on deduction. Unlike the secular view that human beings discover truth by human faculty, the discovery of truth rests on God's prior revelation of his truth to mankind. Science is the solipsism of sensation and rests on the fallacy of coming to the prime mover by induction. To argue from the particular to the general is a fallacy because we can never examine all of reality. Who is to say that all swans are white? This is the formal logical fallacy of asserting the consequence. Because the principle of induction is insoluble, science attempts to rest its case not on induction but on a system of conjectures and refutations. This abandons any claim to knowledge.

Passion for truth now appears narrow-minded to the present culture of evangelicals because many postmodern evangelicals blur the line between subjective interpretation and objective interpretation of Scripture. Their bogeyman is doctrine.

We now turn to evidence that countervails the plague of anti-doctrine and anti-rationalism among evangelicals. No amount of pietism or ecstatic experientialism can daunt the following truths.

The use of "faith" and "believe" in the Bible is not subjective but objective. Belief is not something that arises out of the heart or that flies in the face of reason. Faith always believes something objective, a promise, or extant Scripture. It is a matter of conviction produced by evidence. Faith in the Bible is never irrational faith, but always faith grounded in reason. Biblical faith is not credulity or blind faith.

Faith bridges the gap between evidence or probability and apodictic certainty. Faith is assent to the veracity of knowledge found in the Word of God. Christians believe in the factuality of the death, burial, and resurrection of Christ. We accept and receive this as fact, and then we appropriate it as true to our lives. It is from the object of our faith that we derive faith's value. Faith does not save us, but faith in the object of salvation does—the finished work of Christ for our sins. Don N. Howell, Jr., associate professor of New Testament at Dallas Theological Seminary, in *Bibliotheca Sacra*, shows how faith relates to propositions:

> Faith (πίστις) suggests both an intellectual affirmation of the propositional truths of the gospel, in addition to an internalization of those truths that is manifested most especially in a life of trust in Christ. James and Paul used πίστις in two different senses that are germane to this discussion. Normally πίστις expresses a living and vibrant faith, in which an external profession of assent is coupled with an internal acceptance of and commitment to the professed faith as truth, and this dramatically affects one's comprehensive worldview and subsequent actions.
>
> Πίστις is also used in a more restricted sense to connote an intellectual assent to theological truth, but without the confluence of that assent

with an internal confiding trust in and love of those truths. It suggests a *notitia* and perhaps even an external *assensus* to the gospel, without an internal *fiducia* in the gospel message.

The difference between the two uses may be expressed as the difference between a mere *profession* of faith and a dynamic *possession* of faith. Paul used "faith" in Romans, inherently assuming a true living faith.[210]

We cannot autonomously come to faith in Christ. We need the convincing work of the Holy Spirit to convict us of the truthfulness of Christianity (1 Corinthians 2:13, 14) because Satan supernaturally blinds our minds to the gospel (2 Corinthians 4:3, 4; Ephesians 4:18). The Holy Spirit uses knowledge and reason from the Word of God to convict us (1 Corinthians 2:15, 16). God uses providential means to engage us.

God revealed himself in propositions by words inspired by the Holy Spirit to convey spiritual truth (1 Corinthians 2:13). No one can come to the truth of the gospel apart from the convincing work of the Holy Spirit. As well, no one can accept a gospel that one does not know or understand. Faith and reason inextricably relate to one another. No one can come to Christ apart from the Holy Spirit and no one can come to Christ by reason alone. Nowhere does the Bible present Christianity as an irrational faith.

A truth claim is a proposition, a logical arrangement of truth. A proposition is what a declarative sentence means, affirms, or asserts. A sentence about facts does not assert a proposition. A proposition describes a reality or state of affairs, in other words, a proposition is a truth claim. The statement "The Son of God is God" is a proposition. Denial that the Son is God is a falsity because it rejects objective reality found in Scripture.

There are large portions of Scripture where the idea of a God that acts in history in narrative form does not fit. Note Millard J. Erickson's quantification of the use of narrative versus propositional truth:

> Indeed, if one does a comparative analysis of the content of the Bible, the New Testament books that seem to deal most explicitly with narra-

tive constitute only 56 to 62 percent of the content, depending on whether one treats Revelation as narrative. In the Old Testament, the narrative books (Genesis–Job) constitute 57 percent of the material.[211]

At minimum, a narrative approach that excludes or precludes propositional truth is out of balance and, at worst, outright distortion of Scripture. Stanley Grenz's careless depiction of "card-carrying evangelicals" who cling to propositional truth because they define evangelicalism as mere doctrine is a rash distortion of the movement. Most evangelical leaders take great care to apply truth to experience. However, biblically oriented evangelicals make sure that truth governs experience and not the reverse (unlike postevangelicals). The postevangelical presupposition of pragmatism is neither acknowledged nor addressed. Where do they obtain a functional view of truth? It appears that they are deeply indebted to Kierkegaard's subjective view of truth (existentialism). The idea of existentialism is that there are no absolutes, which is also dialectical.

## Guard Doctrine

God says that the believer is to guard the "good deposit of doctrine." It is the responsibility of every pastor to maintain the faith (1 Timothy 6:12). All doctrinal formation should rest on the content of Scripture. Christianity is more than relationships or mysteries that no one can understand. God reveals himself through propositions in Scripture, using "spiritual words" (words inspired by the Holy Spirit) to express spiritual truths (1 Corinthians 2:13).

> *O Timothy! Guard what was committed to your trust, avoiding the profane and idle babblings and contradictions of what is falsely called knowledge—by professing it some have strayed concerning the faith. Grace be with you. Amen.* (1 Timothy 6:20, 21)

> *For this reason I also suffer these things; nevertheless I am not ashamed, for I know whom I have believed and am persuaded that He is able to keep what I have committed to Him until that Day. Hold fast the pattern of sound words which you have heard from me, in faith and love which are in Christ Jesus. That good thing which was committed to you, keep by the Holy Spirit who dwells in us.* (2 Timothy 1:12–14)

*Holding fast the faithful word as he has been taught, that he may be able, by sound doctrine, both to exhort and convict those who contradict. For there are many insubordinate, both idle talkers and deceivers, especially those of the circumcision.* (Titus 1:9, 10)

*But as for you, speak the things which are proper for sound doctrine.* (Titus 2:1)

The Greek word "to teach" means to provide instruction either in a formal or informal setting. The basic idea is "to cause to learn" or "know." This word occurs about ninety-five times in the New Testament. The word for "doctrine," or "teaching," means "to provide instruction or content of doctrine"—in other words, the content of what the Bible teaches. The New Testament uses this word thirty times. There is also a Greek word for "heretical doctrine" (ἑτεροδι-δασκαλέω); this word means "to teach something different" from what should be taught (1 Timothy 1:3). It is possible to utter a lie or falsehood (1 John 2:21), thus implying it is possible to know what is truth.

Many postconservatives do not believe that the Bible is itself revelation but only a means to revelation. To them, the Bible is a product of the community of faith. There is no one-to-one correspondence between the revelation of God and the Bible, they believe, and the Bible does not reflect information but an ongoing dialogue. The Bible, to these people, is not propositions of what God said but the pragmatic interaction of a community of believers. To them, what is important is not propositions but what the Holy Spirit seeks to do with statements of Scripture. It is true that the Bible is more than propositions, but it is also true that the Bible contains many propositions.

God's truth corresponds to fact. The two key terms for "truth" in the Bible (*emet* in the Old Testament and *alethia* in the New Testament) mean conformity to fact. The Bible warns of false doctrine everywhere.

The Bible is true because it corresponds to reality. A proposition is the content of a sentence. Facts make a proposition true. A fact is a real state of affairs, the way the world actually is. Thus, evidence allows us to determine whether a proposition is true or false. A statement always corresponds to the facts. This is a basis for certainty.

## Propositional Approach of New Testament

We may differentiate between the two uses as the difference between a mere profession of faith and a dynamic possession of faith. Paul used "faith" in Romans, inherently assuming an object of belief.

The Bible clearly presumes that we can know truth and propositions about truth. Christians can witness to objective truth. False teachers bear false witness. Christians can speak to issues of truth as Scripture speaks to truth.

This does not presume that Christians know all things exhaustively. Lack of exhaustive knowledge does not preclude true knowledge. Propositional truth allows us to come to truth truly so that we are not condemned to intellectual futility. The propositional Bible is the locus of authority and its claim is exclusive. If it is not exclusive, of what value is it? Who wants to hold to unsubstantiated hope? Dilution of truth destroys objective revelation of truth. Objective truth stands independent from value-laden perspectives on truth. It can stand independent of cultural conditioning.

The repudiation of objective, external, transcendent authority of Scripture destroys the power of revelation. Relativism prevails. These people cannot escape nihilism. Although postconservatives believe in truths, they cannot come to truth. By deconstruction, postconservatives constantly reformulate truth in a progressive way. This never allows them to come to truth; truth is always elusive (dialectical). There is only relative truth, according to the perspective viewpoint.

Luke tells us in Acts that Paul spent three years "reasoning and persuading" in the synagogue about the "whole counsel of God" (Acts 19:9, 10, 20, 31). The idea that propositional truth is not as important as practicing truth is a false dichotomy. It is not a matter of either/or but of both/and.

Note that the role of a pastor is to teach, in the New Testament. The word "teach" means didactics (*didache*, or didactic propositions in the Greek). This is the key word in the pastorals (1 and 2 Timothy and Titus). Ephesians calls the pastor a "pastor-teacher" in 4:11. Note the Berean view of examined propositional truth:

## Chapter Seven: Is There Certainty Anywhere?

*The brothers immediately sent Paul and Silas away by night to Berea, and when they arrived they went into the Jewish synagogue. Now these Jews were more noble than those in Thessalonica; they received the word with all eagerness, examining the Scriptures daily to see if these things were so. (Acts 17:10, 11 ESV).*

The Bereans clearly operated in a proper mode, for even though they had the apostle Paul himself teaching them, they relied upon Scripture to verify his teaching. Now, it would seem that the Bereans set a precedent regarding verification of the claims of a pastor-teacher and the proper order of relationship between the pastor-teacher and the hearer. After the pastor-teacher has initiated the giving of information, the hearer can respond with verification. The person in the pew has capacity to verify the claims of a pastor-teacher. If verification of a doctrinal teaching from a pastor is not possible, then the hearers would be without recourse to protect themselves against false doctrine, which will inevitably come their way, for no pastor is one hundred percent free from error. Other Scriptures weigh in on this same point:

> *Now we have received not the spirit of the world, but the Spirit who is from God, that we might understand the things freely given us by God. And we impart this in words not taught by human wisdom but taught by the Spirit, interpreting spiritual truths to those who are spiritual. The natural person does not accept the things of the Spirit of God, for they are folly to him, and he is not able to understand them because they are spiritually discerned. The spiritual person judges all things, but is himself to be judged by no one. "For who has understood the mind of the Lord so as to instruct him?" But we have the mind of Christ.* (1 Corinthians 2:12–16 ESV)

> *Do your best to present yourself to God as one approved, a worker who has no need to be ashamed, rightly handling the word of truth.* (2 Timothy 2:15 ESV)

In the pastorals (1 and 2 Timothy, and Titus), the pastor-teacher presents truth didactically (propositionally—the key word in pastorals) from the Word of God. This is very different from the church community coming up with truth by consensus of groupthink. These portions of Scripture do not present the pastor-teacher as absolute authority because the Berean-like believer is to evaluate the formal presentation by the pastor. The Holy Spirit uses the teaching of the pastor-teacher to present God's Word and enables the listener to respond to this teaching.

## Doctrine as Biblical Content

The Greek word for "doctrine" or "teaching" refers to content, propositions, or precepts (διδασκαλία). The idea is to provide instructive content. God wrote Scripture for our "instruction" (Romans 15:4). Christians are to be on guard against winds of doctrine or teaching (Ephesians 4:14). This term "instruction" occurs twenty-one times in the New Testament, and fifteen of those occurrences surface in the pastorals. Note the emphasis on doctrine in the New Testament:

> *And they devoted themselves to the apostles' teaching and the fellowship, to the breaking of bread and the prayers.* (Acts 2:42 ESV)

> *. . . so that we may no longer be children, tossed to and fro by the waves and carried about by every wind of doctrine, by human cunning, by craftiness in deceitful schemes.* (Ephesians 4:14 ESV)

> *. . . the sexually immoral, men who practice homosexuality, enslavers, liars, perjurers, and whatever else is contrary to sound doctrine . . .* (1 Timothy 1:10 ESV)

> *If you put these things before the brothers, you will be a good servant of Christ Jesus, being trained in the words of the faith and of the good doctrine that you have followed.* (1 Timothy 4:6 ESV)

> *Until I come, devote yourself to the public reading of Scripture, to exhortation, to teaching.* (1 Timothy 4:13 ESV)

> *Let all who are under a yoke as slaves regard their own masters as worthy of all honor, so that the name of God and the teaching may not be reviled.* (1 Timothy 6:1 ESV)

> *If anyone teaches a different doctrine and does not agree with the sound words of our Lord Jesus Christ and the teaching that accords with godliness . . .* (1 Timothy 6:3 ESV)

*All Scripture is breathed out by God and profitable for teaching, for reproof, for correction, and for training in righteousness . . .* (2 Timothy 3:16 ESV)

*For the time is coming when people will not endure sound teaching, but having itching ears they will accumulate for themselves teachers to suit their own passions, and will turn away from listening to the truth and wander off into myths.* (2 Timothy 4:3–4 ESV)

*He must hold firm to the trustworthy word as taught, so that he may be able to give instruction in sound doctrine and also to rebuke those who contradict it.* (Titus 1:9 ESV)

*But as for you, teach what accords with sound doctrine.* (Titus 2:1 ESV).

*Show yourself in all respects to be a model of good works, and in your teaching show integrity, dignity . . .* (Titus 2:7 ESV)

*. . . not pilfering, but showing all good faith, so that in everything they may adorn the doctrine of God our Savior.* (Titus 2:10 ESV)

The Spirit of God uses the Word of God to make the child of God like the Son of God. The Spirit of God and the Word of God work together to regenerate (Titus 3:5) and to sanctify (2 Thessalonians 2:13). The Word of God is "effective" (1 Thessalonians 2:13; Hebrews 4:12) because it permanently pairs with the power of the Spirit. Receptivity in the heart of human beings toward this coupling of the Word and the Spirit is a key issue in having mental acuity in the understanding of God's Word. There is no meaning apart from the common understanding of Scripture grasped by the laws of hermeneutics (biblical interpretation).

Although unregenerate people might understand God's Word on a cognitive level, they reject its authority over them. The reason is that they are mere mind, emotion, and will (soulish) with no spiritual capacity (1 Corinthians 2:14). Their problem is that they believe a different system for coming to truth, for "the world through wisdom did not know God" (1 Corinthians 1:21). The gospel is "foolishness" to them (1:18). They have the ability to understand the gospel but not the will to accept it or welcome it. This is an issue of the will. By contrast, the Bereans "welcomed," or "received," the message with great keenness (Acts 17:11), and the Thessalonians did the same (1 Thessalonians 1:6).

The Old Testament has twelve Hebrew words to depict teaching or doctrine. In the Old Testament, "doctrine" occurs chiefly as a translation of *leqaḥ* (חֶקַל), meaning "what is received" (Deuteronomy 32:2; Job 11:4; Proverbs 4:2; Isaiah 29:24). This word occurs in over eighty verses in the Old Testament. It carries the idea of "mandate" or "teaching" as a noun. It means a body of truth. The Hebrew also expresses the body of revealed teaching by *tôrâ*, occurring 216 times and rendered as "law."

Moses says that he "taught" (*lammed*) divine truth in the form of "statutes and judgments." First, Deuteronomy 4:1 says truth is to be appropriated (*sham*), "to be heard consensually." God proposed his truth so that we would appropriate it without negotiation or compromise. Second, Deuteronomy 4:6 affirms that understanding can result from believing and appropriating God's Word. Third, God's Word has lucidity (4:10). It is a clearly written book intelligible to the average person. Finally, God does not obscure his Word (4:14). Once postconservatives abandon doctrine, they abandon God's truth. No amount of subjective sincerity can carry this violation of doctrinal teaching (*lamad*).

## Greek Words for Doctrine

The New Testament uses three primary words for "doctrine." *Didaskalia* (twenty-one occurrences) means both the act and the content of teaching, related to a standard of orthodoxy (Acts 2:42). *Didachē* (thirty occurrences) also can mean either the act or the content of teaching. It occurs in the teaching of Jesus (Matthew 7:28) and where he claimed to be God (John 7:16–17). 3) The final word is *didasko* ("to teach," used to translate the Hebrew *lamad*); the Father "taught" Jesus (John 8:28) a body of truth.

The Greek word "doctrine" or "teaching" (διδαχή) refers to instruction as a fact, an established and formulated doctrine (Hebrews 6:2). The Greek verb "to teach" (διδάσκω) carries the idea of holding discourse with others in order to instruct them, delivering didactic discourses, instilling doctrine, imparting instruction, and explaining or expounding a thing. Jesus taught in the synagogues, temple, and elsewhere (Matthew 5:1, 2). The disciples of Jesus taught (Mark 6:30), and this was part of their commission (Matthew 28:20). The apostles taught in Acts 4. They presented teaching in such a way that people must either accept or reject Scripture. Paul spent a year and a half teaching at Corinth (Acts 18:11). Paul instructed with the purpose of edification: "Him we preach, warning every man and teaching every man in all wisdom, that we may present every man perfect in Christ Jesus" (Colossians 1:28). Paul told Timothy to "command and teach" (1 Timothy 4:11; 6:2; 2 Timothy 2:2). Doctrine began to be formally systematized after the church began (Acts 2:42). God appointed special teachers to give doctrinal instruction (1 Corinthians 12:28, 29; Galatians 6:6).

The Greek word "teach" can refer to the act of teaching or to what is taught. Jesus taught the disciples on the Emmaus road by "explaining" (*diermeneuw*) and "opening up" (*dianoigw*) the Word of God (Luke 24:27, 32). The early church regularly taught its congregation (Acts 2:42). Paul charged Timothy to "teach others also" (2 Timothy 2:2) and to stick true to the Word of God (Titus 1:9). He was to exhort in sound doctrine and refute those who contradicted the Word (Titus 1:9). Paul warned him to pay close attention to his teaching (doctrine) in 1 Timothy 4:16. Paul set the standard for leaders in the local church to Titus: "For a bishop must . . . [hold] fast the faithful word as he has been taught, that he may be able, by sound doctrine, both to exhort and convict those who contradict" (Titus 1:7, 9).

A bishop or pastor is to hold firmly to the faithful Word as he has been taught. This is the basis of the doctrinal task. Doctrine is the foundation for proclaiming the faithful Word. The message is trustworthy, or faithful, precisely because it is in harmony with or conformity to Scripture. The Greek word "as" means "according to the standard of" what he has been taught (by the apostles). "Taught" has the same root as the word "doctrine." This word, when used with the definite article, means that God expects the bishop (that is, the teacher) to be faithful to teaching that is formulated into propositions. By this, the teacher can do two things: (1) exhort by sound doctrine and (2) refute those who contradict sound doctrine. Leaders in the local church must meet these standards of Scripture to lead properly. These passages fly in the face of the narrative and anti-propositional approach.

## Doctrine Demands Clarity and Certainty

God's Word identifies Christianity with the cognitive element but does not preclude the attitudinal or emotional dimensions, as we saw previously.

Doctrine is the first-order dimension. This is far more than "straight thinking" or "right opinion" as Brian McLaren claims in *A Generous Orthodoxy*. According to Paul, some things are clear, but McLaren says that clarity is sometimes overrated. He believes that shock and obscurity communicate better than clarity. He, in effect, denies the truth proclaimed in Titus that we should "guard the faithful word." Truth is not that clear to McLaren. It is difficult to discover orthodoxy in his *Generous Orthodoxy*. He claims to have found a generous third way between conservatism and liberalism, a postmodern modification of Christianity, but he does not attempt to prove this viewpoint.

This search for a "generous orthodoxy" with a huge, accommodating center is impervious to distinctions that differ. Robert Webber, the late professor of ministry and founder of the Institute for Worship Studies, as well seeks to accommodate evangelicalism to postmodern thought. He wants to construct out of tradition a theology that is relevant to present-day culture. All that is important to him is the framework of faith. Religious assertions are true because they are the perspective that is consistent with a particular tradition. In this, he abandons reference to objective revelation.

Jesus warned that false teachers teach "as doctrines the commandments of men" (Matthew 15:9). Truth is not pliable according to preference, but this is exactly how postmodern evangelicals attempt to view it.

1 Timothy refers to "sound doctrine." This is a phrase peculiar to 1 and 2 Timothy and Titus (the books written to pastors). These words occur eight times, six times with "teaching" or "doctrine" and twice with "the faith." It was crucial that pastors continue steadfastly in "sound doctrine"; note the following verses (as well as 1 Timothy 6:3, 2 Timothy 4:3, Titus 1:9, and Titus 2:1 above):

> . . . *the sexually immoral, men who practice homosexuality, enslavers, liars, perjurers, and whatever else is contrary to sound doctrine . . .* (1 Timothy 1:10 ESV)

> *Follow the pattern of the sound words that you have heard from me, in the faith and love that are in Christ Jesus.* (2 Timothy 1:13 ESV)

> *This testimony is true. Therefore rebuke them sharply, that they may be sound in the faith . . .* (Titus 1:13 ESV).

*Older men are to be sober-minded, dignified, self-controlled, sound in faith, in love, and in steadfastness.* (Titus 2:2 ESV).

Sound doctrine is truth balanced and ordered throughout; figuratively, the Greek uses "sound" of doctrinal teaching that is correct, sound, and accurate. Pastors are to be careful with truth; they are to have a sound, or accurate, approach to Scripture. This takes careful study of the text and doctrines that arise out of the text.

Because a proposition is the meaning of a declarative sentence, those who do not believe in propositions declare that God transcends language; so God is not verbal, but they find God in an indefinable experience. This thinking presumes that there is no adequate knowledge of God in propositional form. Though it is true that God is ineffable, this does not mean that we cannot know him propositionally. The assumption that truth is only personal and not propositional runs counter to John 1:1: "In the beginning was the Word, and the Word was with God, and the Word was God."

The "word" (*logos*) means "doctrine, proposition, and logic." John says the Word is God; he does not say that the Word transcends language. God's Word is more than symbols about God; it comprises declarative statements about Him. An ecstatic approach to language denies affirmations and takes them beyond clarity of proposition, making them into something merely metaphorical. In John 5:31, 32, Jesus says that his words are "not true" if he is the only witness to his Messiahship. The word "true" describes spoken statements or propositions about Jesus. The Bible itself never claims that truth is an encounter, an emotion, or experience. Truth is always propositional and intellectual and received by understanding alone. There is no personal truth as distinguished from propositional truth. John was an eyewitness of the crucifixion (John 19:35).

## Illumination of the Spirit

The work of illumination about what the Bible means and its truthfulness is the work of God the Holy Spirit. It is his job to enable the believer to understand and apply the Word of God to experience. We cannot apply what we do not understand. God conditions appropriation of truth on understanding. This is far more than intellectual understanding of the Bible. Not just scholars but any believer can come to this perception on Scriptures. It is true that God specially gifts pastors to understand and teach Scripture, but this does not preclude the individual from studying Scriptures as did the Berean believers.

Illumination by the Spirit does not equate to intuitive insights, although God might give subjective light on the subject. The normal process is careful study followed by subjective reflection. Understanding of Scripture should be verifiable. Study always precedes experience; experience does not precede study. Thus, the illuminating work of the Holy Spirit enables both understanding and application of it.

Not all of the Word is equally clear. There are difficult passages. Peter declared some of Paul's epistles "hard to understand" (2 Peter 3:16). Nor does illumination mean that a believer can reach total and complete understanding of all Scriptures. We know only "in part" (1 Corinthians 13:12) as long as we are finite—and we will always be finite, even in heaven.

Propositions are revelations from inspired Scripture. This is the first principle or axiom of Christianity. It is the epistemological starting point. To start with self or sensation is to leave the foundational axiom of Christianity. If someone starts with self or sensation, then that is one's ultimate presupposition for coming to truth and ultimate basis of belief.

Propositional truth does not reduce God to a proposition. No knowledge of God is possible without propositions that are non-contradictory and logically consistent. Logic does not intrude as a foreign system into propositions about God, but logical propositions are the only way to understand what God says in the Bible.

This is not rationalism but consistent logical process. We cannot present Christianity as true without core propositions inherent in our presentations. We cannot believe in God without believing about God. To reject the law of non-contradiction is to wipe out the notion of truth. The idea of propositions from God presented in sixty-six books is what distinguishes Christianity from all its opponents. If we divorce propositions from Scripture, all we have left is mysticism, and that is where postconservatives end up. Mysticism ends with something not clearly Christian or genuine belief. The close correlation between mysticism and dialectical thinking produces belief in a person without belief in propositions about the person.

Propositional truth is one of the foundations for certainty about truth.

# THERE IS CERTAINTY
# SOMEWHERE
## *Source for Certainty—a Watershed Issue*

In the Old Testament, Job declared at a culminating point in the book, "For I know that my Redeemer lives, and at the last he will stand upon the earth. And after my skin has been thus destroyed, yet in my flesh I shall see God" (Job 19:25, 26 ESV).

Job made a direct statement of certainty.

Certainty is manifestly important to God in the way he communicates biblical parlance. Attempt to marginalize certainty or its associated ideas is to blunt obvious declarations of Scripture. In the following paragraphs, I will focus on key biblical words for certainty to show how the Word of God asserts unequivocal truth. Later in the chapter, I will show how certainty rests on the person and revelation of God.

God makes it patently clear in the Bible that he expects us to take assertions of Scripture with certainty. Luke made this transparent in his prologue to the gospel of Luke. Luke wanted Theophilus to know something for sure: "That you may have certainty [ἀσφάλειαν, literally "no" and "fall"] concerning the things [literally, "words"] you have been taught" (Luke 1:4 ESV).

The Greek word for "certainty" means a state of certainty with regard to a belief—being without doubt. These words will not fall or fail. The concept of certainty in the New Testament carries the idea of stability of statement—presenting facts, real circumstances. Luke's statements through inspiration are reliable; we can count on them. The word "certainty" is emphatic in the sentence because of its position.

The certainty of which Luke speaks (κατήχηθης) came by teaching, by apostolic communication; it means "to resound; to teach by word of mouth." The idea of this word is "received instruction." Theophilus had learned some things from the apostles, but now Luke wanted him to have a factual account (the book of Luke) about what they taught. After Theophilus read the book of Luke, he would have a reliable account and certain knowledge of the truth of Christianity. The word for certainty (ἀσφάλειαν; Luke 1:4) is used again in Acts 2:36: "Let all the house of Israel therefore know for *certain* that God has made him both Lord and Christ, this Jesus whom you crucified (italics mine)"

There was no question whatsoever about God making Jesus Lord and Christ; it was in the plan of God from eternity that Jesus would be the Savior. Luke viewed this as unshakable belief.

Later, in writing Acts, Luke says that Jesus presented himself after the resurrection with "many infallible proofs" (1:3). A proof is, in the Greek, a fixed sign, certain or sure token. It is that which causes something to be known as confirmed or verified. Jesus gave demonstrable evidence that he was alive. The word for "proofs" (*tekmēriois*) is a technical term derived from logic with the thrust of being demonstrative proof or evidence. The idea is proved beyond a doubt. This is exactly what postconservatives do not want to do—to prove something beyond doubt.

Yet another word group carrying the idea of certainty includes the words for "faith" or "to believe." This group connotes "assurance, guarantee." We find the verb form in 2 Timothy 3:14: "But as for you, continue in what you have learned and *have firmly believed*, knowing from whom you learned it" (ESV, italics mine).

Hebrews 11:1 gives another word (Ὑπόστασις) for conviction: "Now faith is the *assurance* of things hoped for, the conviction of things not seen" (ESV, italics mine).

The word "assurance" comes from the two Greek words for "stand" and "under," and it carries the idea of a title deed or of realty that gives a guarantee.

"Conviction" is something based on argument for truth or reality. This is how true faith operates.

The word "persuade" gives the idea of "confidence" in 1 John 3:19: "By this we shall know that we are of the truth and *reassure* our heart before him" (ESV, italics mine).

The word "reassure" (πείθω, *peithō*) means "to convince." It is possible for believers to become persuaded about something.

## Speaking of Indubitable Certainty

Denial of certainty is a denial of God's objective revelation. This way leads to the death of Christianity. If the Bible does not clearly reveal what God wants us to know, but is simply a hodgepodge of mystery, then it is not true revelation. It is a new form of Gnosticism. If God spoke, then he spoke with clarity and certainty.

Certainty is lack of doubt about a state of affairs. If I have no doubt that I live in Saint Cloud, Florida, then I am certain of that fact. There are two kinds of certainty: (1) logical certainty and (2) psychological certainty. Logical (epistemic, propositional) certainty rests on warrant or justification to believe a proposition.

There is no commonly accepted definition of the second kind of certainty. Certainty and doubt admit of degrees; consequently there are psychological levels of relative certainty. Logical certainty gives psychological confidence about a belief. However, psychological certainty must conform to objectivity so that it corresponds to logic. This keeps psychological certainty from resting on pathological understanding or arbitrary viewpoint.

Absolute certainty lacks all doubt. This is pompous to modern skeptical thinking because skeptics' beliefs are never more than probable. Skeptics hesitate to resolve doubt. Classic secular philosophers sought to resolve this issue by philosophical foundationalism—the view that human knowledge rests on "basic" propositions. Current postmodern philosophers reject foundationalism in the latter sense but revise foundationalism to believe that propositions are capable of negation by additional knowledge. Thus, the trend by postmoderns is to reject absolute certainty. Can we know with certainty that the Bible and its claims are true? Paul says it is possible (1 Corinthians 2:4). Luke wanted

Theophilus to know the "certainty" (*asphaleia*) of what the apostles taught (Luke 1:4), and in Acts 1:3 Jesus demonstrated his authenticity by "proofs" (*tekmeria*). These principles rest on the presupposition of special revelation.

Not all doubt is sinful, but doubt of what God says clearly in the Word is sinful. The Bible speaks of doubt with disapproval. Doubt impedes confidence of certainty:

> *Jesus immediately reached out his hand and took hold of him, saying to him, "O you of little faith, why did you doubt?"* (Matthew 14:31 ESV)

> *And Jesus answered them, "Truly, I say to you, if you have faith and do not doubt, you will not only do what has been done to the fig tree, but even if you say to this mountain, 'Be taken up and thrown into the sea,' it will happen."* (Matthew 21:21 )

## Doubt and Certainty

It is true that God accommodates his language so that finite human beings can understand something of who and what he is (anthropomorphism and anthropopathism), and that he speaks in images and analogies for this reason. Humans are limited to a degree of certainty because of finiteness. Evangelicals accept this limitation of human capacity for certainty because God confines absolute certainty to belief demonstrated by propositions of his revelation (1 Corinthians 2). Although we cannot be certain about everything, we can be certain about what God has revealed propositionally.

All honest Christians have doubt, but doubt is not the same as skepticism that questions everything as a matter of principle, or unbelief that deliberately rejects the authority of Scripture. Valid doubt arises from human finiteness— lack of a full grasp of reality. Doubt operates within the realm of certainty or uncertainty of presuppositions. Thus, faith and doubt are not mutually exclusive, but on the other hand, faith and unbelief are exclusive to each other.

There are indeed limits to our understanding of God, but this does not preclude an accurate, reliable, or certain understanding of God. God reveals himself accurately but partially to the limits of finite capacity. God accommodated revelation to the restricted limits of the human being. Although we cannot exhaustively comprehend God, we can know him with certainty. I can know by observation that I lived in Canada for thirty years, and I know a number of other places in the world where I have traveled, but I cannot know with certain knowledge the geography of other places where I have not traveled. Knowing God's revelation is not an issue of being probably true. We can know it with certainty. Having faith in God's Word is not faith without proof; what is at question is the nature of proof.

## Confusion between Confidence and Total Certainty

There is much confusion between confidence and absolute certainty. It is possible to have certainty about the Word of God, even with fallible capacity. This is because the Word of God is the final standard of certainty. What God says is true because it is impossible for him to lie (Hebrews 6:18; Titus 1:2). Abraham believed God's Word in the face of doubt (Romans 4:20–22); God's promise took precedence over everything for him and he deemed God's promise as certain. Therefore, we can have confidence or certainty about revealed truth although we cannot have complete certainty that explains everything about an issue.

God provides historical evidence, such as evidence for Jesus' death and resurrection (Acts 1:3; 1 Corinthians 15). We are to place our confidence in that evidence because it comes from reliable apostolic preaching. Personal certainty comes from the tandem of (1) the Holy Spirit (1 Corinthians 2:4) and (2) the authority of God's Word (vv. 9–16):

> *. . . because our gospel came to you not only in word, but also in power and in the Holy Spirit and with full conviction.* (1 Thessalonians 1:5 ESV)

> *And we also thank God constantly for this, that when you received the word of God, which you heard from us, you accepted it not as the word of men but as what it really is, the word of God, which is at work in you believers.* (1 Thessalonians 2:13 ESV)

The Thessalonians obtained certainty from both the Word of God and the demonstration of the Holy Spirit. Christians of the New Testament era lived "in full assurance of faith" (Hebrews 10:22). Clement of Rome said that the apostles "went forth with the firm assurance that the Holy Spirit gives."[212] Certitude was characteristic of the apostles. Irenaeus made the point that we cannot have certainty without God's initiative: "Without God, God is not known."

Mediaeval Christianity, however, was fraught with uncertainty. Few believed that they had done enough works to gain eternal life. Early on, neither Luther nor Calvin could find release from the uncertainty of their salvation. The Reformation restored certainty because of trust in extant statements of the Word about justification by faith. Under the guidance of Calvin, Nicholas Cop, rector of the University of Paris, said, "God cannot be worshipped in doubt." There was no grand "perhaps" in Calvin or his followers.

The finite capacity of human beings cannot bring us to sure knowledge of God. If we begin with man, the shifting sands of uncertainty will prevail. If we begin with the broad road, we will go nowhere. Finiteness constitutes the limitation of human beings. If we take the narrow road, we will obtain certainty of truth. Mankind's only hope is that God would reveal himself, for God is the source of certainty. God gives us our faith by the power or demonstration of the Holy Spirit. Faith does not begin with self.

## Indubitable Foundation for Certainty

In addition to the words for certainty we studied above, the New Testament sets forth a number of other Greek words such as the word translated "sure." We will view these passages in running fashion.

Christians have a "sure" (ἀσφαλής) and steadfast anchor of the soul (Hebrews 6:19). The word of prophecy was "made more sure" (βέβαιος) than the personal experience on the Mount of Transfiguration (2 Peter 1:10 ff); thus, it is a "more sure" (βέβαιος) word of prophecy. "Sure" implies something trustworthy that we can count on; we cannot trust something about which we are not sure. The Christian is to hold certainty in his confidence: "And we are his house if indeed we hold fast our confidence [βέβαιος] and our boasting in our hope" (Hebrews 3:6 ESV).

We are to hold confidence firm to the end (Hebrews 3:14). This word is used for the act of holding fast to the confidence (βέβαιος) that guards us against apostasy (Hebrews 3:14; 2 Peter 1:10). It is the "sure and steadfast anchor of the soul" (Hebrews 6:19 ESV). The word group carries the idea of permanence and stability for faith. The essential idea of the word (βέβαιος) pertains to that which we know with certainty—known to be true, certain, verified. The verb (βεβαιόω) carries the idea of causing something to be known as certain, such as the gospel (Philippians 1:7). The idea is to prove something to be true and certain—to verify. Peter used this word validating the prophetic word: "And we have something more *sure*, the prophetic word, to which you will do well to pay attention as to a lamp shining in a dark place, until the day dawns and the morning star rises in your hearts" (2 Peter 1:19 ESV, italics mine).

Another form of this word (βεβαίωσις) carries the ideas of ratification, confirmation, corroboration, verification, making sure (Philippians 1:7; Hebrews 6:16). This word is a legal, technical term for furnishing a guarantee. Paul used this word in 1 Corinthians 1:6, 8 for keeping the Corinthians firm in faith. Paul's imprisonment made a "confirmation" of the gospel (Philippians 1:7). It is important that a believer operate with a sense of verification of his faith.

The Greek word for "complete certainty" (πληροφορία) means "full or complete assurance" (Colossians 2:2), "full conviction" or "certitude" (1 Thessalonians 1:5), and carries the idea of being completely certain of the truth of something—to be absolutely sure, to be certain, complete certainty (Romans 4:21). The noun (πληροφορία) means "fullness" and "firm conviction, absolute certainty": "...because our gospel came to you not only in word, but also in power and in the Holy Spirit and with *full conviction*. You know what kind of men we proved to be among you for your sake" (1 Thessalonians 1:5 ESV, italics mine).

The gospel came to the Thessalonians with complete certainty. The apostles reached a state of complete certainty, full assurance, certainty. The gospel team of Paul, Silvanus, and Timothy came with powerful conviction when they came to Thessalonica. They did not waver with doubt but came with clear conviction and willingly committed their eternal future to this message. If we are uncertain about what we believe, we will not convince others of our message. If we change our position with every fad or opinion poll that comes along, we do not have any message but the message of uncertainty. It is crucial to establish personal convictions. If people are unsure about what they believe, they will not commit to our message. Paul uses this same word in Colossians 2:2: "... that their hearts may be encouraged, being knit together in love, to reach all the riches of *full assurance* of understanding and the knowledge of God's mystery, which is Christ" (ESV, italics mine). The "riches of the full assurance of understanding" is sound judgment about the great truths of Christianity. A person with full assurance of understanding no longer calls into question the Word of God. Doubt is no longer the central mode of operation. This believer embraces truth with high satisfaction in the object of his belief. Paul uses the verb for this word in Romans 4:21 (ESV), being "fully convinced" that God was able to do what he had promised.

Another Greek word (πείθω) signifies "to apply persuasion, to prevail upon or win over, to persuade, bringing about a change of mind by the influence of reason or moral considerations." This word carries the idea "state of certainty, trust, confidence." Paul was sure that nothing could separate him from his salvation: "For I am sure that neither death nor life, nor angels nor rulers, nor things present nor things to come, nor powers, nor height nor depth, nor anything else in all creation, will be able to separate us from the love of God in Christ Jesus our Lord" (Romans 8:38, 39 ESV).

This kind of certainty gives stability to the Christian life. The believer is not to shift from confident belief: ". . . if indeed you continue in the faith, stable and steadfast, not shifting from the hope of the gospel that you heard, which has been proclaimed in all creation under heaven, and of which I, Paul, became a minister" (Colossians 1:23 ESV).

The believer is not to lose firm hold on truth: "You therefore, beloved, knowing this beforehand, take care that you are not carried away with the error of lawless people and lose your own stability [στηριγμός]" (2 Peter 3:17).

As we will see in Chapter Ten, in the study of 1 Corinthians 2:4, a key Greek word for certainty (ἀπόδειξις—we get the English word "apodictic" from this Greek word) means strictly "showing forth"; hence "demonstration, proof, evidence." The word signifies pointing to something for the purpose of demonstration, proof. The Holy Spirit's miracle-working power shows the reality of Christianity. A key word for "certainty" (ἀσφαλής) carries the idea of being unshakable, secure.

The Christian faith has an indubitable foundation—the Word of God. It challenges the idea that truth is always open and subject to change, for it is a belief not derived from other beliefs. God does not present his truth as a hypothesis or theory.

The Enlightenment was *a posteriori* in its approach to truth, and so it always carried uncertainty because it could never come to a universal or ultimate truth. Rationalism as an approach to truth was always finite and never capable of ultimate certainty. All credible philosophers accepted the idea that they could not come to ultimate reality. Christianity does not depend on finite humans as the source for truth but transcends the material view of the world; it is metaphysical (beyond the physical) so is *a priori,* from outside material time-space assumptions.

Postconservative postmodernism affects most doctrines of the Christian faith, but the essential idea of certainty about Christian truth is especially at stake. The central thrust of the Christian faith is that it is rooted in absolute, objective truth regardless of cultural trends. If Christians can only approximate understanding of God's truth, then God's revelation is ambiguous and faulty in its communication system. Our knowledge of God would be only probable or possible but not certain. Relativism weakens the authority of Scripture and reduces God's propositional, informational revelation in lieu of open interaction. By beginning with human limitation as the starting point, postconservatives *ipso facto* put humans in authority over against propositions deduced from God. By assuming as their starting point the human delimitation of probability rather than the idea that God adequately revealed himself in propositions, they are lost in a sea of subjectivity.

If we begin with the idea that God adequately revealed himself in his Word, then we can come to a level of certainty about many things. When we abandon the idea that we can know truths beyond the narrative, then humans become the authority and we cannot come to propositional knowledge of God. This latter viewpoint is no longer evangelical because it rests on self-autonomy, and it lacks the "God has said" point of view. Its mentality is the viewpoint of Satan—"Has God said?"

Evangelicalism defines truth as objective (independently true) and absolute (not dependent on cultural context or finite man's view of reality). Biblical truth does not exclusively rest in the mind of the beholder so that the interpreter's context prejudices his view of reality. We can take the Bible at face value as over against the cynicism of postconservatism. There is value beyond the value the individual creates because God gave objective revelation. The tension in this issue is one of authority; does the authority reside in self or in the Word? There is no equivalence in terms of truth; either the Bible is true in counterdistinction to other so-called truths or it is not. The issue revolves around the question of whether man is the center or God and his revealed Word are the center.

If we are only able to approximate understanding of the Bible, then knowledge of God is only probable. What percentage of Christianity is true? Fifteen percent or fifty percent? We would have to honestly witness to an unbeliever with probability: "It is my estimation that Christianity is sixty-five percent true!" Probability would affect most doctrines of Scripture if we accept postconservative postmodern presupposition. This form of relativism produces a skeptical approach to Christianity and cannot produce a vibrant testimony to truth.

We can reduce this issue to the ultimate presupposition of method for approaching truth. Either we begin with limited human perspectives about truth or we begin with God's revelation. If we begin with human viewpoint, then all that remains is our own devices and presuppositions, and we wallow in doubt. The presupposition of postconservatism is self-autonomy found in the dialectical process.

The believer, according to McLaren, must be "open to the perpetual possibility that our received understanding of the gospel may be faulty . . . including our tradition's understanding of the gospel"; in true postmodern form, he says we "must continually expect to rediscover the gospel."[213] In other words, we must hold our understanding of the gospel tentatively because our perception of it might be wrong. If this view were true, then, if he were honest, he would have to say that there is a thirty percent chance that the gospel is true. Thus, gospel presentation would be tepid and uncertain. Who would believe that except the most amorphous types? As well, with this logic we should question the validity of Christ and the Christian tradition. It is duplicity to question perpetually a view of how people become Christians, and not question the very idea of the truthfulness of Christ. Dialectical thinking always questions whether there is a sun in the sky.

## Truth by Definition Exclusive

Truth is by definition exclusive. There is a strong antithesis in North American culture today that asserts there is an absolute God out there, but that there is no such thing as absolute truth. This might be because of cultural uniformity in North America, a society that seeks approval in plurality.

If it is a practical impossibility to investigate the universe by considering all possibilities of all time both potential and actual, both qualitatively and quantitatively equally, and totally without bias, then we find mankind trapped in futile finiteness. Our finiteness precludes us from finding an infinite God. Only an infinite God can give universal and certain information about himself. He has done that through the revelation of the Bible. If there is an absolute God who brooks no other, then we can find universal truth from him if he reveals himself.

Contemporary people cannot choose between two incompatible lines of action because, for them, there are no absolute norms. Because these norms reduce to personal preference, there is no inherent authority without an absolute. The only important value is social harmony or tolerance. Reality is whatever people make it (solipsism). Postmodernism denies absolutes and holds to a divided field of knowledge. No truth can be final because this philosophy rejects the possibility of an objective basis for absolute truth. The group can come to no meaning except for the meaning the group creates for itself. This is belief that exists only in relation to other finite thinking. Truth varies with the situation.

The root of postmodernism is skepticism that denies truth except for the truth of postmodernism. It claims the exclusive right to hold to its assumption for coming to truth (presupposition). Postmodernism's only absolute is that there are no absolutes. Subjectivism, relativism, humanism, and agnosticism are the result. This is a change in the way that people today approach truth. All of this preconditions people to skepticism.

Holding any truth as absolute is an unpardonable error to those who hold to a divided field of truth. They view those who assert truth as biased opinion holders. Bias is anathema to postmoderns. The reason for this view is their system of thinking, the very system by which their reason prohibits them from coming to absolutes.[214] Their preconceived belief system traps them in finite presupposition. In this perception of things, there can be no categorical unity of truth but only disorder when it comes to conclusions about truth. This perception constantly changes within the confines of the finite. What is true today might be false tomorrow. Truth, then, is relative. The only fixed truth is that truth is not fixed.

If there is no truth, then no one can fix responsibility to anything because there is nothing upon which to base such a view. Values wallow in preferences of a group of people at a particular time. If there is no settled truth, then there is no coherence or purpose to life. People must live in a mass of meaninglessness. Academic freedom becomes the *summun bonum,* or final value, for approaching life. Preference for endless finite conclusions over discovery of truth stands as a first principle.

## Certainty Originates in an Absolute God

The evangelical Christian holds to one absolute integrating point—God himself. Humans try to deny an absolute God and build a way of knowing on finite perspective. Human beings, then, become the integrating point for truth. Because people are finite, their conclusions about truth must be finite. Therefore, the very premise or presupposition of postmodernism precludes the possibility of an absolute God. This is a vicious cycle. All that remains is a world of absurdity. All is in flux and nothing is for sure. All this discharges relativism devoid of fixed truth and ultimate purpose for life.

God has no need of human beings (Acts 17:25). He is the cause of creation, so he is the uncaused cause of all things. Further, he is absolute. He has never learned anything because he has always known all things. He has never gone anywhere because he is always everywhere. There is no rock too hard for him to lift because he created, and thus transcends, any rock. God never miscalculates anything; he never naps; no problem confounds him; nothing is too big for God; his authority reaches to the actions and thoughts of people. There is no random universe with an absolute God. Man, on the other hand, can claim no pretense to autonomy for he is dependent on God for truth. He cannot come to truth independent from God, so the mind is not the ultimate regulator for determining truth.[215] Denial of man's right to autonomy is the greatest fundamental offence against finite man, who wishes to have the prerogative of infinite capacity for truth.

Postmoderns live in a vacuum of meaninglessness unless they move to an absolute God who can give them ultimate purpose and meaning. Because God is absolute, he transcends all other truth. He is unrivaled and unsurpassed supremacy—peerless. Everything has denotation and connotation.[216] We cannot separate the ideas of God and good, because all good comes from God. An absolute God stands at the center of Christianity.

Not only is God absolute, he is a personal absolute. Because we are not absolute, we have a problem that confines us to the prison of finiteness. God's absoluteness is transcendent (outside creation), but he is also immanent (in creation). As absolute, God is creator of all things, is over all things, assesses all things, and exerts power everywhere in creation. God participates in time and space (Ephesians 1:11). He acted in history and he acts in our personal lives (concursus). However, if we define God only in relation to creation, then we limit him to creation.

God answers the problem of finite human ability to come to truth by reducing what he wants people to know by revelation, whether by the general revelation of creation or the special revelation of the Word of God. In doing so, he wants us to be certain that the message about Christ is true (Luke 1:4) and, therefore, to be sure of salvation (1 John 5:13). All of this presupposes that God revealed himself in his Word. Beyond what God does in his Word, the supernatural person of the Holy Spirit "demonstrates" the truth of the gospel to us (1 Corinthians 2:4; 1 Thessalonians 1:5). The Holy Spirit supernaturally gives credibility to the Word. In other words, he ignites our presupposition or fundamental belief in the Bible as true. This is not a natural situation but a supernatural state of affairs.

Moral or ethical standards imply an absolute standard. Truth produces ethical value; otherwise, from nothing, nothing comes. There is no distinction of authority from the perspective approach to the Word of God. The Bible presupposes its own authority in complete viewpoint. God is an absolute being who is all encompassing, uncaused, and unconditioned. Because God has no cause and he is the absolute being, all derivative and ensuing truth and morals flow from him. Because God is absolute, his moral absolutes never change. He cannot change himself, who is immutable. Therefore, God's moral absolutes bind all people everywhere in every culture during every period. If God is God, no human being has the option to choose whether to be responsible to conduct life according these absolutes.

Humans can doubt, question, and even deny God's absolutes; we can debate their validity or attempt to change them, but the only way we could change or do away with them is to do away with the absolute God.

No one can assign genuine guilt without a moral absolute. We could not then judge even the most corrupt person by any ultimate norm and would swim in relativism. If we attempt to adapt or accommodate Christianity to cultural norms, we destroy its unity of truth. The believer who carries biblical convictions should attempt to make society relevant to God, not simply make God relevant to society as postconservatives do. Evangelicals who adapt biblical truth to the prevailing culture without a clear understanding of the absoluteness of God tread on dangerous ground. They confuse method and message.

Christian ethics follow theology. Theology begins with the doctrine of God as its foundation because God exists in and of himself. God has no source other than in his being, whereas man has the source of being outside himself. Therefore, man cannot begin with himself as the starting point, for he is limited and thus finite. If he begins with a finite point, he must reach a finite conclusion. How can man straddle both relativism and the idea of an absolute God? Francis Schaeffer makes a telling point about this in *The God Who Is There*: "We are His people, and if we get caught up in the other methodology, we have really blasphemed, discredited and dishonored Him, for the greatest antithesis of all is that He exists as opposed to His not existing. He is the God who is there."[217]

## Self—the Center of Authority

The non-Christian who begins with self to determine truth has no hope because there is no adequate universal norm for finding truth. Such a person is lost in finiteness. This is especially true if one assumes the dialectical method (the scheme of antithesis). An unbeliever assuming autonomy from God is ensnared in this method. There would be no other choice than to begin with some form of *a posteriori* approach. One can never decide on what is true because the method itself precludes one from coming to ultimate or absolute truth. If human beings are finite, one cannot come to infinite truth by oneself. One needs an all-comprehensive reference point. Evangelicals who buy into this method end in postevangelicalism, a belief system without certainty and with a greatly weakened message.

D. A. Carson calls postmodernism "the bastard child of modernism" because it "shares its fundamental weakness: it begins with the 'I,' the finite self. In this sense, postmodernism, like the modernism that spawned it, is methodologically atheistic—or more generously put, it takes no account of God at the beginning of its deliberations."[218] This makes postmoderns argue in a circle and begs the question of whether gaining certainty is possible. They begin with the conclusion of autonomous self and argue from that premise, making it impossible to come to the transcendent God who reveals himself. The ultimate presupposition of beginning with the God who reveals himself resolves all finite perspectives by his omniscience.

If we begin with autonomous man, we will end with autonomous man, with our finite perspective, and can never arrive at certainty. That foundation is shaky, so it is no wonder postmodernism views God as a perspective of a given group at a given time. With this view, no group has any more validity than any other group. Postmoderns confidently assert that there is no way of knowing anything for sure. Any exclusive claim for truth is intolerant bias. Therefore, each group has its own finite story devoid of any universal certainty.

Postevangelicals try to soften the hard implications of secular postmoderns by allowing a place for objective truth. Once they introduce objective truth, they now have a dilemma. What is the origin of this truth? How do they arrive at it? Most postevangelicals soft-pedal even the most innocuous claim of truth. The reason for this is that truth is by nature exclusive, and that is exactly what they do not want, for they want others to perceive them as open and tolerant of other beliefs.

It seems to me that secular postmoderns would not be impressed with this woolly-headedness. They would ask, "Where do you get the unmitigated gall to believe in the certainty of Jesus Christ?" or "Why do you prefer to believe in the Bible?" Postevangelicals have no answer, other than "This is our perspective! We do not have certainty, but please join our little goody-goody two-shoes group and maybe somehow, some way, you might become a Christian by osmosis." If postevangelical postmoderns begin with autonomous self, they end with finite perspective and lack definite answers for our day. Their postmodern system is devastating to the evangelical cause because Christianity rests on a truth claim of certainty—"I am the way, the truth, and the life."

The issue of how we know what we know is true is at the heart of this whole issue (epistemology). The matter of how we know rests on the subject of which presupposition we choose to find truth. If we choose a transcendent God who reveals himself in concursive revelation, then we can have certainty about God. All that is in the Bible is true as to its record, but not all truth is in the Bible. The Bible does not speak to all fields of science, for example. Neither did God exhaustively reveal everything there is to know about himself. That will never happen because we would have to be infinite to comprehend everything there is to know about God.

## The All-Encompassing Reference Point

Only an infinite, absolute God can be the all-comprehensive reference point from which we derive absolute truth and values. No one caused God to do or be anything; thus, God puts all creation in relation to himself and not himself in relation to creation. God is the only one who possesses absolute freedom; nothing binds God except that which is self-imposed, and he is not subject to any restriction other than self-imposed limitations.

Human freedom is a derived freedom, a freedom that comes from God. Therefore, we find our dignity in God. God does not exist for the sake of mankind but mankind for the sake of God. There is nothing greater than to make God the goal for humanity; that is where people find ultimate meaning and satisfaction. Philosophies that do not take God into account reduce themselves to the finite, a place without universal integration of knowledge. Finite philosophies are inevitably incomplete.

As God is the basis for blessedness, so life without God is the core of wretchedness. God's purpose for life stands in stark contrast to the hopelessness of our society today. Postmoderns believe that there is no meaning to life except what the finite individual or group gives. They have no "metanarrative" or ultimate meaning.

The God who exists outside of creation, eternally by no cause outside himself, and who is the sufficient cause of everything, carries great purpose and meaning. A God-centered worldview affects judgment on the worth of life. This gives identity and purpose to time and space. His purpose gives integration to the structure of values. God's infiniteness comprehends any contingency that we might face. Nothing surprises him. He gives meaning to all events, thought, and activity. Activity for its own sake is vacuous, but activity that ends in the ultimate purpose of glorifying God gives transcendent meaning to creatures of God.

An unchanging God cannot adapt to humans. The reality of an absolute God demands that we view life from his point of view. We cannot begin with the perspective of self—the human viewpoint. Divine viewpoint takes on a new field of view, for mankind is no longer lost in the despair of self or a group. We cannot have hope unless we move to a new center—God's Word as the polestar of reckoning all values for life.

## Inability of the Self to Determine Truth

If God is absolute and unconditioned by anything outside himself, all of human beings' acts concur within his sovereignty and permission. Because God is completely self-determined, no other cause influences him. No one influenced him to create the universe. God's ground of existence rests in himself, for he does not depend on anything outside himself. Thomas Aquinas said that God is the first cause, himself uncaused. This does not imply that God's existence is grounded in his will. God is not his own cause! God is independent in himself and causes everything else to depend on him. This includes mankind's ability to come to truth and certainty.

God does not depend on the universe in any sense. There was nothing to compel him to create. Creation does not complete God, for God exists for himself and is wholly sufficient to himself. Yet there is a difference between the outward and the inward constraint of God. Creation was a free decision by God. God decreed creation but he did not decree himself or anything about himself.

God freely relates to his creatures and creation but not because of any necessary relation. His incommunicable attributes (attributes that he cannot share with humans) emphasize his absoluteness.[219] His communicable attributes (attributes that he shares with humans) stress his relationship with creation and mankind. God's relationship to creation is by his plan and not from knowledge outside himself. God planned from all eternity to create the universe. He had prior knowledge to every fact that existed or ever will exist. Every fact of the universe has purpose because it fits into the unifying plan of God.

Because God's plan to create the universe is eternal, and from an absolute being, it is perfect. An imperfect plan would imply a finite god who is not infinite and absolute. If there were a necessity to revamp God's plan, it would not be perfect. God would have failed in some sense. God is an absolute category and cannot adapt to events over which he has no control. If so, he would be equivocal and conditioned upon some limitation within himself. Otherwise, he could not control the universe. He would have to rescue the ruins of his plan as he goes along, attempting to make modifications of an incomplete plan. He would have to concur with things as he finds them and extricate them from their mess. God will, however, ultimately vindicate or justify his permission of the existence of sin in the world.

God's decree is his infinite, eternal, and immutable will concerning future events and their precise order and manner of occurrence within his creation. All events are then certain from eternity. The Westminster Shorter Catechism puts it pithily: "The decree of God is his eternal purpose, according to the counsels of his own will, whereby for his own glory he has foreordained whatever comes to pass." Certainty is not arbitrary from God's viewpoint.

Decree, and the certainty that it implies, is eternal. If God changed his plan by succession as crisis comes, he would be ignorant of contingency or powerless to do anything about it. God willed before he put his plan into effect, so his actions accord with absolute perfection. Psalm 33:11 says, "The counsel of the LORD stands forever, The plans of His heart to all generations [literally, 'one generation after another']."

God vetoes the plots and plans of international politics, and nothing can frustrate his plan; after setting forth God's omniscience, the psalmist rues the futility of trust in human methods: "The LORD brings the counsel of the nations to nothing; He makes the plans of the peoples of no effect" (Psalm 33:10).

Human judgments and God's plan stand in stark contrast. Human methods are finite, not absolute but uncertain and incomplete.

God's decree is not conditional. Nothing ever placed God on the horns of a dilemma. He is not temporal or spatial, so he does not wait for contingencies before he makes a decision (Daniel 4:35). If any part of God's plan would fail, then God would not be absolute or perfect. A perfect plan must stand in every respect. God provides even for the free choice and acts of people in his plan. Whatever God does or allows, he decrees to do or allow. Humans are, therefore, epistemologically under the sovereignty of God's plan.

God knows everything perfectly. This includes concurrence with man's freedom to go independent of him. This is his purpose for creation: the manifest glory of God. Everything about creation is about God; God is the source, sustainer, and goal of creation: "For of Him and through Him and to Him are all things, to whom be glory forever. Amen" (Romans 11:36).

God can express his communicable attributes to free agents who make free choices. God can love the creature because the creature has the choice to receive God's love, making fellowship possible. The doctrine of providence means that God makes all events work out according to his plan. Concurrence is a corollary doctrine to providence. Concurrence means that human will has a range of freedom under God's sovereignty. Freedom of will can operate only with God's concurrence. God interpenetrates human will without stifling it so that he can preserve integrity of choice. Human beings can exercise our will within the sovereignty of God. Thus, God enables us epistemologically to make a transcendent choice, influencing us without intruding into our will.

Two extremes distort the doctrine of decree. On the one hand is fatalism, accepting everything as previously determined: there is no point to choice. On the other hand, some dethrone God from his superintendence over human will. This supposes humans have more choice than we do, and it excludes God's superintendence over every thought and action. If we assume free will, there is certainty in God's decree because God considered every contingency when he declared his decree. We sin only with God's permission. God extends his concurrence to every choice of every person, even to the permission of evil. God works with every human choice to process his plan. Mankind epistemo-logically operates under God's concurrence.

God varies his options for dealing with human volition: (1) he might keep us from doing what we would otherwise do; (2) he might use people, circum-stance, or inner compulsion to fulfill his purpose; (3) God might unilaterally annul our design; (4) he might make our wrath praise him; and (5) God might put no hindrances in our path. Through it all, there are no accidents in the plan of an absolute God. There is no chance or fate in God's economy. He will guide his plan to its ultimate design. Therefore, we do not float on a sea of epistemological uncertainty, for God makes a way for us to come to himself.

God's behavior toward people is not the result of change, chance, or uncertainty. Nothing we could or would do could change his purpose. God cannot change his attributes, but he can change the application of an attribute to meet the need of man. Nevertheless, his immutable, infinite, and absolute decree does not change. God moves the fulfillment of his plan toward his own glory. God's ceaseless activity is toward that end. Creation carries God's design.

## Truth Fixed in the Absolute

Truth existed from eternity, so universal truth rests in the nature of God and not in the contingencies of creation. This fixes truth in the absolute. Biblically, the meaning of the universe rests in the intrinsic nature of God. Truth is intrinsic to the object of God himself. Reality is aimed at a definite end—God. God does not will truth because it is true. If this were true, he would be servant to truth. God wills truth because he is truth. God does not conform to a standard; he is the standard. He is a law unto himself! He is that because he is absolute and utterly independent. Creatures cannot be a law unto themselves because they are finite, limited, and dependent. God's absoluteness means that nothing can affect him outside himself, for there is no sovereignty outside him. The essential problem for human epistemology is that it is finite and not absolute. God's absoluteness secures absolutes for mankind. God's truth is not unstable or relative. Humanity, of necessity, is epistemologically dependent upon God, if God is God.

God directs his will for its own sake because his will is the underpinning for reality. He is eternal, so his will is eternal. God's will stems from his character; the purpose for humans and our ability to come to absolutes finds its source in who God is. From a biblical worldview, truth is not true because it is expedient or pragmatic. It is true because God is absolute truth, and not due to personal preference. Biblical truth inextricably connects with the essence of God.

God's uncaused being determines the true end of creation. Because human beings are caused (i.e., a finite creature under the authority of the Creator), we cannot move beyond our finiteness. We have no way of knowing absolute truth other than through God's revelation. Our finiteness restricts us to our limited world. We can measure truth only within certain limitations. When we violate God's authority, we violate God's essence and plan. The nature of negative volition toward God is a distortion of order and authority; it is no defect, but a violation of God's will. Autonomy of humans makes finite self the center for authority, finds sufficiency in self, and moves independent of the sovereign, uncaused, autonomous God. Rejection of God's authority in revelation is a problem of rebellion.

Absolute truth and norms come from an absolute God. Because God is absolute, truth has objective validity; truth is not relative to different people or different situations. Cosmos does not come from chaos. So long as human beings do not hold to the absolute God, we can fix no truth or value. Because God directs everything in the universe by a plan, all truth and standards rest within divine design. Only an infinite God can understand this; humans can understand it only in a fragmented sense. The human viewpoint is, therefore, distorted and incomplete. Only God can fully understand his plan. We know one thing for sure about this plan from biblical revelation—the purpose of this plan is for God's own glory. The plan does not end in people or in a people-centered purpose. Truth rests on the foundation of the doctrine of God and his plan. Faith in the God of revelation molds viewpoint on life.

## No Equivocation in Nature of Gospel Message

Why do we have the kind of salvation we do? Because we have the kind of God we do. The kind of salvation we have rests on an absolute God. The doctrine of salvation does not center on the problem of sin but on God's absolute character. Sin contravenes God's character of absolute righteousness. Only God can align us with his absolute righteousness because man by nature and action violated his perfect righteousness. We cannot attain absolute righteousness by operation bootstraps. How righteous does a person have to be in order to stand righteous before God? One would have to have the same righteousness that God has—perfect righteousness or, if you prefer, absolute righteousness. If God were to allow us into heaven without being as right in our standing as God is right, he would compromise his absolute character. However, no one is as right as God is right in himself by nature or action.

Paul employs the first three chapters in Romans to show that man is not as right as God is right: "As it is written: "There is none righteous [in reference to God's righteousness], no, not one" (Romans 3:10).

Because no one is righteous as God is righteous, then none can go to heaven by being self-righteous. Paul then advances the idea that we can have absolute righteousness only if God gives it to us freely (Romans 3:21–5:1, especially 3:24). This righteousness originates in an absolute God and not in the person. God "justifies" (declares righteous) the believer into an absolute righteousness. The word "justify" is a causative verb meaning that God does the justifying or causing righteous standing before him. This is a forensic or judicial process whereby the believer has the veritable righteousness that God himself has (forensically). That is an absolute status with God forever.

The heart of the book of Romans defends the character of God (a theodicy). The first three chapters show how every person fell short of God's character. The last half of chapter 3 through chapter 5 shows how God declares a believer right with an absolute God. Chapters 6 through 8 show the Christian how to live in the light of his justification. The ground for sanctification is justification. We can live the Christian life because we have absolute status with God forever. Chapters 9 through 11 defend God's righteous purpose in dealing with Israel (a specific theodicy). The ensuing chapters of Romans show how to live out the truth of who God is.

If the Bible goes to such a great extent to establish a theodicy of God, why do postconservatives Christians minimize this great truth? They are afraid to be true to truth because they fear that postmoderns might deem them too narrow.

## Man as the Gauge for Man

Truth based on the idea that man is the gauge for man can go no further than finite man in coming to reality. The existence of an absolute God establishes the absoluteness of truth by an objectively fixed order. So long as people reject the God of the Bible, they cannot have ultimate truth, ultimate meaning, or absolute norms. They can never reach an all-encompassing reference point (the ultimate metanarrative). What people ought to be depends on their location in God's total scheme of things.

Ethics cannot escape truth. It is not possible to separate how we live from what we believe. When we define good with our own self as its end, we restrict good to mean what we can make of ourselves. This limits us to a natural view of truth. Truth founded in an absolute God produces transcendent meaning, God's assessment on reality. This is a source of truth beyond the autonomous person, finite mind, or human reason.

All certainty rests on who and what God is.

# A PLACE TO STAND
## A Pou Sto

### Point of Reference Beyond Self

In the first chapter of this book, I referred to Archimedes, who sought a place to stand in the universe. He said that if he could find a place to stand, he could "move the earth" with a lever. We need a place of certainty to stand, a point of reference beyond the self. *Pou sto* is the Greek term for "a place to stand." Only God can provide that ultimate perspective for where to stand on certainty; the place that he provided was the Word of God.

God has eternal viewpoint; humans have finite viewpoint. Only God's total transcendent viewpoint can give certainty because it is absolute, universal, and exhaustive. Human knowledge is by nature derivative, but God derives his knowledge from no one. God's knowledge is absolute, but human knowledge is dependent. God has never learned anything because he always knew every-thing, thus there is no fact independent of God.

Unless there is comprehensive knowledge somewhere, there can be no certainty anywhere because absolute knowledge is inextricably interrelated. Finiteness cannot lead to infiniteness. Without universal knowledge from God, human knowledge will forever be a fragmented viewpoint. Humans cannot examine all reality comprehensively and look at all possible relationships of information. We cannot begin with ourselves by detailed induction, for discovery of ultimate reality would take infinite capacity. The process of discovery will perpetually trap us in a process of discovery without ever coming to conclusion about all-inclusive certainty. We can never know any ultimate truth for sure, if we begin with ourselves.

God's knowledge, however, is coextensive with all that there is. Biblically, there is no brute fact, no fact that does not relate to God's purpose for creation. There is no ultimate certainty without God's disclosure of himself. God does not reveal himself exhaustively in the Bible, but he reveals himself truly. Only complete universal knowledge is capable to verify certainty; therefore, God's universal knowledge is prior to man's finite knowledge. Man's knowledge will always be equivocal, but God's is univocal. Most people are unwilling to humble themselves to this fact; consequently, they remain in despair of ever reaching certainty. Because there is no fact in the universe independent of God, we must choose between uncertainty or the Word of God as the source of certainty.

Evidence derived from the assumption that God spoke in his Word provides certainty. Every presupposition is the ultimate belief system that one takes. If we take a presupposition different from revelation, then all that remains is possibility or probability, not certainty.

## No Place to Stand

If we human beings begin with ourselves, we have no place to stand (*pou sto*). We are like the jackass who would not cross the bridge to the other side. Then non-Christians must reject Christ of necessity because they have no adequate universal knowledge; they cannot get beyond their finiteness. In the final analysis, God's revelation of himself must be self-authenticating because only an infinite God can be an adequate witness to himself, the only being who possesses ultimate universal truth.[220]

Admittedly, this is argument in a circle, but it is the only case where arguing in a circle is valid, because only God is sufficient testimony to himself. Human beings are completely inadequate to apply any human test to determine whether truth about God is valid. If we invite people to test Christianity without revelation, we open the door to false methodology to determine ultimate truth. They would begin with humanistic bias, and would not start from a clean slate. Human autonomy is not ultimate and can never become the ultimate arbiter of truth. All we can do is flounder in our limited, incomplete, imperfect, partial, inadequate, and narrow perceptions.

McLaren says that Martin Luther's words "Here I stand" are "the first state-ment uttered in the modern world."[221] McLaren's postmodernism cannot accept modernism's premise of logic, objectivity, and reason because the interpreter distorts meaning. This acceptance of the premise that the fallible person is the starting point in understanding Scripture is McLaren's fundamental flaw. He bases his construct on doubt in counterdistinction to the biblical view that rests on confidence in knowledge about God's revelation. McLaren says,

> How do "I" know the Bible is always right? And if "I" am sophisticated enough to realize that I know nothing of the Bible without my own involvement via interpretation, I'll also ask how I know which school, method, or technique of biblical interpretation is right. What makes a "good" interpretation good? And if an appeal is made to a written standard (book, doctrinal statement, etc.) or to common sense or to "scholarly principles of interpretation," the same pesky "I" who liberated us from the authority of the church will ask, "Who["] sets the standard? Whose common sense? Which scholars and why? Don't all these appeals to authorities and principles outside the Bible actually undermine the claim of ultimate biblical authority? Aren't they just the new pope?[222]

These assertions have been addressed by Christian scholars many times over. There is clear reason to believe that it is possible to know something about literature apart from lurching in self-impressions about a text. Let us look at this point by dealing with self-evident truth.

## Self-evident Truth

Is there such a thing as a self-evident truth? The issue that lies at the bottom of this question is the nature of truth. There are two essential views of truth: (1) coherent and (2) correspondent. The correspondent view maintains that assertion of truth must match factuality of the assertion. This means that we can correct falsity by measuring an asserted truth with facts and can know objective truth. Radical perspectivalism is not able to check its validity against something else. All perspectives are interpretations and cannot be independently true of the interpreter. There is no vantage point to make a judgment about truth or error in this view. However, biblical truth accurately accounts for what is real.

God makes truth "evident" to all (Romans 1:18–20). We can know enough truth to be accountable before him. Truth is plain and apparent from God's viewpoint because the Greek word for "evident" means "cause to be seen, very clear, patent, conspicuous." On the other hand, McLaren believes that the Bible is mostly narrative, so we cannot know things for sure, and that it does not produce a clear theology. He believes that evangelicals bought into modernism (foundationalism) that brought about concepts such as "authority, inerrancy, infallibility, revelation, objective, absolute, and literal."[223] This is another false premise, because it does not follow that narrative always produces uncertainty. The narrative of David's adultery with Bathsheba has a moral message. Psalms 32 and 52 draw the implication of his sinful adultery and murder.

Personal stories (narratives—"Why I am . . .") are rickety underpinnings for overthrowing evangelical theology. McLaren needs unending uncertainty to deliver him from the certainty of modernism.[224] He wants to float in a sea of subjective relativism because he must reject both reason and the Word of God; his dialectical process will not allow him to come to conclusion about truth. That is why he ran pell-mell into mysticism, and escapes from the authority of Scripture in spirituality. Mysticism enables radical emergent thinkers to reject propositional truth and systematic theology.

Postconservatives wish to avoid concrete knowledge of God with all its certain and attendant implications. They need an uncertain salvation, uncertain Jesus, and uncertain knowledge for a postmodern generation; their social kingdom emerges in time. This deliberate ambiguity that values the vague and detests the certain, clear, and objective is at the heart of emergent thinking. It is vacuous of content and definition. Emergent people would rather light candles than hear clarity of Bible exposition.

Postmoderns dethroned objective truth as the arbiter to determine whatever certainty there might be out there. Reality for them is non-rational. Emotion, intuition, and personal and relational ideas rest at the root of their existential thinking. Truth is not objective but relative, indeterminate, and participatory. There is no such thing as a dispassionate, independent knower or universal, timeless, objective truth that transcends culture. Truth for them is not culturally neutral or eternal. Each culture or community has its own limited truth that it shares in finite stories. Postmoderns cannot trust reason and logic. In other words, they live in unadulterated skepticism. All that remains is a world of conflicting opinions.

The biblical claim is that we have an absolute criterion of truth that transcends community, perspective, opinion, or thinking of the finite. This criterion functions above the practical within the world of limited human viewpoint. The unifying center for Christianity is that God spoke into time and space and gave people universal, eternal, infinite, absolute truth. This objective truth evaluates the validity of all other claims to truth. This fact lies beyond the capacity of people to reason beyond themselves to the universal. Christianity transcends the finite capacity to approach truth.

Although training, culture, and many other factors influence biblical Christians, they come to truth that is logical and objective. God revealed truth in propositions that we can readily understand. Thus, we can truly understand correct doctrine and come to certainty about truth, as we saw in the previous chapter. Christianity is far more than a "personal encounter." Objective truth governs our experience. Experience is not the grid for determining truth as Stanley Grenz claims.[225] True Christianity goes far beyond the subjectivity and uncertainty of postmodernism.

## How We Know What We Know Is True

Believer and unbeliever disagree over biblical truth, not because of facts but on assumption about how to find truth. How do we know what we know is true? All approaches to truth ultimately come down to an assumption about how to find truth (epistemology).

A *pou sto* is an ultimate place to stand to find ultimate truth, absolute truth. Modernism took its stand on philosophy (rationalism) and science (empiricism). Postmodernism finds both systems inadequate; in fact, it finds all systems inadequate, including Christianity. To them, all systems break down in their search for certainty. They begin from a presumption of skepticism. Their skepticism goes to both means and end.

The biblical methodology for finding certainty is deductive revelation. The Bible proclaims that Jesus is the light of the world (John 1:5, 9). The Father draws people to come to him (John 6:45), making him the initiator of presupposition for finding truth. God initiates revelation to each person individually, for he sends the Holy Spirit to convict (John 16:8, 9) humans of the right presupposition. Therefore, God is the cause of our methodology for coming to truth.

Fundamental to the issue of certainty is the problem of the universal and the particular. We in our finiteness cannot come to an adequate universal to explain all that is necessary to come to universal certainty. We would need to be infinite to do that. God is the only sufficient and infinite being who can see all things in their completeness; thus, only God can establish a universal.

The universe has an overwhelming number of particulars. No one can claim to have inductively studied everything in the universe qualitatively and quantitatively equally, and with total dispassion, not leaning to one view or the other until coming to a completely dispassionate and objective conclusion. That is a practical impossibility. It is "the sole providence of universals (all-encompassing concepts) to give particulars their meaning."[226] If that is true, then how can finite beings find a true universal?

Only God can provide absolute comprehensive meaning for all possible particulars. No human method is big enough to cover all contingencies of creation. God is absolute, so all contingencies flow from him. God's being determines truth, and nothing is true in itself. There is no law that governs God—he is the absolute universal. A thing is true based on whether or not it is consistent with God. Because God is the infinite reference point, Christians can assert certainty about particulars. A human being cannot begin with self, whether it is with philosophy or science, because neither of those systems is a complete universal. We can never find unity of truth in the diversity of the world. That is why postmodern skepticism throws up its hands in despair. This is the point of 1 Corinthians 1:18–2:16.

God is the universal, the infinite reference point for Christian certainty. All facts integrate under this umbrella. Man became his own *pou sto* after the fall. He turned into his own reference point, wanting autonomy from God (the essence of sin). The price for this finite autonomy is loss of certainty. By exchanging the truth of God for a lie and worshipping and serving the creature rather than the Creator (Romans 1:25), man confined himself to the finite. Man's understanding became the measure of all things, yet from God's viewpoint human understanding was depraved (Romans 1:28) and darkened (Ephesians 2:1–3; 4:18).

The scientist has to assume a method for finding answers in the universe. The fundamental method is materialism (in which the only reality is a physical universe). Presupposition of that method is one's belief system. If there is anything metaphysical, then the method preempts the scientist from finding anything beyond the physical. This mode of operation maintains an open mind toward further discoveries—but strictly in the material realm. Conclusions must remain tentative and provisional because of the finite approach. Brute facts, uninterpreted facts, always remain out of reach for the finite scientist. Chance is always irrational.

## The Anti-Biblical Paradigm

The assertion that the Bible is the Word of the absolute God is either true or false. If it is true, then it is true regardless of personal opinion because truth is a property of propositions. It does not rest on culture, subjective opinion, or personal perspective. As Groothuis says, "The statement 'The world is spherical' was true even when the majority of earthlings believed their habitat to be flat."[227] The following is the biblical view of truth:

> *For what if some did not believe? Will their unbelief make the faithfulness of God without effect? Certainly not! Indeed, let God be true but every man a liar, as it is written:*
>
> *"That You may be justified in Your words,*
>
> *And may overcome when You are judged."* (Romans 3:3, 4)

The Bible is more than narrative; it is propositional and systematic as well. It is the believer's responsibility to understand the truth of Scripture in a logical and coherent way because the Bible is correspondently inerrant (completely and factually without error).

God gave his revelation to communities, but communities were not the source of revelation. Belief that communities are the source of revelation confuses cause and effect; a community does not reveal truth but receives truth. Whether anyone knows a given truth does not affect its truthfulness.

When postevangelicals attempt to reduce truth to language perspectives and render the Bible subjective, they reduce truth to something uncertain. This treachery of distorting biblical revelation will render Christians incapable of hearing God's Word accurately and will keep them from sharing the gospel aggressively.

For example, Stanley Grenz believes that evangelicals should not articulate the gospel in a propositional manner. His view is that we should see the gospel in personal experience with God in a community context. Doctrine applies only to a given community. If this is correct, then one community cannot correct another community. If we did not obtain theology from Scripture but derive it from community and experience, it would not be possible to come to objective truth, and Christians would then wallow in competing perspectives. On the other hand, only propositions can convey truth. Scripture gives truth for everyone, both within and without community. God's Word is more than propositions, but without propositions the ideas God wants us to know of him are without meaning or purpose. Without objective truth, evangelism, missions, and theology would not have purpose.

The biblical paradigm is didactic (the key word in the pastoral epistles—*didache*), not dialectical. God fixes and presets principles of revelation in didactic truth. Satan did not want didactic truth but dialectical process (Genesis 3:1–6). God said, "You shall not" but Satan whispered, "Has God said?" This was a temptation to become "like God" by rationalization. Postconservatives want transformational (dialectical) ministries. They try to move the church from didactic propositions to dialectical process orientation—the very tool Satan used to deceive Eve. This is extrapolation (picking and choosing and then redefining) of truth into a relationship paradigm. Aversion to the closed didactic paradigm of inerrant, inspired revelation is at the philosophical heart of radical emergent thinking. Their massive philosophical presupposition of dialectical theology moves them away from evangelicalism. "There is a way that seems right to a man, But the end is the way of death" (Proverbs 14:12).

Paul warns believers to avoid the antithesis that is involved in the dialectical process: "O Timothy! Guard what was committed to your trust, avoiding the profane and idle babblings and contradictions of what is falsely called knowledge" (1 Timothy 6:20).

Christianity rests on what God says, not on how people think.

Postconservatives reject the correspondent view of truth (in which propositions must conform to facts); instead they hold to the coherentist view of truth (where beliefs rest on other beliefs and propositions are not justified by derivation from foundational propositions). The coherentist view merely holds to the comprehensiveness of the idea, the cohesive consistency of propositions.

Hundreds of passages in the Old Testament use words that carry the idea of correspondent truth. The primary terms for "truth" in the Old Testament (*emet*, Isaiah 45:19) and in the New Testament (*alethia*) both carry correspondent meaning. In addition, many passages explicitly contrast true propositions with falsehoods. Repeatedly, the Old Testament warns against false prophets whose words do not correspond to truth (Deuteronomy 18:22). Facts make a proposition true because there is a correspondent relation between a proposition and relevant fact.

The dialectical view of truth rejects correspondence and presumes personal assertions. Yet postconservatives' assumption that their "assertions" are true destroys the dialectical approach to truth, for they assume a didactic form of argument to establish their dialectic. We can never have confidence or a certainty of truth by the dialectical process.

The didactic view of truth puts us in contact with reality. Truth has consequence and falsity has consequence. Didactic truth holds to a clear notion of antithesis; belief and unbelief stand as polar opposites. If something is true, then its opposite is untrue. Postconservatives hold antipathy to this kind of antithesis because they are relativists about propositional truth, about conclusions of truth. Truth always corresponds to reality and postmodernism always results in skepticism. This has been true from the days of Protagoras, Socrates, and Plato. Postmodernism itself has a corresponding truth—that there is no consensus on truth. Postmoderns abandon knowable absolutes and conclude that we mediate all truth through the subjective perspective of the knower.

Brian McLaren believes that systematic theology should be an "ongoing dialogue in search for truth."[228] That is a combination of a dialectical belief system with the philosophical instrumentalism of William James, who held that the process of finding truth was more important than to discover truth. As well, McLaren holds to a coherentist rather than a correspondent view of truth.[229] According to him,

> Jesus taught us that the way to know what God is like is not by
> determining our philosophical boundary conditions/definitions/

delineations before departing, but rather the way to know is by embarking on an adventure of faith, hope, and love, even if you don't know where your path will lead.[230]

This is foundational dialectical instrumentalism. McLaren maintains two fundamentals of the faith, "to love God and to love our neighbor,"[231] which, of course, are not fundamental in the normal sense of the term but are primary life goals for the believer. Doctrine reduced to these two is *reductum ad absurdum* when it comes to claim for truth.

Before the introduction of dialectical thinking, people thought in terms of antithesis and carried a unified field of knowledge, the law of logic called the law of non-contradiction. Dialectical thinkers do not think in terms of cause and effect but in terms of synthesis. They seek truth in synthesis rather than antithesis. Synthesis undermines the whole idea of certainty and of how we know what we know (epistemology). To them, there is truth in thesis and antithesis. This makes all assertions of truth relative. This dialectical methodology assumption is at the heart of postconservative fallacy. Synthesis as over against antithetical methodology forms pseudo-Christianity. Instead of setting Christianity in stark contrast to heterodoxy, postconservatives offer a synthesis with other religions via dialogue, and that synthesis leads to an emergent view of truth.

The Bible presents logical consistency regarding truth, a coherence of truth that is true to facts. The problem is that man is finite and cannot come to truth as a whole, so his views are tentative and provisional if he comes to truth through his finiteness. Dialectical and coherent thinking is true if we begin with finiteness. There will always be a dynamic tension between thesis and antithesis; both are inadequate as a self-contained approach. Indeed, humanity is in an endless process of discovery if there is no objective starting point, no *pou sto*. No unbeliever can justify or warrant any view as true. Any approach to ultimate truth by finite humans is foolish. The problem is that mankind stands in enmity (antipathy) against God. There is a massive difference in worldview originating from that enmity. "Where is the wise? Where is the scribe? Where is the disputer of this age? Has not God made foolish the wisdom of this world?" (1 Corinthians 1:20).

The Bible presents truth in an objective sense and not in the way one constructs understanding or how one interprets a position. Postmodernism perceives truth not as objective but as personal, subjective, and pragmatic.

McLaren believes that not only should methodology change, but the message should change as well.[232] He represents himself as offering not only a high change in method but a high change in *message* as well.[233] The ongoing change of mission demands that we change our message.[234] This requires "new content" and "new truths."[235] He says, "These new messages are not incompatible with the gospel of the kingdom Jesus taught, and asserts that the Holy Spirit will guide them into new, previously unknown truth.[236] This has major implications for the closing of the canon of Scripture. There is a significant distinction between the progress of doctrine and revelation of new truth.

## Circular Reasoning

Universal, absolute knowledge raises the question: Where is the starting point for this universal knowledge? The presuppositional approach to truth rests on the premise that God alone can reveal himself because he is transcendent, but that people are confined to the immanent world around them. The presuppositional approach is not mystical in its methodology because it submits itself to verification by logic and evidence. Yet Christianity is a call to final truth, not to a probable theory. It rests on one assumption—that the Bible is the Word of God. All other approaches to truth rest on assumptions of philosophy, science, mysticism, subjectivism, skepticism. Every chain of argument begins with a starting point. That starting point is self-evidencing.

Any approach to truth that does not begin with the Word of God will result in a relative view of truth, a relative ethic, and will negate the possibility of certainty. Humans, even in an unfallen or in an eternal state, will never carry infinite understanding. We will always have something to learn about God. Sin added further incapacity to understand universals.

Man needs spiritual birth to understand spiritual things; otherwise, he remains spiritually dead. He cannot in himself come to truth or know truth. Certainty eludes him without universal revelation from God. In his finitude, chance becomes prevalent, contingency rules, and nihilism and skepticism are the result. There is no neutrality in the non-Christian, for he holds the bias of human viewpoint against God. Belief in a non-biblical worldview precludes knowing God. The Bible constantly challenges human autonomy as an adequate way to certainty.

Both Scripture and Jesus Christ are self-attesting. People dead in trespasses and sin cannot attest to the truth that is in Christ because they do not have the capacity to do so. They are pure soul and without spiritual capacity (1 Corinthians 2:14). Neither do they possess the valid tests of truth, Scripture, or Jesus himself. That is why they need "the foolishness of the thing preached" (the gospel message) to believe (1:21). That witness does not come in persuasive words of human wisdom but in the demonstration of the Spirit and power. This boils down to the self-attesting Word of God versus the self-attesting autonomy of the self-commended autonomy of rebellious mankind.

As God is self-contained and self-sufficient, so is his Word self-contained and self-sufficient (1 Corinthians 2:11). The God of the Bible can only be self-revealed and knowledge of him depends on his self-disclosure (Matthew 11:27; 1 Corinthians 2:11). It is self-attesting because only God is a valid witness to himself.

Self-attesting Scripture is an argument in a circle, but it is necessarily the case because God is the final source of ultimate truth if he is absolute. If we apply an extra-biblical test, such as philosophy or science (rationalism or empiricism—modernism), then we limit God to the finite capacities of people. This test would assume that it already knows by the assumptions of philosophy and science what God can and cannot reveal. No, the necessity of God's absoluteness requires that he reveal himself independently of the finite creature. That is the only way people can possibly know the God of the Bible. Who God is determines the conditions for knowing him. We are left with Anselm's presupposition—"I believe in order to understand" (*credo ut intelligam*). However, this belief requires God's revealed content. "By faith we understand that the worlds were framed by the word of God, so that the things which are seen were not made of things which are visible" (Hebrews 11:3).

# Ten

# SOURCE OF CERTAINTY

*Extant Statements from Scripture about Certainty*

In this chapter I will change my argument to an expository method to address the issue of certainty. God has much to say about certainty and objective truth. God's method to communicate specifics of transcendent truth is by didactic propositions. He uses narrative literature to communicate more general revelation. I will show how God in 1 Corinthians chapters 1 and 2 views the fallacy of postconservatism.

We clearly see God's didactic approach to truth in 1 Corinthians 1:17–2:16. This section shows that the message was not exclusively for the intellectual and that the method of approach did not accommodate their assumptions about truth (1:18–25). Second, Paul used the simple, unadulterated, certain gospel to reach people (2:1–5). Third, because God's wisdom comes by revelation, inspiration, and illumination (2:6–16), we can know what God said with certainty.

> *For Christ did not send me to baptize but to preach the gospel, and not with words of eloquent wisdom, lest the cross of Christ be emptied of its power.* (1 Corinthians 1:17 ESV)

Paul transitions from explicitly dealing with divisions in the church to explaining what causes divisions—the Corinthian church's lack of focus on the central message of the cross (1:18–2:16). Often Greek culture of the first century did not care about the content of what was said, as long as it was said beautifully. To Paul, content mattered, not simply the manner of delivery. Paul did not use clever speech of human wisdom. His method did not use human viewpoint to convince his hearers of the gospel. He did not use rhetoric so that people would focus on the messenger's style rather than on the gospel itself.

> *For Christ did not send me to baptize but to preach the gospel, and not*
> *with words of eloquent wisdom, lest the cross of Christ be emptied of its*
> *power.* (1:17 ESV)

It is the ministry of the Holy Spirit to win people to Christ by the power of
the message of the cross. The gospel of Christ can be "emptied of its power."
Human technique and presupposition can neutralize the power of the gospel.
"Emptied" means "to render void." "Eloquent wisdom" will void effectiveness
in presenting the gospel. If we begin with the presupposition of human viewpoint, we will end in human viewpoint. If we leave the message of the cross out
of the gospel, we negate and vacate its true power.

Paul and his team used a countervailing system of evangelism. They kept the
message of the gospel central in their presentations even at a cost. They clearly
understood that this message would be viewed as "folly" to their hearers. This
did not daunt them from presenting the message unabashedly. The attitude of
Paul's team was that the gospel itself carried the power in evangelism.

> *For the word of the cross is folly to those who are perishing, but to us*
> *who are being saved it is the power of God.* (1 Corinthians 1:18 ESV)

The Holy Spirit radically distinguishes the wisdom of human viewpoint
against the wisdom of God. Greeks formed their culture around philosophy.
They had scores of countervailing philosophies. Above all, they were in love
with wisdom. Their ultimate view of life revolved around philosophy (love of
wisdom). This gave them a sense of certainty, meaning, and purpose. A plurality of viewpoints pervaded Corinth (pluralism), none of which provided an
absolute view of truth. Some Greek Corinthian Christians brought their philosophies to church. This desire to add human wisdom to truth caused schism in the
Corinthian church (chapters 1 through 4). The central problem was the disloca-
tion of Scripture as the focus of viewpoint. Christians cannot permit themselves
to become divided over human viewpoints; true unity comes in unity of truth
(divine viewpoint).

The word "for" indicates the reason Paul did not come to Corinth in the wisdom
of words. Human wisdom ruins the content of the message. That is why there
are two reactions to the cross. The cross always offends philosophical pluralism

because the message of the cross demands exclusivity. God's wisdom is the only true wisdom. The word "wisdom" occurs thirteen times from 1:18 through chapter 2. Throughout this section of Corinthians the Holy Spirit sets divine wisdom over against human wisdom. Those who are in the process of perishing use human wisdom to appeal to human wisdom. There is nothing supernatural in it.

In the phrase "For the word of the cross is folly to those who are perishing," "word" means the message or content (revelation) of the cross, not the act of preaching the cross. "Word" carries the idea of "message." The message is God's plan that Christ would die for our sins. This is foolishness to the non-Christian. Their first reaction to the cross is that it is "foolishness."

Paul sets "who are being saved" in sharp contrast those to "those who are perishing." Everyone falls into one of these two classes of people. On the one hand, the message of the cross is the power of God to the believer—the true and essential means of evangelism. Paul contrasts "power" to the "wisdom" of the previous clause. We would expect that Paul would say that the gospel is the "wisdom of God," but he says it is the "power of God." The gospel is more than a good suggestion, because it produces a dynamic effect. It is fit to attain its end. We can have confidence in its efficacy. However, that is the problem today—many do not believe in the gospel message as supernaturally powerful.

We live in a pluralistic society where people prefer relativism to absolutes. No one has the truth, and pundits revel in opinion rejecting divine authority and certainty. The church today falls prey to the prevailing idea in society that the self is the only source for meaning, so Christians accommodate Scripture to prevailing subjective opinion. When the believer accepts human philosophy as ultimate, that inevitably exchanges the truth for a lie (Romans 1:25).

There are only two kinds of people, and the differentiating point between them is the cross. We understand this difference when we grasp the meaning of the cross. The cross indicates that God has absolute righteousness and cannot compromise with sin. That absolute righteousness condemns our righteousness. This is an offense to our pride and good works. We cannot obtain God's wisdom through human cunning, for there is no compromise in the cross. Those who perish take offense to the cross because it is the only way to heaven.

Now the Holy Spirit turns to argue extensively against the idea of trusting human viewpoint. Verses 19 through 25 give three reasons for why we cannot trust man's wisdom: (1) Scripture (vv. 19–20); (2) finiteness of reason (v. 21), and (3) a spiritual issue (vv. 22–25).

First, God will "destroy" human viewpoint. For evangelicals to trust in human faculty is a dangerous thing because it is something that God will demolish.

> *For it is written, "I will destroy the wisdom of the wise, and the discernment of the discerning I will thwart."* (1 Corinthians 1:19 ESV)

To prove his point that human viewpoint will end in destruction, Paul appeals to Scripture by quoting from Isaiah: "For it is written." Paul argues from the Bible to prove that we cannot trust man's wisdom or reason (Isaiah 29:14). At the time, Sennacherib the Assyrian threatened Judah with an invasion. Isaiah declared that deliverance would come by God and not through alliance with pagan Egypt. Assyria had already conquered the northern kingdom and Syria. Judah was tottering and about to fall. The politicians of Isaiah's day used human wisdom to form an alliance with Egypt rather than trust God to address their problem. That is why God said, "I will destroy the wisdom of the wise"; God will overthrow human-centered wisdom. Political brain trusts are not adequate to do God's work. God does not depend on human ingenuity.

God challenges human discernment when he says, "And the discernment of the discerning I will thwart." "Discernment" means to "bring together," and it denotes the ability of bringing the parts to a whole; hence, it carries the idea of comprehension or insight. God does not need our finite comprehension. "Thwart" means "to set aside, reject." God brings to nothing those who trust in human ingenuity or political schemes. God sets aside the prudent or the brilliant. Rulers of Israel sought the help of Egypt. This was rebellion against God's policy of depending on God alone. God delivered Judah without Egypt's help (Isaiah 37; 2 Kings 17). When the Assyrian army surrounded Jerusalem, Hezekiah prayed about it and God answered by destroying 185,000 Assyrian soldiers in one night (Isaiah 37:36). God saves souls by special revelation of his Word and the person of Christ. He does not join other worldviews in doing so. God does not operate on relative truth or pluralism. He does not ask counsel from human wisdom.

To develop the idea that God will render human faculty ineffective, Paul fires four machine-gun-like rhetorical questions to make emphatic the finite perspective on reality:

> *Where is the one who is wise? Where is the scribe? Where is the debater of this age? Has not God made foolish the wisdom of the world?* (1 Corinthians 1:20 ESV)

Human wisdom is not permanent. It ebbs and flows, for its theories go back and forth like a pendulum. First comes a view; then a countervailing view follows. Finite wisdom has a problem of instability and constant change. This verse alludes to Isaiah 33:18. Because human viewpoint is finite, it cannot get to the root of reality or find ultimate answers. God views finite wisdom as transient in nature. This wisdom is a short-lived show. God not only disregards the wisdom of the world, he designates it as foolish. The first question Paul asks—"Where is the one who is wise?"—is a reference to Greek philosophers. Stoicism and Epicureanism (antithetical schools of thought) were the dominating philosophies of Corinth at the time.

The second question—"Where is the scribe?"—could refer to the scribe that the Assyrians sent with their army to record the battles and booty or, alternatively, to the Jewish scribe who interpreted the law.

The third question is "Where is the debater of this age?" The Greeks loved to argue. Paul asks where all the clever arguments of philosophy are in the light of God's eternal truth. Finite philosophers bring us finite truth. The debater of this age uses the dialectical approach that debates all the incompatible viewpoints of the day. That gets nowhere.

Finally Paul asks, "Has not God made foolish the wisdom of the world?" The infinite wisdom of God puts human wisdom into finite irrelevance. The strong negative in the Greek shows the utter foolishness of the finite wisdom of this age, for God proves human wisdom to be diminished and minuscule. Humans by human wisdom and effort can never provide certainty. Humans are not autonomous from God and it is ridiculous from God's viewpoint to think otherwise.

The polytheistic gods of the Greco Roman culture made that culture pluralistic. Zeus governed the gods and chased women on the side. Mercury carried messages. Aphrodite was the goddess of love. Each played a role without a unifying truth. Pluralistic polytheism sustained antithetical and competing viewpoints in Corinth.

Some believers at Corinth turned from the viewpoint of God's Word to seek solutions in human wisdom. This was the cause of the Corinthian division problem; the church began to divide into varying positions. They turned from God's plan to man's plan. They wanted to accommodate their culture, time, and philosophies and did not fancy a system of absolutes. They preferred a more flexible viewpoint, as do postconservatives today. The Bible presents the gospel as absolute. God does not permit equivocation on the truth of the gospel. The debater does not tolerate the believer who comes to a final view of truth. Absolute truth flies in the face of the predominant bias of today's thinkers who are people without conviction. However, God is absolute, and anything that comes from God is absolute. Our understanding of God's Word is not absolute, but neither is it eclectic; it is definitive. Definition comes from didactics, as we will see later. Note the following passages where Paul answers three of the above questions: he deals with the philosopher in 1:21–29, with the scribe in 1:30, 31, and with the debater in 2:1–16.

Christianity stands in mutually exclusive counterdistinction to relativistic pluralism. A strength of Christianity is its certainty, its truth. It is strong because it comes to conviction and is not a flexible system that neutralizes conviction. Believers with strong conviction do not fall for plurality and relativism. The "wisdom of this world" is the satanic system, worldliness. Because human wisdom is finite, it cannot come to certainty, for finite philosophy can find no ultimate answers; thus, God views finite wisdom as transient and foolish. The Bible presents the gospel as absolute. God does not allow equivocation on the truth of the gospel.

The wish of the debater or dialectical thinker is to offer varying viewpoints without conclusion; however, God's desire is that we come to conclusion about truth. God's perspective on the universe is entirely different from the viewpoint of finite humans. God proves human viewpoints foolish. It is impossible for a perfect, absolute person to devise an imperfect plan. This galls pluralistic, relativistic thinkers of our day.

Paul now turns to the second reason we cannot trust man's viewpoint—finiteness of human reason (v. 21). Man in finite capacity cannot know God:

> *For since, in the wisdom of God, the world did not know God through wisdom, it pleased God through the folly of what we preach to save those who believe.* (1 Corinthians 1:21 ESV)

Humans cannot know God in our own capacity. When Paul says, "For since, in the wisdom of God," the word "since" means "inasmuch as"—that is, inasmuch as the reality of God's wisdom is a different domain than the wisdom of humans. Paul here responds to his own rhetorical questions of verse 20.

All human philosophy operates in the realm of the finite soul, not in the realm of an infinitely wise God—an omniscient God. Both philosophy and science rest on human beings' capacity to understand with a finite brain. God's wisdom is omniscient, encompassing both time and eternity, both space and beyond space (that which is transcendent). God's wisdom demands that humans depend on God for knowing eternity and everything transcendent (beyond time and space). This is humbling for humans. Most people do not want to submit to the wisdom of God.

People cannot come to God through the presupposition of philosophy, for "the world did not know God through wisdom." In the realm of wisdom, the world, by employing human wisdom, did not know God. The only way anyone can know God is by the supernatural means of God revealing himself (1:18–2:16). Human wisdom breaks down in its attempt to know God; it is utterly futile for finiteness to try to find infiniteness.

No one can become a Christian solely from the Adam's apple up. Neither can anyone become a Christian without information. It is the nature of the information whereby a person becomes a Christian—God's revelation of the gospel in the Bible. No one would know God if God did not reveal himself. Because God is infinite, no one can know him by finite means. God reveals himself by nature, by the person of Christ, and by the Word of God.

Christianity epistemologically depends on God to reveal himself. It is a system of faith based on unadulterated grace to show God in Jesus Christ, in nature, and in the Word. There is no success to finding truth by operation bootstraps. The only way to come to infinite (absolute) truth is through an infinite God who reveals himself. Finite humans must depend on God to reveal himself. Humans are not autonomous, so there is no sense in asking people to come to God independently. If the Bible is true, then we human beings must humble ourselves to accept God's grace in showing himself to us.

Humans want to hang onto a system of independence from God. This is *kosmos diabolicus*—the satanic system that seeks wisdom about God independent from God. Satan's system is an organized scheme that pivots around the autonomy of humans. God's system is entirely different; his truth transcends time and space and, accordingly, only he can give us truth about himself.

There is a method that pleases God, for the verse under consideration says that "it pleased God." The absolute God has a right to determine which methodology saves us. It is totally his prerogative because he created the world. His method is to give mankind a message received by faith.

God's method is completely different than human methods; it is "the folly of what we preach." God's system is entirely different; he chooses to use a foolish system of declaring the message preached. Note again that this refers not to the act of preaching but to the content preached. Literally, "the word preached" is "the thing preached." It is not the act of preaching but the message preached that reaches people. It is the message that Jesus died for our sins—past, present, and future—and that all that is necessary is for us to believe it.

The phrase "those who believe" shows that salvation is entirely a work of God engaged by faith. God's purpose is to save eternally anyone who believes the message. All systems that approach truth come to belief by faith, including the systems of philosophy and science. This is also true with the current skeptical movement about knowing truth (postmodernism), which accepts by faith that no one can come to an absolute truth. By faith, the philosopher accepts the methodology of philosophy (rationalism). By faith, the scientist accepts the method of approaching truth by data (empiricism). Every approach to truth has an assumption of faith. That choice of a faith system is where the issue lies from God's viewpoint; that is, we accept either a human system or God's system.

Choice of a faith system is where the issue lies from God's viewpoint; either we accept our system or God's system. Thus, the third reason why we cannot trust human viewpoint is a truth issue, a refusal to accept God's way of coming to truth (1:22–25).

> *For Jews demand signs and Greeks seek wisdom.*
> (1 Corinthians 1:22 ESV)

Here we find two classes of unbelief and two false criteria for determining truth: (1) The Jews asked for supernatural evidence (a miracle); they wanted supernatural evidence before they would believe in the authenticity of the message. (2) The Greeks sought after wisdom (philosophy); they wanted to use a human method in order to believe.

The word "for" means "seeing that." This verse shows how the message preached was deemed foolish by both Jews and Greeks.

The Jews "demand signs." They possessed revelation in the Old Testament and believed in truth, but they wanted their own, supernatural system of verification. They wanted supernatural evidence manifested in a miracle as the ground for their belief. The Jews wanted something to stimulate and cater to their emotions, which is a false criterion for coming to God.

On the other hand, the Greeks (Gentiles) "seek wisdom." Deeming the message preached as foolish, they sought after wisdom (philosophy); they wanted to presume human philosophical assumption in order to believe. They required God to submit to their conventions. Greeks pursued truth; they did not possess it.

Because they did not have a Bible, the Greeks lurched in philosophical speculation; that is, they "seek after wisdom." They sought wisdom, but they did not find it. Like a countervailing pendulum, one system of philosophy contradicted another system so that all that remained was skepticism. They sought but did not find. Their skepticism was very much like the skepticism of today (postmodernism). One system of ideas abrogated another system. Even Pilate called out, "What is truth?" This was also a false criterion in order to believe in God.

Paul now turns to the Christian approach to truth which countervails the two previous systems for coming to truth:

> *But we preach Christ crucified, a stumbling block to Jews and folly to Gentiles.* (1 Corinthians 1:23 ESV)

The word "preach" here is the action of a herald, so the message is God's, not the preacher's. The word "preach" means "to make an announcement or declaration" of something important. The Christian method is to "preach" something revealed by God.

The Romans crucified thousands of people. There was nothing unique about the idea of crucifixion itself, but there is something unique in Christ's crucifixion. He was the God-man who came to die for sin. The Greek for "crucified" indicates that the work of Jesus stands as permanent in its effect and efficacy. This is the heart and soul of the message of Jesus Christ. Final truth was a problem to both Jews and Greeks.

The crucified Christ was a "stumbling block" to the Jews. A stumbling block was an occasion of offense. The finished work of Christ was a hindrance to Jewish doctrine. They expected a triumphant Messiah who would establish a kingdom for them, but Christ was a crucified Messiah who delayed his kingdom until a later time.

The Greek view of the cross was different from that of the Jews; the Greeks viewed it as fallacious. There was no way they could squeeze a crucified Christ into their system of thinking. Biblical evangelicalism is a declaration of the crucifixion of Christ for our sins. God's method for winning the lost does not cater to the Greeks' system or criterion for coming to truth. God uses his own system for reaching people. The content of the cross convicts of sin and supernaturally touches the heart. This flies in the face of much of evangelism today. We want to do anything but tell the essential meaning of the gospel.

We find the antithesis to the Jews and the Gentiles in Christ, who was God's power and work:

> *But to those who are called, both Jews and Greeks, Christ the power of God and the wisdom of God.* (1 Corinthians 1:24 ESV)

In this verse, the "called" stand in contrast to those who do not know God by their own methodologies. "Called" means "effectually called," so that these people actually became believers (Matthew 22:14; 1 Corinthians 1:1, 2; Romans 8:30).

By the phrase "both Jews and Greeks" (Gentiles), we know that people of any stripe can find God by God's means.

The name "Christ" is in the emphatic position in the Greek phrase "Christ the power of God and the wisdom of God." This means that "Christ and only Christ" is the power and wisdom of God. Christ is God's answer to the issue of salvation. Christ is the means whereby both Jews and Greeks can connect with the power of God and the wisdom of God. He and his work are the highest expressions of the power and wisdom of God. God's power and wisdom originate in his eternal counsel and decree.

Christ is the personal instrument of our salvation. God's wisdom and power extend far beyond the finite capacity to comprehend. We can find this only in God and from God because it comes from his eternal counsel before the world began. God's plan centers on the person and work of Christ. This plan so transcends human capacity to understand that God does not attempt to stoop to finite method for determining truth. Because God's capacity is infinite and our capacity is finite, there is no way we can fully comprehend God, so God reduces his plan to the simple message of Christ crucified. Acceptance of the death of Christ for the individual is the beginning of the plan of God for us. God's plan is, therefore, based on his essence and character. That is why it is foolish for finite man to try to figure it out. There is self-sufficiency in God, but there is no self-sufficiency in man.

Verse 25 shows that God's foolishness is wiser than finite man's wisdom, and his weakness is stronger than finite man's strength:

> *For the foolishness of God is wiser than men, and the weakness of God is stronger than men.* (1 Corinthians 1:25 ESV)

The "foolishness of God" is the gospel of "Christ crucified." The words "the foolishness" are literally "the foolish thing" (neuter). This is yet again the foolish message of God (not the act of preaching).

The "weakness of God" is stronger than the greatest of human might. The words "the weakness" are literally "the weak thing." This again says that the foolish message of God is stronger than the greatest power of philosophy or science man might concoct. The rationale of God's philosophy is the revelation of Christ and his finished work on the cross. As people believe this, they see God's wisdom and power. No futile philosophies can match this.

It is humbling to realize that God does evangelism his way and does not depend on finite devices. This is a hard pill as well for Christian leaders to swallow today. Beyond all church growth and understanding of our target audience lies God's simple message of the cross. Obviously, believers should grasp everything they can about how to reach people, but if we forget that it is the content of Christ crucified that wins people, then we have missed God's boat. Vision planning, building church-growth constructs, and understanding the values of people of our day pale in light of the content of the gospel. The gospel transcends any human reason, philosophy, or device.

Verse 26 begins to demonstrate the nature of those who come to certainty about truth. God does things by his method, not by human method:

> *For consider your calling, brothers: not many of you were wise according to worldly standards, not many were powerful, not many were of noble birth.* (1 Corinthians 1:26 ESV)

This verse shows that God does not depend on nobility or might to accomplish his purposes. God does not count on philosophy, or power, or nobility itself to win people to Christ. He uses frail instruments to carry out his ends. God does things according to his provision, his providence, and does not depend on education, philosophy, science, or any human device for doing his will.

In the phrase "for consider your calling brothers," the word "for" indicates further proof of verse 25: "For the foolishness of God is wiser than men, and the weakness of God is stronger than men." The Corinthians could "see" their calling by looking around at the Corinthian congregation. Evidently, there were some human greats among them, but not many. The majority were ordinary people.

The word "calling" is the focus of the entire section. Christianity is a divine act, not a human act. The New Testament never uses the Greek word for "calling" to refer to human employment or vocation. It is always an act of calling by God's initiative. If God chose us in his calling, there is no place for human pride.

If God takes the initiative and makes the provision, then there is no place for works. God does the work, and God does the epistemological calling. "Brothers" needed to take a close look at this.

In saying, "Not many of you were wise according to worldly standards," Paul modifies the word "wise" with "according to the flesh." God does not use human norms and standards to establish his plans. He conveys wisdom but not the wisdom confined to time and space or human wisdom, the criterion of human rationalism or empiricism, or even postmodernism.

God's call does not include many "powerful" people. He does not put his plan for the gospel at the mercy of the mighty—the influence of great leaders, politicians, or military strategy. The glory of God's conquest does not depend on mighty messengers who wield authority but on the power of his message supernaturally revealed.

In the phrase "Not many were of noble birth," "noble birth" refers to aristocrats, blue bloods, families of high descent. God does not try to make the gospel fashionable before people can receive it. The gospel is not a product of human machinations or devices; rather, God uses methodology different from our expectation. He turns our viewpoints upside down by using the scandal of the cross. The issue at stake is God's power, not human power. The questions asked earlier in this chapter were "Where is the wise man? Where is the scribe? Where is the debater of this age?" What real value is there in their systems? We can put no trust in their epistemological systems.

The issue addressed in this passage is not anti-intellectualism or irrationalism. The issue at hand is that we are at the mercy of God to reveal himself. We cannot find infinite things by finite methods. Note T. S. Eliot's warning of elevating human wisdom too far:

> All our knowledge brings us closer to our ignorance.
> All our ignorance brings us nearer to death.
> But nearness to death, no nearer to God.
> Where is the life we have lost in living?[237]

God's ways "seem" foolish to man (1:25) but the most minimal thing God ever thought is greater than the best thing man ever thought. That is why God uses the weak things of the world to "confound" the great of the world (1:26–28). God does not choose human greatness to do his work—he rejects it as a value in itself. He does not reject great people, but he rejects their greatness as a means of reaching people for Christ. This runs counter to the world's system. God chooses the weaker and less noble to prove the power of his message. Human methodologies preempt God's method of truth—the gospel of Christ. Humility to accept God's message is a first prerequisite in becoming a Christian. God always works by giving grace to the humble.

In presenting a radical distinction between God's infinite wisdom and finite wisdom, verse 26 shows three things the Corinthians were not and, in verses 27 and 28, what they were.

> *But God chose what is foolish in the world to shame the wise; God chose what is weak in the world to shame the strong.*
> (1 Corinthians 1:27 ESV)

The context of verse 27 shows the radical distinction between God's infinite wisdom and the finite wisdom of humans in coming to truth. This shows the fundamental difference between God-confidence and self-confidence. Verses 26 through 31 take a hard look at the Corinthians themselves. Verses 29 through 31 explain why God uses the weaker. In 2:1–5, Paul reminds the Corinthians of the one-and-a-half years he spent with them. Neither those who listened nor those who presented the gospel did so by self-confidence.

The word "but" in the phrase "But God chose what is foolish in the world to shame the wise" is a conjunction of strong contrast. God's wisdom is set in strong contrast to human wisdom. God chooses simple trust in the gospel message to accomplish his purpose. The reason for this is that human philosophy is bankrupt in its attempt to find infinite truth by finite means.

The phrase "God chose what is weak in the world to shame the strong" shows the power of Christianity is in its message, not in its messengers. The power of the gospel does not reside in recognition by the high and mighty but in the power of the gospel message itself. Note the three-fold use of the words "has chosen" (twice in this verse and once in the next). God makes it abundantly clear that his work is his work, not that of the human being. His chosen weak things put to shame mighty things and expose the pretentions of the academy to reveal it as a shallow show. God is in the business of disgracing it, and he does this to demonstrate the power of the message of the gospel, not the power of the evangelist. God is independent of human power.

In verse 28 God renders human systems for certainty inoperative by a super-natural intervention of the Word of God into time and space:

> *God chose what is low and despised in the world, even things that are not, to bring to nothing things that are.* (1 Corinthians 1:28 ESV)

The word "low" in this verse means "ignoble, of no family, low born." It does not refer to evil but to humble persons, people of low pedigree. God chooses nobodies to achieve his purposes. The word "despised" means "considered as nothing." The world brands believers with contempt because of their naive acceptance of the gospel, yet this is the very kind God chooses. God's system epistemologically is the polar opposite of the system of the world.

God's system is a paradox to human systems, for what is epistemologically weak is strong in God's economy. God will "bring to nothing the things that are;" these "things" are pure human systems for knowing and certainty. God will render them inoperative for knowing in the infinite realm. Finite philoso-phers cannot see beyond time and space. They can only come to conclusions that reside in the finite brain. That is because they have only a soul (mind, emotion, and will) and do not have a capacity to relate to God. They are spiritu-ally dead epistemologically.

The simple believer knows something beyond time and space because God revealed himself in the Word. Unbelieving PhDs confine themselves to their own assumptions about how to know truth. They choose human systems with human results. Yet the lowly believer with the message, viewed as of no repute in the estimation of the philosopher, will render inoperative all philosophical systems.

Verses 29–31 explain why God chose the ignoble to confound the noble, why he chose the weak to render inoperative the strong, and why he chose those with less academic credentials to confound those with high academic achieve-ment. The reason? God, not humans, will receive glory for God's work.

> *So that no human being might boast in the presence of God.*
> (1 Corinthians 1:29 ESV)

In the phrase "so that no human being might boast in the presence of God, the word "that" is a term for strong purpose and ultimate end. God shows that by rendering inoperative the philosophical systems of this world and choosing lesser powers for his purpose, all glory should go to him. He is totally self-sufficient and needs nothing, but humans are finite and need God epistemologically.

God negates human pride. The word "boast" means pride in self-confidence, self-glory. It carries the idea of "brag." That is why we do not boast or glory in the messenger but in the message. Everything in our society points to human achievement and pride. God takes full responsibility for his epistemological system of truth. Human pride rests on the illusion that people can find ultimate truth. We cannot independently come to God, so God does not give us the option of doing so. God shatters all our pride and self-sufficiency. If God does the epistemological doing, God gets the glory. If we autonomously seek salvation by our own means, then we get the glory.

In verses 30 and 31, God gives the reason why he uses lesser folks to advance his kingdom. Our identity is an unadulterated gift from God in Christ. God's wisdom pivots around the believer's position in Christ. This kind of wisdom produces righteousness, sanctification, and redemption.

> *And because of him you are in Christ Jesus, who became to us wisdom from God, righteousness and sanctification and redemption.*
> (1 Corinthians 1:30 ESV)

God's salvation comes from God, in contrast to those who seek God by human methods. The source indicated by the words "of him" is literally "out of him"—God the Father is the source of what follows. God is the epistemological original cause of our salvation in Christ. Salvation comes from God, not from something that originates in the self.

In the phrase "who became to us wisdom from God, righteousness and sanctification and redemption," the word "became" means "to become something he was not before." What Christ was before was eternal God. Then he stepped foot on earth into a human body to die for our sins. Christ became the source of our salvation by his incarnation, death, and resurrection. This did not happen when we believed but when Christ came in the first century.

God made Christ "our wisdom"—with "wisdom" the ruling word in the Greek sentence. "Righteousness, and sanctification, and redemption" expand what God's wisdom means—God's system of salvation. Every believer accepts "wisdom from God" in becoming a Christian. Christians become Christians by God's wisdom, not human epistemological method. God's wisdom is unattainable by a human method of seeking. This wisdom involves righteousness, sanctification, and redemption. It is a wisdom of a different viewpoint—God's viewpoint. God personifies his thoughts (wisdom) in what he did in Christ.

"Righteousness" here is not our personal righteousness but Christ's righteousness (imputed righteousness). It is the quality of being right in God's eyes; we stand in perfect conformity to God's standard of righteousness. "Sanctification" means "set apart." God sets each believer apart unto himself; we hold special deference with God and are his unique possession. This is imparted sanctification, positional sanctification. "Redemption" means "to buy something back." Christ delivered our souls from the penalty of sin and its curse. Therefore, God views our identity as being in Christ; we hold the same status quo as Jesus holds before God. Because God alone is the source of our salvation, this points to his glory. God gets the glory because God does the doing. Verse 31 excludes all human achievement in God's plan of salvation:

> . . . *so that, as it is written, "Let the one who boasts, boast in the Lord."* (1 Corinthians 1:31 ESV)

The words "so that" point to the purpose of God's wisdom of salvation: to glorify God through providing a simple message in Christ.

The words following "as it is written" are a free quotation from Jeremiah 9:24. Jeremiah does not want Israel to brag about human wisdom, strength, or riches, for these things are temporary. Instead, Israel should brag only to the degree that they understood and knew God.

The focus of our boasting should be "in the Lord." The true basis for glorying is God's grace in providing salvation from his viewpoint. The believer's boast is in God, who works from something already known and self-evident to reveal conclusions in the Bible (*a priori*). We can never experience all that God knows and experiences; that is why we must accept God's deductive conclusions, for we cannot discover them with finiteness. God reveals his grace through the wisdom of the person and work of Christ, a concept that comes by pure revelation. We cannot brag in the finite limitations of humans who seek to discover truth inductively (*a posteriori*).

We cannot work our way from the effect to the cause, because the cause is finite and God is infinite. We do not have the capacity to comprehend God exhaustively in order to evaluate him fully. We must accept God's deductive conclusions from the revelation of Scripture. That is why we glory in the Lord rather than glory in finite human capacity.

Paul turns to how he keeps the message the core of his ministry in chapter 2. He did not allow method to displace message. He first states how he did not minister when he came to Corinth:

> And I, when I came to you, brothers, did not come proclaiming to you the testimony of God with lofty speech or wisdom. (1 Corinthians 2:1 ESV)

Paul met a diversity of viewpoints (pluralism) when he came to Athens (Acts 17:18–21). When the Athenians heard of the resurrection, they sneered at Paul (17:32). The natural mind views the resurrection as unacceptable. Paul, in the face of this skepticism, determined to know nothing but Jesus Christ and him crucified when he came to Corinth (1 Corinthians 2:2) and did not accommodate truth to meet their need. They did not need one more opinion. The supernatural power of the cross would countervail human viewpoint.

When Paul writes "and I, when I came to you, brethren," he harks back to when he first came to Corinth. He did not come with philosophy but with an announcement of a message. He depended on God's system of transcendent, objective truth rather than a human perspective approach to truth.

Paul did not come to Corinth with "lofty of speech or wisdom." "Lofty" carries the ideas of "preeminence, rising above." Paul did not seek to rise above Corinthian culture by trying to outshine them with rhetoric of philosophical display, which would have been right in their wheelhouse. That might have appeared impressive, but it is vacuous in comparison to God's mighty concrete revelation in the Bible.

But Paul came "proclaiming" the "testimony of God." The word "proclaiming" means "to announce, declare, make known, proclaim publicly, publish." A proclaimer for Christ is to present the facts of the gospel stated in the Bible and his personal experience with those facts. A witness in court does not presume, speculate, or suppose. Paul did not speculate about philosophical theories about life but came with the testimony of God and nothing more. Evangelicals today are impressed with the latest and greatest methodology that comes along. These new machinations always sound very impressive. Like a pendulum, these phases come and go. Today's philosophical emphasis on postmodernism will one day disappear; this is especially appalling in that postconservatives change their message to adapt to this philosophy. Will they change their message again for a newer philosophy?

Paul proclaimed biblical truth to the Corinthians. He did not speculate about philosophical theories about life but came with the testimony (truth not hitherto revealed; that is, the New Testament) of God and nothing more. Paul did not come with dialectical process. He came with a proclamation of the objective gospel. He simply announced the facts. He added no properties to the gospel but presented it in an unvarnished fashion. There is a correlation between the very essence of the gospel message and its method of delivery. The Corinthians came to Christ through declaration of the content of the person and work of Christ. As long as the message was not changed, Paul was willing to change the method (1 Corinthians 9).

The reason Christians buy into these philosophies is that they look at them through the eyes of their culture. Culture rife with relativism and pluralism blinds them to stark statements of Scripture. They reinterpret and make Scripture in the likeness of culture (deconstructing the Bible).

In verse 2 Paul moves to the focus of his message. It was message, not method:

> *For I decided to know nothing among you except Jesus Christ and him crucified.* (1 Corinthians 2:2 ESV)

In deciding "to know nothing" among them, Paul set up a policy for himself. This protocol did not allow him to be sidetracked by philosophy in presenting the simple gospel message. Paul did not address or adapt to the philosophies of

Pythagoreanism, Epicureanism, Stoicism, or any other philosophy. He simply presented the gospel of the person of Christ and him crucified.

Paul resolved to keep the one great central truth of the gospel message primary in any evangelistic approach used to reach the Corinthians—the person and work of Christ: "For I determined not to know anything among you." Paul intentionally set aside anything that might prop up the message of the gospel. He did not seek any other means of communication. The reason for this was that the cross was a verdict on human wisdom and philosophy. This is God's foolish methodology. People do not seek God because they have a stake in not doing so:

> *As it is written: "There is none righteous, no, not one; There is none who understands; There is none who seeks after God. They have all turned aside; They have together become unprofitable; There is none who does good, no, not one."* (Romans 3:10–12)

Paul determined to know nothing "except Jesus Christ and him crucified." The content of the cross is what counts in God's eyes. Biblical evangelism is an unembellished setting forth of the unvarnished gospel of Christ. God blesses an unpretentious and simple gospel message. The reason Paul centered on the person and work of Christ is that this is the heart of the gospel whereby one becomes a Christian—"except Jesus Christ and Him crucified."

Paul placed his trust in the sufficiency of Christ's work on the cross to save and did not clutter his message with philosophy. A simple gospel presentation is a foolish approach in the eyes of the world and in the eyes of some postconservatives as well! Any approach that belittles the unadulterated gospel message obscures the gospel. Because the gospel constitutes absolute truth, philosophy or human methods cannot defeat it. This is in stark contrast to the popular method today of taking the dialectical approach to truth. The biblical principle is to declare the message and let the Holy Spirit work on the heart (1 Corinthians 2:4). We do not have to know everything about a Muslim to witness to a Muslim; we do not have to know philosophy to witness to a philosopher; we do not have to be a scientist to witness to a scientist.

Paul came to Corinth with a sense of apprehension because he did not have confidence in human technique:

*And I was with you in weakness and in fear and much trembling.*
(1 Corinthians 2:3 ESV)

Paul sensed personal inadequacy to minister in Corinth, especially because he
had not received a warm welcome in Athens (Acts 16:22–17:32). His fear and
trembling had to do with how the Corinthians would accept the gospel from an
inadequate person.

## The Spirit's Testimony to Certainty

Although Paul went to Corinth with a personal sense of inadequacy, that did
not mean he had no sense of confidence; his confidence was in the power of the
Spirit to demonstrate certainty to a pluralistic society.

> *And my speech and my message were not in plausible words of wisdom,*
> *but in demonstration of the Spirit and of power.*
> (1 Corinthians 2:4 ESV)

When Paul came to Corinth, he did not come with human persuasion or try
to coax and convince with the human point of view. He did not conciliate the
Corinthians by accommodating his message to their philosophy. The Corinthians were famous for putting a premium on the facade of false rhetoric.
The word "speech" refers to the style of delivery, and "message" refers to the
gospel. Paul adjusted neither to suit the Corinthians; rather, he presented the
simple gospel message of Jesus Christ and him crucified.

Paul "came in the demonstration of the Spirit and of power." He depended
on the Holy Spirit to minister in antagonistic Corinth and did not rest on his
intellect or speaking ability. The Holy Spirit took the content of his message
and won a number of Corinthians to Jesus. The Holy Spirit supernaturally
persuaded the Corinthians to come to Christ. Paul proclaimed, and the Holy
Spirit persuaded.

The word "demonstration" carries the idea of manifestation or proof. The Holy
Spirit presents evidence that convinces. This is the polar opposite of the façade
of false rhetoric. The Holy Spirit shows by demonstration and exposition that
something is factual—proof, evidence, verification. The Greek term "demonstration" means proof that is necessarily or demonstrably true—incontrovert-

ible. This word carries the idea of something evident beyond contradiction by expressing absolute certainty; it is true with mathematical certainty. This was a term of didactic Aristotelian logic opposed to dialectical thought. The Holy Spirit proves the Bible true through demonstration of his power by making the propositions of Scripture unassailable.

The word "demonstration" is an etiologic term (a figure of speech known as *apodeixis* for rendering a full reason for what is said or done). The Greek word for "demonstration" indicates clarity produced in the hearer's mind by lifting of the veil of darkness (2 Corinthians 4:3, 4). The Holy Spirit produces in the hearer a conviction from the force of a sovereign move of God, the Holy Spirit. The Holy Spirit powerfully reveals the truth of salvation.

If Paul wanted to use a term for probability, he could have used another term in the Greek: πῐθᾰνολογία—use of probable arguments. It is plausible, but false, speech resulting from the use of well-constructed, probable arguments—convincing speech, plausible language. The word carries the idea of plausible argument in Colossians 2:4: "that no one may delude you with plausible arguments." This term is opposite to our word "demonstration" (ἀπόδειξις—we get the English word "apodictic" from this word).

Probability speaks of a degree of belief less than certain. The Bible asserts a certainty of belief to the point that the individual is culpable for what is known (Romans 1:19, 20). John speaks of the argument in the writing of the gospel of John, saying that we can "know" and "believe" that Jesus is the Son of God (John 20:31).

The claim that there is no uncontaminated interpretation that is independent from bias flies in the face of extant statements of Scripture. This is an attempt to shed the very essence of what the Scripture is all about—objective and certain truth. The Bible does not present truth as situational and bound by culture or experience. Contrary to this premise, postconservatives cannot come to conclusion about God's revelation with confidence—because they deem that people always ascribe meaning to the text. According to them, we must constantly dialogue with other theological viewpoints and restrict formal and even practical certainty to the Word of God. We must especially restrict individual understanding in favor of the community and downplay absolutes in lieu of a dynamic or flexible perspective on truth. There is openness toward the salvation of people in other religions. Tolerance and saccharin sentiment prevails in this thinking. It is almost a mirror reflection of present culture and a desire to accommodate that culture. In this shift from the Bible, truth and certainty are at stake in a compromise of the faith.

"Demonstration" stands in opposition to plausibility. The noun form of this word occurs nowhere else in the New Testament. God expects us to be certain of convincing truths about Christ.

Paul explains that he went to Corinth in fear and trembling that he would not have an adequate presentation of the gospel for the intellectual Corinthians. He went with a sense of dependency on the Lord to do the work. Verse 4 explains that dependency.

The point of this passage is to demonstrate that knowledge of God depends on God conveying his knowledge into time and space so that man can understand it. People cannot find the transcendent and infinite God by finite means. We need the Holy Spirit to reveal an infinite God. In logic, we call this the *a priori* approach to truth. People cannot come to God by studying the universe inductively (*a posteriori*). That is why there is no certainty in human systems for finding truth. There is peril in taking a human approach to understanding God because it rests on the false presumptions of human reason to demonstrate certainty.

The Holy Spirit sets forth God's Word by evidence and certainty. The issue at hand is the certainty of premises. Only God knows premises that are transcendent, so only he can know whether those premises are true. The Holy Spirit shows the ultimate causes of truth within God's sphere of knowledge. All other knowledge is subordinate to these reasons.

Dialectical knowledge starts from uncertain and non-evident premises of human beings. Thus, the apodictic knowledge of the Holy Spirit stands in opposition to the prominent system of thought today—dialectical process. Apodictic (certain) knowledge rests on two kinds of properties: definitions and assertions. Definitions present the object of what God says in his Word; assertions present the connection between the objects. These definitions and assertions create a system whereby definitions are justified by assertions justified earlier, resting on ultimate premises of the Word of God—axioms revealed by God through the Holy Spirit. An axiom is the most general assumption for finding truth.

The only way we can find God is through God revealing himself deductively. That is why God uses the term "demonstration" (*apodictic*) in this verse. This is a Greek term for deductive knowledge. A deductive syllogism's validity rests unconditionally on the relation of the facts inferred to the facts posited in the premises. The premises of God's syllogism depend upon existence of knowledge that comes only from God. A syllogism whose validity rests partly upon the non-existence of some other knowledge is a probable syllogism. Only the Holy Spirit can give knowledge that rests solely on transcendent knowledge.

Apodictic truth is self-evident truth. An apodictic truth is a working fact but not a hypothesis. Apodictic truth needs no justification by reason or argument, or evidence. It is truth based on judgment by the Apprehender, for only God apprehends infinite truth. When God revealed himself, all pursuit of truth about him outside of revelation came to a dead end. God's truth is external to evidence or philosophy.

The Holy Spirit demonstrably or indisputably shows that Christianity is true. Humans cannot autonomously come to God, because finiteness cannot comprehend infiniteness. We are at the mercy of God revealing himself through the Holy Spirit.

> *And even if our gospel is veiled, it is veiled only to those who are perishing. In their case the god of this world has blinded the minds of the unbelievers, to keep them from seeing the light of the gospel of the glory of Christ, who is the image of God.* (2 Corinthians 4:3, 4 ESV)

The issue here is not that the Christian should follow personal feelings to connect with the Holy Spirit. The concern is in responding to the convicting work of the Holy Spirit's testimony to the objective Word of God. There is a norm, or standard, of truth that confirms the Holy Spirit's convicting work. That is what Scripture warrants or justifies. This is coming to understand what God wants us to know deductively.

The Bible never presupposes that communicators are infallible in preaching the Word of God. However, to the degree that we faithfully expound God's Word, the Holy Spirit takes that Word and confirms it to the heart. Insofar as we accurately communicate the content of Scripture, we communicate the certainty of that evidence. This is the only sense whereby we can claim communication of certainty.

The presuppositions of an argument are not among the premises of the argument. Therefore, the circularity in view is not what we normally call circularity in logic textbooks.[238]

Paul rejects the prevailing philosophical culture of Corinth for the convincing work of the Holy Spirit. The Corinthians knew nothing of the realm of the Holy Spirit. Paul sets in stark contrast the demonstration and power of the Holy Spirit against vacuous philosophy. The Holy Spirit can give apodictic proof of the truthfulness of the gospel. He establishes the gospel by conviction (John 16:8) and illumination of the finite perspective with divine viewpoint. The role of the Holy Spirit in convincing the unbeliever is clear from Scripture.

> *And when He has come, He will convict the world of sin, and of righteousness, and of judgment: of sin, because they do not believe in Me; of righteousness, because I go to My Father and you see Me no more; of judgment, because the ruler of this world is judged.* (John 16:8–11)

The Holy Spirit convicts the unbeliever in three areas: (1) the sin of non-belief, (2) God's absolute righteousness, and (3) the fact that Satan has been judged. Without the authenticating ministry of the Holy Spirit in these three areas, no one would become a Christian, for no one "seeks after God" on one's own (Romans 3:10, 11). If people seek God, it is because God the Holy Spirit has already sought them. God takes the initiative to "draw" people to himself (John 6:44). We love darkness rather than light (John 3:19). Satan blinds the mind of the unbeliever (2 Corinthians 4:3, 4). The unbeliever is spiritually dead about the premises of God (1 Corinthians 2:14) and even hostile to God (Romans 8:7). Rejection of Christ is not because of insufficient drawing by God but because of spiritual darkness of the soul. At root, the unbeliever's problem is darkened negative volition. It is a matter of volition whether a person responds positively to the gospel.

> *Jesus answered them and said, "My doctrine is not Mine, but His who sent Me. If anyone wills to do His will, he shall know concerning the*

> *doctrine, whether it is from God or whether I speak on My own*
> *authority."* (John 7:16, 17)

## Apodictic Truth and Logical Syllogisms

Aristotle distinguished apodictic truth from logical syllogisms. Logical syllo-gisms depend on premises. The problem is the warrant or veracity of the prem-ises. In apodictic logic, the premises are known to be true and are therefore certain. Therefore, there is an issue higher than mere logic. The Holy Spirit establishes certainty in a way that finite premises can by no means do.

The word "power" in 1 Corinthians 2:4 complements the quality of the Holy Spirit's "demonstration"—it denotes the mode of the Spirit's action. Paul came to Corinth in power as well as demonstration. The Holy Spirit takes possession of the understanding and will by the inward power of truth. The "demonstra-tion" of the Spirit takes place in conjunction with the Spirit's power; thus, it is God's power that saves, not man's:

> *So I am eager to preach the gospel to you also who are in Rome. For*
> *I am not ashamed of the gospel, for it is the power of God for salva-*
> *tion to everyone who believes, to the Jew first and also to the Greek.*
> (Romans 1:15, 16 ESV)

> *For the kingdom of God does not consist in talk but in power.*
> (1 Corinthians 4:20 ESV)

> *. . . because our gospel came to you not only in word, but also in power*
> *and in the Holy Spirit and with full conviction. You know what kind of*
> *men we proved to be among you for your sake.* (1 Thessalonians 1:5 ESV)

> *And we also thank God constantly for this, that when you received the*
> *word of God, which you heard from us, you accepted it not as the word*
> *of men but as what it really is, the word of God, which is at work in you*
> *believers.* (1 Thessalonians 2:13 ESV)

## Testimonium and Certainty

The two occurrences of "my" in 1 Corinthians 2:4 ("my speech" and "my message") emphatically contrast Paul's message and method with the philosophers'. Paul's method was to depend on the Spirit of God to convict about the truth of the gospel. This is what the Reformers called the *testimonium*. This is the relationship between the Word and the Spirit. The Holy Spirit relates to Scripture in inspiration, illumination, application (conviction), and *testimonium*. Inspiration refers to the Spirit's superintending the writing of Scripture (2 Timothy 3:16). Illumination enables the reader of Scripture to understand with clarity (1 Corinthians 2:10, 14). Application is the Spirit's work in appropriating principles of Scripture to experience.

The concept of *testimonium* focuses on certainty. The Holy Spirit authenticates the reliability of Scripture to our souls, bestowing certainty about its veracity. The *testimonium*, not subjectivism or mysticism, is the ultimate ground for certainty in the veracity of Scripture. It transcends reason but does not contradict reason. Only God can verify his words. Only infiniteness enlightens infinite truth. Therefore, the *testimonium* is transrational.

There is then both objectivity and subjectivity in the demonstration of the Spirit. The believer clearly understands with reason (logic) what the Scripture says but also concurs with that truth through the "demonstration of the Spirit and power." The Holy Spirit offers no new truth but convicts with the statements already made in Scripture. He brings compliance to the truth of Scripture with a sense of certainty. This is unqualified yielding to the truth of Scripture with assurance of its truthfulness.

This *testimonium* does not function in a subjective vacuum but with the objectivity of the Word of God. This demonstration of the Spirit does not go against evidence and is not separate from the evidence but works in conjunction with the evidence in God's revelation. The Spirit gives certainty that the evidence is true, and he supernaturally impels us to submit to the truthfulness of Scripture. Submission is a subjective trust in the objective evidence. Negative volition against the evidence of Scripture countervails the ministry of the Holy Spirit in verifying the truthfulness of Scripture.

The ultimate truth of Christianity does not rest on anything posterior to revelation or on some sensory experience. It is definitely not *a posteriori* in that it rests on science or some sense experience. It is a deduction from fixed premises ("demonstration"). This is apodictic truth, truth based on established premises.

God's arguments from Scripture transcend human experience by Scripture's very nature. This is correspondence between the knower and the object known at the most supreme level.

No inductive argument can establish anything. Something that has only the possibility or probability to be true has the possibility or probably to be false. Hence, inductive argument cannot give certainty to the reality of Christianity. Only arguments that flow from right premises are true and can give formally valid "demonstration."

The first principle, or ultimate presupposition, for finding truth is the starting point for the person committed to revelation. Finding ultimate truth by induction is a pragmatically hopeless task. Thus, finite humans must assume the first principle without proof from induction if they are to become Christians. The Bible does not grant to human knowledge the self-sufficiency to arrive at God's truth autonomously. Finiteness can never find transcendent truth. That is why mankind is epistemologically under the authority of God. This is an undeniable, intransigent starting point, but without it we wallow in our own schemes. Without it, we can never arrive at truth with validity and certainty.

Every system begins with a presupposition; even inductive approaches to truth begin with the assumption about how to know what is known. It is that presupposition that controls all assessment of truth from that point forward. The Christian presupposition is that the Spirit of God reveals the Word of God. Unless we begin with this, we will never end with this. Unless we begin with the assumption that the Bible is the Word of God, we will never end with confidence or certainty that it is absolute truth. That is the fundamental axiom of the Christian faith, for only the infinite God can know all things qualitatively and quantitatively. Ultimately, the Holy Spirit authenticates the Word of God in a self-authenticating way. Unless we begin with God, we will not end with God; nor will we be able to verify anything as absolute truth. Because God is absolute, only he can bear witness to himself. God's Word and the Holy Spirit inherently carry their own evidences.

The conviction of the Holy Spirit transcends our opinion or the opinion of others. No human system can evaluate the testimony of the Spirit. This unassailable truth does not lean upon probabilities or human judgment.

If one assumes an inductive approach, the data of inductive logic is never finished. That is why the only way to certainty is through the self-attesting conviction of the Holy Spirit in the objective Word of God.

> *It is written in the Prophets, 'And they will all be taught by God.'*
> *Everyone who has heard and learned from the Father comes to me.*
> (John 6:45)

## Kinds of Certainty

Because the *testimonium* concerns certainty, we need to define what we mean by that term. Theologian R. C. Sproul indicates that there are three different kinds of certainty: (1) philosophical, or formal, certainty, (2) confidence as certainty, and (3) moral certainty.[239]

Sproul first identifies philosophical certainty as a tight, formal argument based on logic. This argument rests on the "formal relationship of propositions," such as in syllogisms. Syllogisms require the veracity of the premises of the syllogisms. There is no certainty without demonstrating the truthfulness of the premises. The conclusion could be properly valid but not essentially true. We can never achieve this kind of certainty if we limit ourselves to induction.

If we try to find ultimate certainty by induction, until we examine all reality exhaustively and completely dispassionately for all time and in every situation, we cannot make an absolute claim to know something with absolute certainty. We cannot come to absolute truth inductively (*a posteriori*). Absolute certainty is restricted by relative and conditional formal relationships of propositions. This is the problem of a finite human being. As long as we are finite, our ability to achieve absolute certainty philosophically is impossible. Only infiniteness can comprehend infiniteness. Only God can possess philosophical certainty.

Sproul's second category is "confidence as certainty," which he says is "not the same as technical philosophical certainty." This form of certainty is a matter of degrees. Confidence is an attitudinal state of assurance with a mixture of doubt.

The third form of certainty mentioned by Sproul is "juridical" certainty, which is confidence "beyond reasonable doubt." A doubt might be rational but not reasonable. This is a distinction between formal and juridical certainty. Juridical certainty is certainty "from the weight of evidence." This kind of certainty is the certainty of Scripture. It does not carry philosophical certainty but a certainty of culpability.

The subjective condition of mankind means that humans cannot come to certitude by our own means. This condition makes the *testimonium* necessary. Without God, the heart is adverse to God's Word. The testimony of the Spirit to Scripture is a subjective grounding of the heart (mind, emotion, and will) with a temper to receive the objective Word of God.

The dialectical method proposes another explanation of the internal witness of the Spirit. The neo-orthodox perspective of dialectical thought shifts the *testimonium* from Scripture to the person of Christ as the incarnate Word. Neo-orthodox thinkers do not want to view the Bible as objective revelation but as dynamic revelation. Scripture, in their view, is not itself revelation but is a witness to revelation. Revelation becomes revelatory as the Holy Spirit speaks through it dynamically. The only objectivity is in the person of Christ, not in biblical writings.

Contrary to neo-orthodoxy, orthodoxy argues that concursive Scripture is the only place where we know about Christ. There is no person of Christ without the Word that tells about Christ. Scriptures are not the ultimate object of our faith, but they are the means of faith. All truth is personal in that we must respond to truth, but truth is also propositional. We have objective revelation to which we can reply.

If we divorce the content of revelation from objective truth, then we end in the subjectivism of finite human beings. God's objective authority in the Bible is above human experience, not in the authority of private human experience. There is an experience, but that experience is a subjective answer to the objective Word of God from incentive of the Holy Spirit.

## Relation of Faith to Certainty

Now Paul explains why he rests his case in the demonstration of the Spirit; he did not want to depend on human faculty but on the power of God:

> *That your faith might not rest in the wisdom of men but in the power of God.* (1 Corinthians 2:5 ESV)

Paul came in the "demonstration of the Spirit" rather than in the power of his speaking ability, that "faith might not rest in the wisdom of men." The word "that" indicates Paul's basis for coming to Corinth in the "demonstration of the Spirit."

The principle is clear: All the human ability and power in the world cannot persuade one person to trust Christ as Savior. Only demonstration from the Holy Spirit can break through to the soul. Faith comes from Christ, not from the ingenuity of philosophy, oratory, or human persuasion. This refutes the idea that a person must be a success in order to witness. Human attraction does not bring people to Christ. It is not necessary to be intellectual to introduce intellectuals to Christ. We do not have to know all philosophies to win them; all we need to know is the gospel message. If we base faith on philosophical argument, we can refute our faith by philosophical argument.

The nature of faith includes the idea of certainty. Any degree of lack of faith undermines faith. Faith always rests on certainty, not on a suggestion of probability. Otherwise, chance is final and probability is empty. The very idea of probability precludes certainty and places chance at the core of a system. A probable belief is of no more value than an improbable belief. That is why God's self-attesting Word transcends all probable approaches to truth. It is impossible to verify truth by probability because the finite mind can never come to infinite truth. No one can come to truth *a posteriori* but only through *a priori* revelation. Conclusion about truth must come from a higher source than the human being. Christianity does not rest on opinion, as most non-believers presume. The testimony of the Holy Spirit transcends the finite world of beliefs and perspectives. He is superior to philosophy and reason.

Every ultimate belief must begin with an ultimate presupposition, a first principle somewhere. Every system always assumes that presupposition without proof. The axiom that God revealed himself in the Word is Christianity's first principle. Unless we begin with this, we will not arrive at this. The genesis of Christianity about choosing the first principle or presupposition is that God the Holy Spirit "demonstrates" the first principle to us. That is, it does not rest on finite humans choosing a finite presupposition for finding truth.

The Holy Spirit characterizes God's Word by evidence and certainty, but the issue at hand is the certainty of premises. Only God knows premises that are transcendent, so only he can know whether those premises are true. The Holy Spirit shows the ultimate causes of truth within God's sphere of knowledge. All other knowledge is subordinate to these reasons. Only God has infinite as over against finite knowledge. He has the true perspective on the universe.

> The highest level of justification-rationality for the human mind exists when a person has attained truth by reliable belief-forming mechanisms that are in keeping with biblical norms. At this level, all true beliefs, and only true beliefs, are justified and hence rational.[240]

Belief in the truthfulness of God's Word is an ultimate presupposition and the controlling approach to truth. God's revelation in Scripture is our deepest commitment for truth. It is a strategic error to appeal to autonomous human reason because that will confine the conclusion to the finite realm. It will make chance ultimate because chance is the outcome of probability, with the best chance of belief in the Word of God then only probable. But God reveals himself in self-attesting revelation (Hebrews 1:1–3).

## Atypical Wisdom of the Word Not Understood by Human Faculty

From verse 6 to the end of the chapter, Paul addresses believers so that they can understand revelation, inspiration, and illumination.

> *Yet among the mature we do impart wisdom, although it is not a wisdom of this age or of the rulers of this age, who are doomed to pass away.* (1 Corinthians 2:6 ESV)

The "we" in this verse refers to the apostles. When the apostles spoke the wisdom of the Word of God, they spoke to Christians. The "mature" are simply Christians. Maturity recognizes God's wisdom as superior to man's wisdom because only those with positive volition toward the gospel can understand divine viewpoint.

God's wisdom is not temporal or transitory as is the "wisdom of this age or the rulers of this age." All that leaders of this world know is the passing wisdom of human thought and "are doomed to pass away." These leaders "are coming to nothing." These leaders and their philosophies will not last into eternity. Christians operate in the realm of eternity when it comes to truth; our view of truth comes from eternal decree.

> *But we impart a secret and hidden wisdom of God, which God decreed before the ages for our glory.* (1 Corinthians 2:7 ESV)

God's wisdom is emphatically superior to the puny brain of man. The Greek for the word "secret" means a truth not hitherto revealed. It does not mean spooky, puzzling, or mysterious. It is truth infinitely higher than we can attain by our finite faculties.

God's wisdom is prior to creation—"decreed before the ages." There was no place for input from people at that time, for God hid his wisdom in eternity past. God's wisdom was no afterthought, nor was it contingent on circumstance. Unlike the wisdom of the world, the Word of God is eternally designed for "our glory." We possess this glory currently and will enter into a state of glory (blessedness) when we get to heaven, where God will glorify body and soul. Our bodies will have no defect; our souls will be completely set apart unto God without sin. All this is in the realm of eternal truth. If non-Christians would have understood this, "they would not have crucified the Lord of glory" because he conveys his glory to us.

> *None of the rulers of this age understood this, for if they had, they would not have crucified the Lord of glory.* (1 Corinthians 2:8 ESV)

Leaders at the time of Christ did not know that the glory of the Christ came in flesh. Pilot, Herod, religious leaders, and the Sanhedrin all failed to recognize the glory that was in Christ at his first coming. The phrase "Lord of glory" refers to the deity of Christ and all that that entails; he in every respect is almighty God.

Turning to the Bible itself to demonstrate the glory of God's revelation, Paul draws inferences from Isaiah 64:4 and 65:17:

> *But, as it is written, "What no eye has seen, nor ear heard, nor the heart of man imagined, what God has prepared for those who love him."* (1 Corinthians 2:9 ESV)

The context of Isaiah 64 and 65 speaks to Israel in captivity. God put Israel in captivity to Babylon because of her rebellion and located her in a place of discipline. Israel cried to God to deliver her from captivity, and he delivered the

Israelites after seventy years of exile. Isaiah gives words of encouragement for present deliverance. Paul draws on the authority of written revelation to make the point that God delivers believers in time by promise. This is documentation from the Word of God that we can know transcendent truth only by revelation.

The "eye" that has not seen and the "ear" that has not heard indicate empirical ways of knowing. People cannot find the nature of this truth by empirical evidence independent of revelation. No one can observe the content of Scripture in nature or creation. We can know some things by creation, but we can know nothing of God's love or God's provision in Christ by nature or science. Likewise, neither has "the heart of man imagined," for we cannot comprehend transcendent truth from something within ourselves.

In this context, "what God has prepared for those who love him" is not the glory of heaven but the glory of the Word of God. God reveals his truth in the Word of God in the here and now (note verse 10). We do not seek God by external or internal evidence naturally; however, God bestows his unexpected grace on us solely by revealing himself in the Word of God through the convicting work of the Holy Spirit. It is utterly impossible for us to find God by science or philosophy. Postconservatives are right in this.

## Ways to Know Transcendent Truth and Certainty

From verse 10 to the end of the chapter, Paul shows three ways the believer can know God: by revelation (2:10, 11), by inspiration (2:12, 13), and by illumination (2:14–16).

*Revelation* is the first way we can know God:

> *These things God has revealed to us through the Spirit. For the Spirit searches everything, even the depths of God.* (1 Corinthians 2:10 ESV)

"Revealed" (unveiled) here refers to Scripture, an end product of revelation. The Holy Spirit is the author of Scripture. He used human agents to place Scripture in written form; the Holy Spirit disclosed Scripture to the human authors. The Holy Spirit is the agent who unveils God in written form. The Greek stresses the words "to us"—to the apostles in contrast to the rulers of the world. Leaders of the world use science and philosophy but cannot come to ultimate truth. They can find only human perspectives of truth, but God revealed eternal, absolute truth to the apostles so that they could write Scripture.

The Greek word for "searches" is the report of a professional researcher, such as someone who investigates custom issues for the government. The Holy Spirit searches the attributes, work, and counsels of God and selects from "all things" truth appropriate for the believer. He does not search to discover but to select what is appropriate for the writing of Scripture. He searches the "depths of God," so there is nothing that he does not penetrate to formulate the final product of Scripture. Therefore, we can know supernatural truth through the Holy Spirit's work.

> *For who knows a person's thoughts except the spirit of that person, which is in him? So also no one comprehends the thoughts of God except the Spirit of God.* (1 Corinthians 2:11 ESV)

Here Paul set up an analogy of the Holy Spirit's revelation of Scripture to a personal knowledge of oneself in a self-conscious sense. We can never know another person as we know ourselves. We cannot even know a mate as we know ourselves. The Spirit of God can know God thoroughly because he is God and thus knows himself.

Human authors of Scripture were not left to themselves to write Scripture. The Holy Spirit who "comprehends the thoughts of God" knows everything about God because he is God. The Word of God is the product of God himself. He used human agents, but he supernaturally superintended the writing of every word of Scripture so it became fully inspired. There is a distinction between revelation and inspiration. Revelation is the process whereby the Holy Spirit gave the content of Scripture, whereas inspiration is the superintending process of the Holy Spirit to ensure that every word of Scripture is without error and accurate.

> *All Scripture [that which is written down or scribed] is breathed out by God and profitable for teaching, for reproof, for correction, and for training in righteousness, that the man of God may be competent, equipped for every good work.* (2 Timothy 3:16, 17 ESV)

*Inspiration* is the second way the believer can know God:

> *Now we have received not the spirit of the world, but the Spirit who is from God, that we might understand the things freely given us by God.*
> (1 Corinthians 2:12 ESV)

The Holy Spirit first revealed truth to the apostles (writers of Scripture), then he inspired their writings (12, 13).

The human authors of Scripture could not find God's wisdom through human faculty—through "the spirit of the world." The spirit of the world is the prevailing principle working in mankind today. This principle is autonomous from God and alien to God, a knowledge limited to the realm of the world.

The only way the Bible's authors could know God's transcendent wisdom was by revelation through the Holy Spirit—"the Spirit who is from God." Note the contrast: There is the spirit of the world but then there is the spirit of God. The Holy Spirit gave us the Word of God by revelation and verbal, plenary inspiration. God did not leave writers of Scripture to themselves to write Scripture.

The "we" in this verse refers to the apostles. The "things that have been freely given by God" is the Word of God—Scripture. Inspiration of Scripture is an act of the grace of God.

> *And we impart this in words not taught by human wisdom but taught by the Spirit, interpreting spiritual truths to those who are spiritual.*
> (1 Corinthians 2:13 ESV)

"This" in verse 13 is divine wisdom, or "the things freely given us by God" of verse 12. Scripture is not human wisdom or a compilation of human thoughts.

Inspiration of Scripture came in "words," not merely in thoughts—"in words not taught by human wisdom." The Holy Spirit did not give general thoughts to the human authors of Scripture and then let them put down whatever words they wanted. He guided them to use each word.

The Holy Spirit teaches truth consistent with what Scripture says in words. The idea of inspiration is that the Holy Spirit combines divine revelation with words guided by him personally—"interpreting spiritual truths to those who are spiritual." The apostles did not source their knowledge from human means but from the Holy Spirit.

*Illumination* is the third and final way God can be known. Paul takes up this subject in verses 14 through 16.

> *The natural person does not accept the things of the Spirit of God, for they are folly to him, and he is not able to understand them because they are spiritually discerned.* (1 Corinthians 2:14 ESV)

Illumination is God's intervention on our behalf to help us understand the Word of God.

First, Paul deals with why the non-believer cannot understand divine phenomenon. The word "natural" means "soulish." We get our word "psychology" from this word (*psuchikos*). The "natural person" is all soul, pure psychology, and no spirit. In this state, non-Christians have natural capacity but no spiritual capacity. They do not have capacity to relate to God because they have had only one birth and not a second birth. They might outwardly be very moral or righteous, but inwardly they are dead to God. Soulish people do not "receive the things of the Spirit of God." In this state, they have no capacity to appreciate divine truth. God's Word does not penetrate their thinking. The word "receive" means "welcome." They do not welcome the Word of God into their souls because they are self-sufficient and independent from God.

The "things of the Spirit of God" (revelation) are "folly" to the natural person. Such a person has negative volition toward divine, deductive, didactic truth.

In the phrase "he is not able to understand [Scriptures] because they are spiritually discerned," the word "discerned" is the word "judged." A judge makes distinction as to who is innocent or who is guilty and distinguishes between opinion and fact. Non-Christians do not have the faculty to make judgments about the Word of God because they are spiritually dead; therefore, they have no transcendent discernment.

Non-Christians exist purely at the human or material level. They have a perception handicap to spiritual things and, therefore, lack adequate faculty to know God. They begin with self and end with self, and exist in a purely human condition without recourse to connect to God. Non-believers are spiritually blind, like a sightless person who cannot see the sun. They believe that self is the measure of a person—that all that they need is their own perception of reality. Operating in pure self, they are kind as long as they can have their own way.

> *For the mind that is set on the flesh is hostile to God, for it does not submit to God's law; indeed, it cannot.* (Romans 8:7 ESV)

The Christian, on the other hand, has a special capacity to discern truth by illumination:

> *The spiritual person judges all things, but is himself to be judged by no one.* (1 Corinthians 2:15 ESV)

The believer has a built-in Bible teacher—the Holy Spirit. This stands in contradistinction to the non-believer, who cannot decipher spiritual truth (see previous verse). It is the ministry of the indwelling Holy Spirit to illumine the Bible to the believer. God gave revelation and inspired the writing of the apostles, but he as well illumines the Word of God to all believers.

Believers then can "judge" or assess spiritual things by their true standard. They can come to believe properly and apply truth to experience. They can judge "all things," in contrast to the non-believers, who cannot discern spiritual things. They can come to conclusion and certainty about truth.

> *...having the eyes of your hearts enlightened, that you may know what is the hope to which he has called you, what are the riches of his glorious inheritance in the saints.* (Ephesians 1:18)

Paul says to the believer that he is "judged by no one." Non-believers try to pass judgment on believers, but they do not have capacity to do so because they are spiritually dead, incapable of connecting to the believer's orientation to divine revelation. They might accurately assess our faults, but they cannot accurately assess our faith. Unbelievers cannot figure us out because we march to a different drummer than they have the capacity to perceive.

Non-Christians have no built-in Bible teacher. Non-Christians can understand facts and objective phenomena of Scripture, but they cannot truly grasp the spiritual significance of its truth, being spiritually blind.

Finally, Paul quotes from Isaiah 40:13 to establish his point that the Bible is transcendent phenomena:

> *"For who has understood the mind of the Lord so as to instruct him?"*
> *But we have the mind of Christ.* (1 Corinthians 2:16 ESV)

The "mind of the Lord" is the Word of God. Isaiah was Old Testament Scripture. No one knows the mind of God except God, so natural man does not have the capacity to assess the mind of God autonomously.

The word "mind" refers to the seat of consciousness, the faculty of perception and judgment; here the "mind" is the "mind of the Lord." To pronounce false what God reveals to the believer from his "mind" is to pronounce false the "mind of Christ," Christ's perception and judgment about truth. Believers have the mind of Christ because we have the Bible, the revelation of God's mind.

Believers have the capacity to understand inspired books of the Bible because the Holy Spirit illumines our minds to do so. The Holy Spirit will guide us into all truth. Believers must first understand truth before we apply truth to experience. We have the ability to apply truth to experience because we have the "mind of Christ." We do not flop around in our convictions but stand firm on what we believe. We have certainty that comes from God. The Bible stands in polar opposition to the prevailing and dominant view of man today.

# *Eleven*

# EVANGELICAL IDENTITY CRISIS
## *Redefining Evangelicalism*

## Loss of Biblical Identity

In its February 7, 2005, edition, *TIME* lists Brian McLaren as one of the 25 most influential evangelicals; yet McLaren would be better classified as a postevangelical. Postevangelicals view evangelicalism as oppressive and adolescent. They are especially suspicious of proclamations of certainties in evangelicalism. This movement draws many disaffected evangelicals into its domain.

Postevangelicals have no way to stand for truth to the world once they buy into postmodernism. They have no adequate doctrinal place to stand. David Wells asserts that much of so-called evangelicalism today cannot even declare itself Protestant:

> In eviscerating theology in this way, by substituting for its defining, confessional center a new set of principles (if they can appropriately be called that), evangelicals are moving ever closer to the point at which they will no longer meaningfully be able to speak of themselves as historic Protestants.[241]

Postevangelicals label evangelicals as fundamentalists, neo-fundamentalists, and rigid conservatives. They claim that evangelicals have bought into the assumptions of modernity with its emphasis on propositions and forced harmony of the Bible. Implied in this claim is that postevangelicals come from an open viewpoint. However, postmodern assumptions pervade their thinking; the presuppositions of postmodernism condition their assumptions. The postevangelical assumption that Scripture must link significantly with tradition and culture as authoritative sources of theology is exceedingly dangerous to its ability to uphold its truth.[242]

Postevangelicals look upon evangelicalism as a particular movement in time, and they deem evangelicals as rooted in modernism (philosophy and science). They see themselves as postmodern; accordingly, they desire to strip evangelicalism from its historical and cultural baggage and adapt it to postmodernism.[243] This theological view wants to retain commitment to the person of Jesus and his generic message. Postevangelicals regard evangelicalism as immature intellectually, and therefore consider it a stifling system. They are suspicious of certainty and have no consistent way to represent the truth of Christianity to the world; they do not want to identify with those who hold to truth with conclusion and clarity. Thus, they have no coherent system of theology or system for knowing truth. (That is, they do not have a systemized epistemology.) It appears they want to move into a system of truth without knowing what it is!

This is unadulterated disaffection and disillusionment with evangelicalism without clear alternative. They languish without coherent understanding of truth because they are adverse to truth and conclusion. Postevangelicals are people without substantive conviction, a transparent difference from evangelicals of the past and many of the present. One thing is patently clear—they want to differentiate themselves from evangelicalism as we know it. With this, they want the Bible to be the normative way they establish faith and community with the people of God. To do this, they must realign the way they interpret Scripture. Interpretation will come out of different perspectives of community by conversation, which is hermeneutical pluralism. The result is that "distance" from the text will produce ambiguities that do not allow for clear distinctions upon which they stand. Postevangelicals must move away from propositions to stories of the Bible on order to justify their argument; their framework is narrative rather than systematic. The narrative approach puts interpretation of text into disjointed fragmentation. Thus, postevangelicals are moving away not only from evangelicals but also from the evangelical way of interpreting Scripture.

If a question admits of any number of plausible and mutually conflicting answers, then there is no certainty and no way to get to certainty. All alternatives are equally true, so we must grant tolerance to all views uniformly. No assertion can claim to be true. Postevangelicals must place all claims to religion on equal footing. There is no valid claim to exclusive truth but simply the perspective that it is "true for me." If this is so, then no Christian should assert that Jesus is "the truth" (John 14:6). In an attempt to move away from the traditional view of what an evangelical is, postconservatives try to avoid the appearance that they hold certainty about something.

We live in a day when postconservatives obscure biblical Christianity with current cultural priorities, whether political, philosophical, or social. On the other hand, true Christianity rests on the foundation of truth uniquely revealed by God. It is sad that evangelicals have now lost trust in the "living and operative" Word of God and have begun a long and relentless slide from biblical truth. Christianity has no message without the starting point of the Word of God; nevertheless, this aberrant form of evangelicalism has lost its biblical identity.

Postevangelicals hail the success of postmodernism and the demise of doctrinal formulation. They want to oust from the market of ideas evangelicals who appeal to Scripture and view Scripture as inerrant. Postconservatives want to formulate doctrine in community and not by individual interpretation; this positions doctrine in the language of community rather than Scripture itself. They rebuff the evangelical view of continuity of Scripture and doctrine. By this, they can accept mutually exclusive beliefs as equally true or, at least, acceptable to their fraternity of ideas.

Roger Olson, a postconservative, wants to distinguish postconservatives from conservatives. Postliberals such as George Lindbeck, with whom Stanley Grenz associated himself, attempt to stiff-arm evangelicals as well. Lindbeck wishes to portray the idea that not all evangelicals are conservative, and to assert that many evangelicals are shedding theological conservatism.[244] Millard Erickson says Stanley Grenz's historical judgments are "deeply tendentious, in need of serious qualification, or simply mistaken."[245] Grenz's attempt to characterize the Reformation or the stance of Puritanism as indifferent in doctrine is specious. He does not want to define evangelicalism within the boundaries of theology or doctrine. In defining evangelicalism by social or historical approaches, he enfolds sundry scholars and movements that, as D. A. Carson says, "no evangelical thinker would have admitted as 'evangelical' a mere half-century ago."[246] Grenz places John Sanders in the evangelical camp, whereas Carson is not sure whether Sanders is evangelical.[247] Wells shows how the term "evangelical" has lost its definitive meaning:

> As evangelicalism has continued to grow numerically, it has seeped through its older structures and now spills out in all directions, producing a family of hybrids whose theological connections are quite baffling: evangelical Catholics, evangelicals who are Catholic, evangelical liberationists, evangelical feminists, evangelical ecumenists, ecumenists who are evangelical, young evangelicals, orthodox evangelicals, radical evangelicals, liberal evangelicals, Liberals who are evangelical, and charismatic evangelicals. The word *evangelical*, precisely because it has lost its confessional dimension, has become descriptively anemic. To say that someone is an evangelical says little about what they are likely to believe (although it says more if they are older and less if they are younger). And so the term is forced to compensate for its theological weakness by borrowing meaning from adjectives the very presence of which signals the fragmentation and disintegration of the movement. What is now primary is not what is evangelical but what is adjectivally distinctive, whether Catholic, liberationalist, feminist, ecumenist, young, orthodox, radical, liberal, or charismatic. It is, I believe, the dark prelude to death, when parasites have finally succeeded in bringing down their host. Amid the clamor of all these new models of evangelical faith there is the sound of a death rattle.[248]

R. Albert Mohler, Jr. makes a telling point regarding the current evangelical identity crisis: "A word that can mean anything means nothing. If 'evangelical identity' means drawing no boundaries, then we really have no center, no matter what we may claim. The fundamental issue is truth . . . there is nowhere else for us to stand."[249]

## Sola Scriptura—Source for Evangelical Identity

Evangelical identity and the authority of Scripture are closely linked. *Sola scriptura* is the formal principle of Christianity that gives direction and framework to all that follows in Christianity. The mutually exclusive Word of God cannot accommodate itself to something that undermines its truthfulness or inerrancy. Those who reinterpret the Bible or neglect the Bible in their notions of reality violate the formal principle. Many reject the absolute truth of the Bible and others go a step further and reject absolute morality. The nature of truth is at stake in doing so.

Stanley Grenz undermines the doctrine of Scripture in the classical evangelical sense, causing Carson to say: "I cannot see how Grenz's approach to Scripture can be called 'evangelical' in any useful sense."[250] The heart of evangelical identity has been *sola scriptura, sola gratia*, and *sola fides*. Mohler identifies the doctrine of Scripture as the foundational truth of evangelicalism:

> An Evangelical Christian is pulled in two directions here. We believe in justification by faith *alone*, and we believe that this doctrine is indeed the *articulus stantis et cadentis ecclesiae* ("the article by which the church stands or falls"). Thus, while we hold without compromise that theology matters, we do not believe that we are saved by theological formulae. But we really do believe that theology matters, and that a sinner must believe that Christ is Savior, and that salvation comes through Christ's work and merits alone. We do not claim to be able to read the human heart—that power is God's alone. We must, on the other hand, evaluate all doctrinal claims—ours and those of others—by a biblical standard of judgment. Evangelicals came to our understanding of justification by faith alone the hard way, and we defend it as central and essential to Christianity itself. This is the doctrine of salvation, the *kerygma*, as preached by the true church.
>
> Without this doctrine, no church is a true gospel church. Many Evangelicals, myself included, remain unconvinced that any consensus on salvation now exists between those who hold to the teachings of the Reformers and those who hold to the official teachings of the Roman Catholic Church. As a matter of fact, the embrace of an inclusivist model of salvation by the Catholic Church at Vatican II (and expanded thereafter) has served to increase the distance between the Evangelical affirmation of salvation through faith *alone* by grace *alone* through Christ *alone* and the official teaching of the Catholic Church. Central to the Evangelical doctrine of justification by faith is faith *in Christ—*

and this faith is a gift received consciously by the believer through the means of the proclamation of the gospel.[251]

Mohler also argues that Roman Catholics, evangelicals, and Orthodox Catholics must concede that their doctrinal disagreements are not incidental but carry significance for eternity. He says that each must have honest disagreement in postmodern culture and irrationality that does not allow difference. The evangelical principle of *sola scriptura* is non-negotiable, whether it is the Roman Catholic understanding of Scripture as interpreted by tradition or the popular evangelical deviation of interpreting Scripture by personal experience.[252]

Mohler further asserts in the same article that evangelicals should stand with Roman Catholics and Orthodox Catholics as "co-belligerents in the culture war" because all three groups believe in transcendent truth. The three together must commit to the unity of truth that they have in common and deny the relativism of postmodernism. They should stand against the postmodern English departments of universities that promote deconstructionism, which declares the text of Scripture to be dead, with the idea that interpretation is up to every reader's perspective.[253]

Criticism against identifying evangelicalism with the Reformation is not valid because it is not merely the defense of the Reformation *per se* that is at stake, but the argument of the book of Romans and other books of the Bible that define the identity of an evangelical. It appears that these critics are long on church history and short on the Bible. It is true that the Reformation was a response to the context of its time, but it is not true that that response was purely historical or cultural.

Another aspect people use to negate the Reformation in defining an evangelical is globalization of missions. The charge is that Western evangelicals carry Western theology arising out of Western culture. The fallacy of this assumption is the idea that Western evangelicals have derived their theology from culture. No doubt, this is true to some degree; however, careful exegesis and exposition does not necessarily imply a Western read on the Bible. It appears that these critics want to reject a concept such as justification by faith alone as somehow Western. No, this charge is a rejection of the Bible itself. There is no need to find a new way to understand the gospel.

The error of postevangelicals is that they assume the fallacies of postmodernism and then reject propositional truth based on that assumption. It is the propositional truths in Romans, for example, that define what an evangelical is. Postevangelicals, in rejecting the propositions of Romans and Galatians, leave evangelicalism itself. They turn into something other than what it means to be an evangelical. They have lost identity with evangelicals and with the idea of the Bible itself.

## Inspiration and Inerrancy—Core Issues of Identity

The issue of whether the doctrine of inerrancy defines an evangelical is crucial. Harold Lindsell, in *The Battle for the Bible,* years ago drew the line on inerrancy as to what in part identifies an evangelical. However, Carl Henry and J. I. Packer contended that inerrancy was an issue of evangelical consistency rather than identity.

The true Christian cannot start anywhere but at the Bible's attestation of itself. Although this is circular reasoning, all systems that approach truth begin at a presupposition of method for finding truth. The skeptic begins with the method of suspicion about coming to any truth at all. The scientist begins by assuming that the physical is all that there is, so one only has to examine the phenomena to come to truth. The philosopher begins with belief that the finite mind can find truth. All these are circular by choosing an independently credible method, the presupposition of an essential *modus operandi* for coming to truth.

The Bible claims for itself "inspiration" in 2 Timothy 3:16. The idea is that God breathed out from his realm into time and space. God took the initiative as the only source of ultimate truth. Biblical inspiration has to do with words (*graphe*—that which is written down concursively), not simply the message. Revelation has to do with the process of getting God's Word into time, but inspiration has to do with the end result of revelation. The Holy Spirit under God's concurrence supernaturally guided the writing of each word of Scripture so that it is without error.

Jack Rogers and Donald McKim, from Fuller Theological Seminary, challenged the inerrancy of Scripture.[254] They consider that the idea of inerrancy was of recent origin theologically. They view the historical position on Scripture as accommodation to human form, so biblical facts might fail but God communicated general ideas of truth effectively. It is generally recognized among scholars that John Woodbridge laid bare their faulty approach to history by showing their selectivity in choosing materials and their use of secondary sources for their own purposes.[255] Even Clark Pinnock (an errantist) concedes that Woodbridge's analysis was right.

Rogers and McKim view themselves as evangelicals like John Calvin, Martin Luther, Gerrit Cornelis Berkouwer, James Orr, C. S. Lewis, Donald Bloesch, and I. Howard Marshall because these figures did not accept the doctrine of factual inerrancy (although they cannot substantiate this claim for Calvin and Luther). Their argument is that, because these figures did not believe in inerrancy yet were accepted within the evangelical camp, why do evangelicals today not accept errantists into the camp?

The issue of inerrancy is a safeguard against inadequate views of Scripture but not a ground for totally negating errantists' identity as evangelicals. It is necessary, therefore, to classify errantists as an aberrant form of evangelical. However, postevangelicals who relinquish the idea that the Bible is totally accurate cannot be classified as clearly with the evangelical camp.

## Correspondent View of Truth—Stability of Identity

Postevangelical postmodernism rejects the correspondent idea of truth—that is, that facts must correspond to assertions in Scripture. They do not define truth in relation to reality but in relation to community or culture: "What is true for you is not true for me." This is blatant rejection of the exclusivity of truth and leads to rejection of objective truth independent of anything else. There are only beliefs and opinions but no independent truth. There is no universal certainty but only "narratives" (worldviews) of perspectives (atheism, Christianity). This makes "truth" relative and makes the self absolute. Tolerance becomes the controlling norm for discernment. Refusal to pass negative judgments has a problem with making judgment on those who hold true beliefs.

Liberals for years have claimed that the Bible contains the word of God but that it is not the Word of God in its words. Some portions of the Bible are sheer cultural expressions, they contend. So-called evangelicals began to adopt this position as indicated by Fuller Seminary professor of theology Paul Jewett in his book *Man as Male and Female.*[256] Jewett believed that Paul imbibed his view of women through rabbinic tradition so that Paul's passages on the submission of women were not the Word of God.

Fuller Seminary launched a committee to investigate Jewett's views, and

> a majority concluded that Jewett was wrong in his interpreta-
> tion of Paul. They also indicated that they believed that Jewett
> was sincere in his subscription to the school's affirmation that
> the Bible is the only infallible rule of faith and practice.[257]

The only way Fuller Seminary could conclude that Jewett could affirm "the Bible as the only infallible rule of faith" was that the seminary itself denied factually inerrant Scripture. It became apparent in later years that Fuller would hold to a coherentist view of inerrancy rather than a correspondent view; that is, the Bible gets its idea across but fumbles in the facts.

## Change View of God and Salvation
## —Loss of Identity in Beliefs

Postevangelicals changed their view of both God and salvation. Clark Pinnock's writings support a belief in a limited God in some sense; that is, God does not know choices men will make in the future.[258] Pinnock thinks that evangelicals embraced an omniscient God through Greek philosophy.

Others no longer believe in justification by faith alone. Some advocate that evangelicals move away from the substitutionary atonement, imputed righ-teousness, and forensic justification by faith alone. They believe we should reject the doctrine of hell and the traditional view of God. Because of this, it is time to draw lines. D. A. Carson gives four reasons for doing so:

(1) truth demands it

(2) the distinction between orthodoxy and heresy models it

(3) the plurality of errors calls for it

(4) the entailments of the gospel confront our culture—and must be lived out[259]

## Differentiating Evangelical Viewpoint from Other Viewpoints —Keeping our Identity

Every "breed of cat" now wants to call itself "evangelical" because evangelicalism has gained a place in North American society. If evangelicals do not define themselves by Scripture, what is their norm for defining themselves? If it is tradition, then evangelicalism will lose itself in the wash of the plethora of viewpoints. If it revolves around *sola scriptura*, then the Word of God defines the evangelical as the legitimate source of truth. Postevangelical authority rests in the church's recognition that the Bible is inspired and thus authoritative, but epistemology based on tradition is tenuous.

Under postmodernism, evangelicalism's desire to be true to the doctrines of the Bible will undergo great pressure, for postmodernism is at heart anti-doctrine. Associated with this is diminished certainty based on the Bible. Postmodern evangelicals look askance upon exposition of propositions of Scripture and question objectivity in Scripture. They challenge truth itself. Postevangelicals view claims of exclusive truth as odd because postevangelicals are subjectivists in approach and thus question the need for teaching or exposition. Pressure for tolerance of other ideas and for openness to aberration put evangelicals into the obscurantist viewpoint. Presentation in propositional form, such as use of *The Four Spiritual Laws*, will become more difficult.

All of these issues create obstacles of communication between truly biblical Christians and non-Christians. Methods of communication that focus on openness to others will get a hearing. The need to help non-Christians see the philosophical assumptions of philosophical tolerance will be imperative. We need to challenge such statements as "I believe everyone has a right to believe what they want" and "How dare you judge what someone else believes?" We need to help non-Christians view truth as more than someone's subjective opinion. They have to see something of the absoluteness of God and therefore the existence of absolute principles for life. They need help in seeing universal truth and that this truth delimits their freedom of ideas. They should see what biblical freedom really means and that true freedom must of necessity involve critique of other viewpoints. A strong conduit to postmoderns is biblical spirituality and integrity of walking with God. They must see how genuine Christianity works in day-to-day life.

Christian leaders who minister to culturally postmodern Christians will undergo a difficult task. Christianity without doctrine will be a vacuous affair. There will be few norms or principles whereby Christians differentiate themselves as biblical believers. People will do what their subjective opinion drives them to do. They will do what is right in their own eyes as long as it is "true for them."

Postmoderns are changing the doctrinal content of evangelicalism because they are caught up in culture; culture dominates their doctrine. Evangelicals are gradually losing their identity by losing commitment to truths of Scripture. The badge of identification is no longer biblical belief but "spiritual experiences." This anti-truth mentality is a desire for assimilation and accommodation to culture. They do not want to be viewed as people at odds with the prevailing ideas of society. The question at hand is, Do we allow culture to set the agenda, or does the Word of God set it?

Old fundamentalism rejected both the good and bad of society because it wanted to set up an antithesis to society, making Christianity distinctive from the world. However, in doing so, fundamentalism developed cultural aberrations and taboos not consistent with biblical truth. It developed a legalistic and biblically distorted separatist worldview. Evangelicals distanced themselves from this viewpoint. Harold Ockenga and Carl Henry made the break from fundamentalism. A new danger came with this change—the old fundamentalists carried hostility to culture but the new evangelicals accommodated assimilation into culture.

Today's evangelicals think they can rush to embrace postmodernism with impunity. By pragmatism they change the transcendent God to an almost immanent god, losing the sense of his majesty. The church loses its message by taking its cues from the world and becomes indistinguishable from the world system. Spiritual dissipation results from such wandering. If this happens, the church will lose its distinctiveness and, thus, its relevance to society and individuals. The church will have little to offer non-Christians.

Postevangelical postmoderns simply formalize what culturally happens in evangelicalism. The prime example of this is Stanley Grenz's writings. According to him, the Christian has three sources for theology: Scripture, tradition, and culture. His adaptation to culture is raw subjectivism and cultural pragmatism.

## Gauging Evangelical Identity

David Wells shows the difficulty in defining an evangelical in the twenty-first century:

> In the 1950s and 1960s, defining evangelical faith was not hard, because evangelicals were anxious to say exactly who they were and what they believed. But in the 1990s, when the movement has become a sprawling empire in which the left hand has no idea that the right hand exists, definitions of who the evangelicals are frequently reflect the movement's disintegration and, on occasion, the special interest of the authors who offer the definitions.[260]

Western Christianity has historically defined an evangelical by the Reformation (sixteenth century); that is, essentially by justification through faith alone. Now some evangelicals want to change the identity of an evangelical to one who does not necessarily believe in justification by faith.[261] Some believe this definition is judgmental and fear mongering.

A complicating factor in evangelical identity is the third-world evangelical perception of what is an evangelical. Third-world Christians deem Western evangelicals to be adherents to individualism and philosophy (rationalism). Many Western evangelicals believe the West is out of touch with post-Christians so they want to redefine what an evangelical is. This could fragment evangelicalism into syncretism, which would cause the movement to lose its identity and doctrinal distinction.

Alister McGrath, in defining six distinguishing doctrines of evangelicalism, leaves out justification by faith.[262] Kwame Bediako draws on history to show that Christianity formed its identity as a reaction to second-century philosophy and that the situation in Africa is not that different from that of the second century.[263] Michael Cooper, of Trinity International University, has moved into postevangelical postmodernism by re-identification with the Christian past and with world Christianity. These arguments are irrelevant to the arguments of Romans and Galatians, which define a believer as someone who is justified by faith. In other words, identifying the evangelical by justification by faith is not a cultural issue but a biblical issue. This issue of discontinuity with false doctrine from other cultures is irrelevant to the Word of God. The *solas* should define evangelicalism (*sola fides, sola gratia, sola scriptura, sola Christus, sola Deo Gloria*).

Use of the term "evangelical" requires responsibility to define the term. It is important to know what it is to be evangelical. Frank Beckwith recently resigned as president of the Evangelical Theological Society because he believed the Roman Catholic Church was more in line with the early church fathers, which he calls "the great tradition."[264] This placed him outside the framework of an evangelical because he no longer believes in justification by faith alone or by grace alone. He said that he still considers himself an evangelical but no longer a Protestant. A key issue for him was that his personal virtue counted for something in justification. He said in a *Christianity Today* interview, "I just think if you hold to a highly cognitive, almost legal model of justification, there is no component for God's grace working out salvation within you."[265] In the *Associated Baptist Press*, he said,

> I became convinced that the Early Church is more Catholic than Protestant and that the Catholic view of justification, correctly understood, is biblically and historically defensible. Even though I also believe that the Reformed view is biblically and historically defensible, I think the Catholic view has more explanatory power to account for both all the biblical texts on justification as well as the church's historical understanding of salvation prior to the Reformation all the way back to the ancient church of the first few centuries.[266]

Evangelicals since the Reformation defined themselves as those who believe in justification by faith alone through Scripture alone. These two doctrines are the irreducible minimum of being an evangelical. If evangelicals lose these two doctrines, they will go down into a bog of accommodation to this world system. Accommodation of truth will take evangelicalism down a very dangerous road in its churches, parachurch movements, denominations, and academies.

We can see the Evangelical Theological Society's commitment to Scripture in their doctrinal statement: "The Bible alone, and the Bible in its entirety, is the Word of God written, and hence free from error in the autographs."[267] However, even this organization—using word games—allows errantists and open theists into their membership. Evangelicals have formally fought for the inerrancy of Scripture for a quarter of a century, since the International Council for Biblical Inerrancy.

Postevangelicals now challenge the two fundamental doctrines as essential to their identity. They apparently want to identify with evangelicals but change the foundation upon which evangelicalism stands. They challenge the idea of propositional, objective truth. All that remains is our own personal, subjective viewpoint on truth. This is a crisis of enormous proportion. Postevangelicals fear the label of intransigence in standing for truth. They value cooperation at the sacrifice of truth because in a postmodern culture it is hubris to claim to have a final answer about anything.

The Bible is the standard by which true evangelicals measure truth. Postevangelicals want to go back to tradition as a measuring stick for the church. Evangelicals have always valued history and tradition, but they never conceded that tradition held any ultimate authority for belief.

Some extremely right-wing evangelicals (fundamentalists) connect present customs with Scripture. This is not an acceptable standard to define evangelicalism. There are differences among fundamentalists, evangelicals, neo-evangelicals, and postconservatives who are so-called evangelicals. We can draw a huge boundary around the first three to separate them from the last. Some postconservatives are no longer evangelicals by the definition of justification by faith alone and by Scripture alone.

David S. Dockery also addresses this subject as editor of *Southern Baptists and American Evangelicals*.[268] Carl F. H. Henry admonishes evangelicals that if they do not answer the issue of what an evangelical is, they will be nothing more than a cult in the wilderness in a secular society with no more significance than the outcast Essenes living in a remote part of Israel near the Dead Sea.[269]

## Inability to Stand on Truth

Postevangelicals are unable to take a stand on truth because they have lost their identity in postmodernism. They guide by consensus of the group, for there is no objective authority that speaks to the group. Rather, the group speaks to authority, even the authority of the Word of God. They yield to the autonomy of the self or group subjectivism. This is the coup of the audience. The listeners are sovereign because they reject objective authority. Their authority is prevailing public opinion. Validation comes from the authority of self and the public. This is what the Bible calls worldliness—conformity to the values of culture and the satanic world system. There is no fundamental or obvious truth. Values find authority in the market. The only right is the right of pluralism, where everyone advances personal perspective. Heaven forbid that anyone study the Word of God in such a fashion as to speak with authority about it. This is apostasy to a therapeutic community of believers. Wells deals with this issue:

> In these three decades [1959–1989], the laity had apparently moved from a doctrinally framed faith the central concern of which was truth to a therapeutically constructed faith the central concern of which was psychological survival. Christian truth went from being an end in itself to being merely the means to personal healing. Thus was biblical truth eclipsed by the self and holiness by wholeness.[270]

Again, Wells shows how evangelicals are losing their identity to culture:

> Therapeutic spiritualities which are non-religious begin to look quite like evangelical spirituality which is therapeutic and non-doctrinal.
>
> These two developments—the emergence of the postmodern ethos and the growing religious and spiritual diversity—are by no means parallel or even complementary but they are unmistakably defining American culture in a significantly new way. And they are defining the context within which the Church must live out its life. Already there are some signs that this engagement with culture is not exactly going the Church's way. It was certainly noticeable that following September 11 the Church was mostly unable to offer any public reading on the tragedy which did anything more than commiserate with those who had lost loved ones. There was virtually no Christian interpretation, no wrestling with the meaning of Evil, little thought about the Cross where Christians contend its back was broken.[271]

The idea behind this is what they deem as universal authority in truth. Because postconservatives have lost their identity in postmodernism, they wallow in the authority of culture, a universal authority in truth. However, not everyone understands the Word of God equally, and not everyone can lead the Christian community equally. Christianity by its very nature is authoritative, and those who have the responsibility of leading it have authority by nature of position, have an inherent grasp of truth, and have ways to deliver that truth to society. Not all viewpoints of evangelicalism are equally valid or true, and thus are not all equally useful. Legitimacy of leadership does not rest in the community but in the objective Word of God.

Evangelicals often distort what "servant leadership" means. They take it to mean lack of leadership, which somehow appears more pious than having authority based on knowledge of the Word of God and a role that comes from God. Biblical leadership involves the right to lead without consulting the prevailing opinion in the evangelical community. True Christian leadership does not put the finger to the prevailing wind. It must at times go counter to culture and counter to prevailing Christian opinion. The Christian leader's responsibility is first to the God of truth and all that he represents. Truth prevails over experience and triumphs over self-ruled faith. Principles of truth via biblical exposition prevail over autonomous opinion. An autonomous faith driven by the desire to kowtow to culture will generate a subjective church without norms for life. It takes a stand on truth to lead properly.

Truth cannot be enslaved to any individual or group. But this is the problem of both evangelicals and postevangelicals—they are held captive by the world system. Christian truth is not a means to an end; it is the end. Truth is the source from which we do ministry. The dominant worldview should never take the Word of God captive; the Word should take the world system captive. Conformity to the world system undermines truth; it does not advance it. As Wells says,

> Without theology, however, there is no faith, no believing, no Christian hope. And the Church's loss of preoccupation with theology goes a long way toward explaining its current weakness: it has inadvertently exchanged the sensibilities of modern culture for the truth of Christ.[272]

## Tolerance—The Controlling Identity

Tolerance is a core belief of postevangelicals, and this belief becomes the controlling norm for discernment. Refusal to pass negative judgments has a problem with making judgment on those who hold true beliefs. Postevangelical authority rests centrally on tradition of the church; an epistemology based on tradition is tenuous.

Under postevangelical postmodernism, desire to be true to the truth will endure great pressure, for postmodernism is essentially anti-doctrine. This philosophy will undermine certainty based on the Bible. Postevangelicals look askance upon exposition of propositions of Scripture. They question objectivity in Scripture. They challenge the certainty of truth itself. These subjectivists view claims of exclusive truth as odd. Pressure for tolerance of other ideas and openness to aberration will put evangelicals into the obscurantist viewpoint. David Wells indicts the evangelical world for accommodating its distinctive identity to the world:

> Without a sharp, cogent, differentiating identity, evangelicals, no less than the Liberals before them, are simply absorbed into the conventions of the modern world in which they live. It is no mystery, therefore, why they are failing to out-think their cognitive opponents. The reason is that they are not that different from these opponents, and the motivation to out-think them is no longer compelling.[273]

Wells calls truth-diminishing evangelicals "amicable partners" with society because they are banishing "theology from its place in the center of evangelical life and relegating it to the periphery," going on to say,

> Behind this banishment is a greatly diminished sense of truth. Where truth is central in the religious disposition, theology is always close at hand. As theology has become dislodged, contemporary evangelicals have become progressively more remote from their forebears in the faith whose courage and fortitude produced the rich heritage of historic Protestant orthodoxy. They are, in fact, now beginning to retread the path that the Protestant Liberals once trod, and they are doing so, oddly enough, at the very time when many of the descendants of the Liberals have abandoned this path because of its spiritual bankruptcy.[274]

Unless evangelicals closely identify with the truth of the Word of God, they will end on the ash heap of subjectivity, uncertainty, and loss of aggressive belief and evangelism.

# *Twelve*

# REACHING THOSE WITHOUT A PLACE TO STAND
## *Reaching Postmoderns*

Many emergent church leaders resist highly polished approaches to evangelism, as in the seeker church movement. They believe their practices are more "authentic" and "other worldly."

Some return to ancient practices of the church past; the late Robert Webber is an example. "The Chicago Call," with theologians Donald Bloesch and Thomas Howard, also attempted to appeal to a form of ancient church history. In 1988 Richard Foster introduced Roman Catholic mystics to Protestants and promoted a mystical approach to evangelicalism. It is interesting that these leaders do not go back to definitive apostolic teachings but to some aberrant teachings of the church flying in the face of the message of the gospel.

Critique of those involved in postmodern methodology is always difficult because the movement is purposefully diverse, curiously amorphous, and constantly in change. It carries no clear uniformity in doctrine, theology, or practice.

Merging postmodernism with the Bible is tricky business. By holding truth claims with suspicion, something has to give; invariably, it is the gospel message itself, especially the certainty and knowledge of truth given by God. Postconservative equivocation is capitulation to postmodernism.

## Postmodern Modalities

The worldview of the emergent church is decidedly postmodern and overwhelmingly uses postmodern modalities. Each message is filtered through that grid.

Some postconservatives hold to deconstruction of the Bible. We cannot know what the author of Scripture meant, they say; the important thing is our experience with it. This guts the Bible of its original meaning.

For Christian postmoderns to be consistent with the absence of unconditional truth in the secular world, they must dispose of biblical unbending truth claims (doctrine). They minimize the idea of an exclusive gospel that exposes the need to deal with sin before God. They replace doctrine and extant statements of the Bible with question and mystery. The reason they want to emphasize these ideas is to move away from certainty and the clarion call of unquestioned truth. Reality for them is mysterious and without clarity. They replace certainty with the elements of dialogue, dialectical thinking, conversation, search, and intrigue as though these ideas were ends in themselves.

The emergent church attempts to frame the gospel message in a way that meets the unique challenges of postmoderns. (This, of course, is a valid issue.) We acknowledge them for addressing this concern. However, accommodating the message itself, rather than only adjusting approach, has allowed uncritical assimilation of postmodern philosophy to seep into the gospel message itself.

Rather than speak a clear gospel message, more radical emergents turn to messages with uncertainty, ambiguity, novelty, mystery, and latitudinarianism masked as "tolerance." They do not want a closed arrangement of truth tied together by facts and logic. Some call for an open theology with room for obscurity. I am not arguing here that messages directed at postmodern types should communicate in a style other than their genre; my concern is solely with what they do to the message.

Gutting the message of its clarity and certainty stands in polar opposite to such passages as Acts 20:28–31 that speak of protecting the church from error in message. Postmodern Christianity holds the message with skeptical negligence and prompts the question as to why we would campaign at all for a message that does not have the crucified Christ at its center. But, then again, that itself is a rigid boundary!

The secular postmodern view is that if nobody is right, then everyone is right. This is pluralistic relativism. Emergent leaders are reluctant to accept this conclusion, but they have not resolved this problem to my knowledge.

Many postconservatives mischaracterize proclamation as a hard, "in-your-face" presentation, as though evangelicals have an "us against them" mentality and are ready to bang the gospel over the heads of their listeners and grab them by their lapels. This obviously is an unfair depiction of how evangelicals actually carry out evangelism. Most evangelicals exercise contextualization in their methods of presenting the gospel.

Some emergents try to set up a dual gospel (both a corporate gospel and an individual gospel); that is, they want to preach a social gospel of the kingdom as well as a gospel to the individual.[275] However, the gospel of the kingdom relates to the nation Israel, to her future as a nation. It has nothing to do with present social justice that seeks to right the ills of national entities. This is a misleading modality that confuses how a person truly comes to Christ and how God will ultimately deal with the world structure.

## Experience Over Truth

Some emergent church thinkers leave rational, systematic thought and logic for experience. This thinking prefers the mystical and spiritual rather than the evidential and fact-based approach. They are high on culture and minimalist on gospel communication. They believe that those under thirty years of age are profoundly spiritual and are interested in religious experience, even mystical experience. They fancy the personal and relational sense of the supernatural. By attraction to mystery, emergents deduce that baby busters and mosaics (those born between 1984 and 2002, who embrace postmodern thinking and are comfortable with contradiction and non-linear thinking) are opposed to the seeker church model (which is oriented to baby boomers). The seeker church meets "felt needs" but the emergent church meets "spiritual experience." Emergents covet the transcendent, and their church services are designed to give them that experience.

Some emergents go so far as to make Scripture only one of the participants in communication of the gospel; because members of the Christian community have an equal role to play through the preaching event, the Bible becomes only one contributor in the communication process.

Yet others simply minimize the gospel so as to mute clear statements of Scripture, even the gospel message itself. Erwin Raphael McManus, pastor of Mosaic

Church in Los Angeles, California, mutes the gospel message by obfuscating the message. He thinks that postmoderns do not care about knowledge or truth.

Communicators of Christianity such as McManus trifle with truth, doctrine, and clarity of the gospel message because they employ a tone of uncertainty about God's declarations. God's Word and gospel knowledge are always pertinent to any presentation of the gospel.

Attempts to trim truth from the postmodern mind have the opposite effect. Wolfhart Pannenberg, a German theologian, warns about those who muddy God's Word:

> The absolutely worst way to respond to the challenge of secularism is to adapt to secular standards in language, thought, and way of life. If members of a secularist society turn to religion at all, they do so because they are looking for something other than what that culture already provides. It is counter-productive to offer them religion in a secular mode that is carefully trimmed in order not to offend their secular sensibilities.[276]

We can see concession to postmodernism's sense of uncertainty about truth in this statement by McManus:

> Are we searching for truth? For God? For clarity? For Life? Together let's abandon the well-worn path of search for truth in the midst of information and even reason. . . . The journey is filled with mystery, uncertainty, wonder, and adventure. To hear the voice and follow is to know him and find little need to know everything else.[277]

Later McManus speaks to his uncertain view of truth:

> We must never allow ourselves to be deluded by our *own sense of accuracy or rightness.* Whatever the culture, era, or generation, it is essential that we examine our practices, rituals, dogmas, and traditions and measure them against God's intent as communicated through the Scriptures (italics mine).[278]

Does this sense of "rightness" carry over to confidence about the gospel itself? Assault on certainty is at the heart of the way some address the issue of postmodernism. This is completely inconsistent with the way God commanded the church to present the gospel; after proper contextualization, God expects us to declare his answer with certitude. At the heart of biblical propositional communication is knowledge that needs to be conveyed. The gospel always conveys truth, and truth requires propositional statements. It is God's method that the Holy Spirit works with the propositions of the gospel message to transform people in Christ.

In postmodern postconservativism, there is a shift away from thinking in generational approaches to ministry and toward grappling with postmodern thought, to the point that the message is lost in the process. Postmodern culture has become so pervasive in the extreme form of emergent methodology that it no longer has a biblical message. As D. A. Carson writes,

> At the heart of the emerging reformation lies a perception of a major change in culture. . . . Is there at least some danger that what is being advocated is not so much a new kind of Christian in a new emerging church, but a church that is *so submerging itself in the culture that it risks hopeless compromise*?[279] (italics mine)

There is no doubt that the church today has to address a radically new culture; Paul wrestled with cultural issues in Antioch and in Athens. However, this does not mean that culture should dominate our thinking as a non-negotiable authority. The gospel cannot be embodied in culture in an unqualified fashion without affecting the message, fear of obsolescence notwithstanding. This is precisely what led pariah liberalism into apostasy. The disaster that fell on the church in the past century was incalculable. Obviously there are discontinuities between then and now, yet postconservativism is a new pariah itself on evangelicalism and evangelism. We need an unadulterated gospel that is biblically driven, not culturally driven, because the gospel is true regardless of culture.

When the gospel resonates with the sound of culture, we lose the gospel in a vague message and the church becomes assimilated by the message of culture; the gospel becomes entrapped in culture. The radical emergent church does not blatantly deny the gospel but rather distorts, downplays, and recasts the gospel for culture. There is little unequivocal presentation of the substitutionary death of Christ. Equivocation of truth ends in captivity to culture.

Christians cannot divorce themselves from culture, but at the same time, they cannot let their message absorb culture. Taking cues from culture is not the same as refusing to proclaim a clear message to a given culture. Our methods should indeed clearly contextualize with the culture of our day.

Because defining culture is far more than taking signals from prevailing thought patterns, there is nothing more relevant for our times than the changeless message and living out that message within culture. Jesus was under no illusion about how his message would affect culture. He warned his disciples not to be surprised if the world would reject and persecute them for their message. People will reject the truth for being the gospel no matter how we culturally contextualize it. That is inescapable. If we do not make the content of the gospel presentation central, we put an evangelistic movement in danger.

Cultural pluralism disavows exclusive truth. With the shriveled sense of truth underlying evangelical life and practice, evangelicalism has little remaining that will withstand this onslaught. Theology remains on the outer edges of church life, and objective truth has been dislodged from the center.

## Dialogue versus Proclamation

Postconservatives prefer dialogue over didactics. The didactic message never changes; culture changes. Postconservative dialectical belief demands dialogue over teaching or communication of fixed truth. The Greek word for examine (συζητέω) means "to seek, to examine together" (Acts 17:2). The Greek word for discuss (διαλέγομαι) means "to speak through, to ponder" (Acts 20:11). Thus, indeed, there is a process, or journey, in these terms. However, there is a vast difference between the meaning of these words and how the emergent church views them. Biblical dialogue always directed the message toward a particular end; it was not endless conversation, narrative, or story. In Acts 17 Paul argued that the Messiah suffered on the cross and rose again, and this was his pre-established conclusion for his dialogue. The Greek word "proclaim" (κηρύσσω) means "to announce like a herald," carrying the idea of authority behind the message (Mark 16:15; Luke 24:47; Romans 10:14, 15; 1 Corinthians 1:21, 22; 2 Timothy 4:2). The Greek word "teach" (διδάσκω) carries the idea of propositional teaching; that is, it is systematic in an organized fashion, presenting knowledge and principles of God's Word (1 Timothy 3:2; 2 Timothy 1:13,

14; 2:2). This word for didactics, with its various cognates, is the key term in the three pastoral epistles (1 and 2 Timothy and Titus). Acts uses this term for communicating the gospel message itself (Acts 5:42). This is doctrine-oriented preaching, propositional preaching. Emergent preachers do not essentially operate within the borders of these words because some of them mute the message and strip it of its content. Most emergent leaders claim fidelity to Scripture but, after they filter the Bible through postmodernism deconstruction, what remains is something unrecognizable from what the Word of God says. On the other hand, the Bible declares with certainty thousands of propositional thoughts.

It is not enough to tell people that God loves them or that they can find that idea by looking within themselves. The heart of the gospel is not solely that God loves people but that God loves them by sending his son to die for their sins. If they never get that message, then there is no gospel presentation. There is nothing more paramount than this when presenting the gospel: "For I decided to know *nothing* among you except Jesus Christ and him *crucified*" (1 Corinthians 2:2, italics mine).

People left to themselves do not have the right judgment to come to God (Romans 1:32), and they carry personal revolt against the light of truth (Romans 2:14, 15). They reject divine revelation, much less some subjective idea of God within themselves. Sin warped their capacity to know God. They are not able to ascertain God's propositions reliably: "But the natural [*pseukekos*: having only a soul but no spiritual capacity] man does not receive the things of the Spirit of God, for they are foolishness to him; nor *can he know them,* because they are *spiritually discerned*" (1 Corinthians 2:14, italics mine).

Exchanging propositional statements of Scripture for doubt and mystery is at the base of this fallacy, which holds that because we cannot know anything for sure, we must embrace mystery. This is why thoroughgoing emergents do not define doctrinal boundaries but prefer a creedless Christianity that puts ethics and ethos above doctrine.

## Propositional Truth versus Mysticism

Erwin McManus juxtaposes Scripture with something more important to him: connection with a living God devoid of the Bible:

> The real issue facing the church is not essentially about methodology
> [I agree] or even the preserving of the message [I disagree—this is a
> major issue of the church]; the real issue is why the church is so unaf-
> fected by the transforming presence of the living God.[280]

How, pray tell, do we know about this "living God" without Scripture? We
cannot know about the love of God in the general revelation of creation. McManus tries to establish some form of living revelation in the person of God apart
from the written Word when he says that "Jesus lives in every time and place in
human history. He both makes himself known and manifests himself through
the body of Christ."[281] True, the Holy Spirit convicts the world of sin, but that
is not the same as contemporary connection to the person of God without the
Bible. He continues:

> We should give up our role as preservationists [his previous definition
> of those who go back to the Bible for primary belief]—the church was
> never intended to be the Jewish version of the mummification of God.
> God is not lost in the past; he is active in the present.[282]

The idea of connecting to a present voice of God apart from propositional revelation is to confuse understanding the principles of the Word of God, applicable
to any generation anywhere, with false experiential engagement with God in the
present, separate from biblical truth. In not accepting the principle and application of Scripture, McManus sets up a false dichotomy by placing Scripture in
opposition to what he sees as the current voice from God.

McManus introduces mysticism as a way to connect to God because his theory
rests on a low view of the adequacy of Scripture. He establishes his thinking on
the "voice of God": "Well, I build my life *not* on the Word of God, but on the
voice of God"[283] (italics mine). He does not believe that the content of Scripture
is the best way to approach people. His idea is the postmodern philosophy of
telling personal stories "through the Scriptures." This method puts forth Scripture as advice-giving material rather than truth to be proclaimed.

Therefore, his attitude toward Scripture leads him into mysticism. McManus
says, "The emerging demands of a pluralistic society informed by Eastern and
not Western culture challenges us to create dramatically different expressions

of our faith."[284] No doubt we need to change "expressions of our faith," but he does so by stepping into the falsity of mysticism. He believes that an "elemental essence" will reach a generation without belief in biblical content (propositions of Scripture) and that somehow this will "open the eyes of the world to the reality of God evident in all of creation."[285] But it is the gospel message itself, not a subjective or mystical experience, that "is the power of God unto salvation" (Romans 1:16). McManus joins together the ideas of truth as the personal and the mystical.[286] Propositions represent truth or falsehood. Irrationalism talks of inner meaning without propositions. Non-propositional inner meaning has no meaning at all. Knowledge always consists of propositions, of predicates related to subjects. There is no basis for revelation as non-propositional, personal truth.

There is a direct correlation between mysticism and experience. Some postmodern evangelicals falsely view the old paradigm as claiming that, if you have the right teaching, you will experience God. Their new paradigm is that if you experience God, you will have the right belief. This is a movement in search of experience, not truth. Experience based on experience is a mirage. There is a proper place for experience, but that is only under the principles of the Word.

McManus wants to exchange reason (doctrine) for mysticism. In an interview with *Relevant Magazine*, McManus explained the "core" of his book *The Barbarian Way*: "So, I think *Barbarian Way* was my attempt to say, 'Look, underneath what looks like invention, innovation and creativity is really a *core mysticism* that hears from God, and what is fuelling this is *something really ancient*'"[287] (italics mine).

Again, in *The Barbarian Way* he writes: "We may find ourselves uncomfortable with this reality; but the faith of the Scriptures is a *mystical faith*. It leads us beyond the material into an *invisible reality*. . . . We are *mystic warriors* who use weapons not of this world"[288] (italics mine).

Mysticism dominates emergent thought. Overemphasis on experience in theology and "what works for me" in ethics is the underlying fallacy that drives mysticism. Subjective religion or religious consciousness becomes the source and standard for religious ideas. This is faith without doctrine, a faith that cuts its ties with its object. All that is left is a body of subjective opinions in which one is as good as another. All that remains is window dressing and externals.

If we leave it to the subjective, how do we know whether our mysticism is from God or is demonic? Maybe it exclusively rests in the psychological. Without information from God giving boundaries to our experience, we end in no-man's land. Apart from cognitive information, we cannot know that it is God who speaks. All subjective, experiential approaches to God lead to skepticism and away from valid knowledge of God.

The Bible is essentially propositional revelation formed in cognitive truths by sentences. Scriptures are a body of information expressed in propositions. Thus, the Bible is propositional revelation about God's truth. This self-disclosure reveals God's person and work, his thinking itself; this is supernatural information. This knowledge is far more important than subjective human experience. All extra-verbal communication from God in the Bible belongs only to revelation (closing of the canon).

McManus's "voice of God" speaking in mysticism is very dangerous, especially with his minimalist approach to Scripture and the gospel. Believing we interpret the voice of God by what we experience or feel, his view devolves into unadulterated subjectivism.

## Implications for Evangelistic Ministry

If evangelistic ministries push in the direction of postmodern evangelicals (who demean doctrine and minimize truth and the gospel), where is the protection against heresy, the anchor for doctrinal stability, and the guide to sound interpretation of Scripture? Where is the clarity and certainty of the gospel? If we marginalize, neglect, or reject truth, this will lead to a vacuous ministry at best and an organization that enters into error at worst. This is why truth-friendly emergent leaders, who do not minimize or negate truth, hesitate to identify with the more radical emergent church of postconservatives.

Do ministries want to identify with those who carry enormous skepticism over whether the biblical text and words accurately convey meaning? If we buy into the idea that all texts are constructions of meaning, we negate our message, or at least the power of the gospel. In the end, emergent thinking jettisons truth, doctrine, and gospel. Gospel presentations become more about cultural norms used to transport the message than about the gospel content itself. In the end, we lessen the gospel. This is what missiologists call "nominalism"; the norms surrounding the gospel take the place of the gospel itself. Biblically, the gospel never changes. The creed of being without a creed ultimately becomes self-defeating.

This is why postconservatives emphasize "authenticity." Authenticity to them means that we do not have sure answers about truth. They put priority on doubt, differences, and difficulties. This is contrary to the heart of Christianity, with its clear denotations of truth. We cannot revise a faith "once for all delivered to the saints" (Jude 3). No one quibbles with the idea that we are to live out our faith in an authentic way. Either we find authenticity in the Word or we do not. Either the Bible is authentic (that is, true in its propositions, not subject to revision) and we need to be transformed, or the Bible is not authentic—in which case we should cast it off on the garbage heap of falsity. It is also imperative that we live out the principles of the Word authentically.

To place emphasis on the construction of meanings of our own choosing causes us to dilute the gospel in a strikingly subjective appropriation. It is a short step from the constructability of meaning to the constructability of truth itself. This has far-reaching implications on presentations of the gospel. Emergents are more anxious to affirm what culture affirms, but in doing so they change the gospel from a message to a way of life. This changes the truth of the gospel itself and is a repeat of the liberal Friedrich Schleiermacher's attempt to save the Bible from the Enlightenment by conflating description with prescription; he abandoned doctrine for metaphysics and read the gospel off the cultural milieu. Among postconservatives there is little answerability to either the Bible or tradition, as Mark Devine points out in *Evangelicals Engaging Emergent*:

> The ease with which some Emergents equivocate on an array of traditional readings of Scripture and either question the use of doctrine or abandon doctrine altogether is astounding. . . . Emergent thinkers are much more likely to argue that our actual comprehension of the gospel itself must change in a postmodern world. Thus, the Synoptic Gospels and parenetic passages come to rule the hermeneutical roost, while the apostle Paul with all his head-heavy theologizing becomes marginalized, and objective views of the atonement are displaced with subjective ones.[289]

Doctrine-friendly emergents are growing unreceptive to the doctrine-wary movement because, although they agree that communication to culture affects the conveyance of meaning, they want to reach their culture effectively with the true gospel. Ministries that equivocate truth will lose one of their greatest assets—the confidence of the general evangelical community that they are faithful to the gospel and trustworthy in its methods.

## Direct Evangelism

A wonderful feature of dynamic evangelistic ministries has been direct evangelism. Are these ministries now going to develop a new kind of "patience" before they present the gospel? The gospel delayed is the gospel denied. By insisting on building a context of idiosyncratic personal spirituality before they present the gospel, they introduce unnecessary complications into evangelism. Pre-evangelism is important, but pre-evangelism without direct appeal to the gospel at some urgent point is pointless. The gospel in its least common denominator is not culture, spirituality, or morality; it is acceptance of the finished and saving death of Christ for our sins. Unduly delayed evangelism will take the urgency, felicity, and movement out of spreading the good news.

There is no mandate in Scripture to be politically or culturally correct. Acquiescing to the world system without Christian distinctives undermines the power of the gospel. We cannot tolerate diversity to the point that we are not distinct or "peculiar," as 1 Peter says. We need not fear rejection of the gospel message by the crowd.

Ministries must test both the message and method by Scripture. Neither the Bible nor its content is some arcane book of mystery. The gospel is patently clear. We do not need to displace the text of Scripture with "story" (not that story is without validity). God's revealed truth is objective in the sense that truth is a correspondence, or a matching up, of a proposition with how things are in reality, regardless of whether anyone believes that proposition to be true. Although Christianity is more than proposition, it is not less. As Devine again says, "Emergent talk of narrative, authenticity, story, and mystery often seems to involve radical forms of retreat and reductionism vis-à-vis anything recognizable as historic, biblically grounded Christianity."[290]

Do forceful evangelistic ministries want their staff to be spineless communicators of the gospel message without boldness to proclaim the truth of the gospel itself? Will these ministries abandon presentation of the claims of Christ in propositional form? Will they avoid event presentation of the gospel altogether? Will they enter relationship building to the point where they only vaguely present the gospel somewhere, somehow down the line?

The biblical approach to evangelism is always proactive first, not reactive first. Contextualization without proclamation voids God's message. Evangelism is never less than proclamation of the propositions that Jesus died in the place of our sins and that by faith in his work we have forgiveness of sins.

## Say Something

The postconservative approach to evangelism is not to persuade people to believe promises from God but to befriend people to join a Christian community. Because they assume that there is little certainty in what we believe, they ask people to come to dialogue. For them, there is no need to choose between belief systems. However, the biblical approach is to use words, and words or propositions divide; propositions challenge people to choose. The Thessalonians proclaimed words from God to such a point that the apostles did not have to "say" anything: "For not only has the word of the Lord sounded forth from you in Macedonia and Achaia, but your faith in God has gone forth everywhere, so that we need not say anything" (1 Thessalonians 1:8 ESV).

There is an imperative to "say" something about the gospel to effectively present our message. All rejection of propositional preaching with certainty is against the many passages challenging us to proclaim a clear message.

The Bible says that the world is in darkness and under the "dominion of Satan" (Acts 26:15–20; John 3:19). No unilateral understanding by the non-Christian can come to knowledge of truth without proclamation of the gospel in words (1 Corinthians 2:14). Satanic deception preempts the postconservative methodology because non-Christians do not seek God due to the darkness of their hearts (John 3:19). Truth set forth in the conviction of the Holy Spirit and by words of the gospel frees people from darkness in their hearts (John 8:31, 32).

## Different Paradigms

The postconservative movement eviscerates the dynamic of evangelism because it rips the heart out of burning conviction to share the gospel. No longer do postconservatives have confidence in the message, believe in hell, or know for sure that one stands vindicated before God eternally. The essence of the post-modern movement is the negation of certainty, yet it is certainty that is the catalyst for flaming conviction to present the gospel.

Dean Kelley, an official of the liberal National Council of Churches and a United Methodist minister, wrote the book *Why Conservative Churches Are Growing.*[291] His answer is that they believe the Bible and the gospel with conviction. The more truth people believe, the more commitment they have to evangelism in their church, and the more congregants are willing to give and serve sacrificially for what they believe about God's Word. But today, more-radical emergent leaders simply invite their people to casually connect to their religious communities. By this principle they build their approach to postmoderns, which is in part a concession to relativism. No wonder their people are allergic to sharing the message.

Liberals tried to accommodate their message to the prevailing philosophy of a previous day. They yielded to modernism's idea that the self was the starting point for finding truth—man is the measure of man. This led to anti-supernaturalism, rejection of miracles, and an undermining of the Bible itself. The institutions of the church became so doctrinally corrupt that evangelicals left these organizations in massive numbers and formed their own ministries. When liberalism infected the church in the later part of the nineteenth and first half of the twentieth centuries, church attendance dwindled to a few faithful souls huddled together in hollow, large church caverns. A biblical, vibrant church then rose out of the ashes of the corrupted apostate institutions and denominations of liberalism. It is patent that churches with conviction about truth grow, and those with weakened conviction decline. Conservative churches grew in numbers, sent missionaries, believed truths of the Bible with burning conviction, and advanced vibrant church life.

Postconservatives now follow the same trail as old liberalism. They are in a reversion from universal, objective truth to a personal view of truth (as we saw with McManus, earlier). They have low tolerance for anyone who claims to have the doctrinal truth or has deep conviction about truth.

Postconservatives believe that certainty about almost anything is futile palaver. They limit truth to communal or personal perception. All communication is limited, insular, and particular. They are left with personal preference and personal experience. This view of truth stands in stark contrast to a biblical worldview that pivots around the existence of a God who reveals himself in propositional revelation. The postconservative belief system has a serious, negative impact on aggressive evangelism.

Modernists place trust in objective philosophy and science, but postmoderns put significance on subjective understanding. Postmoderns ask whether "it is true for me" and care little about what "is true for you." They hate judgment or conclusion about almost anything and view judgment as intolerance. Their only intolerance is intolerance itself; therefore, tolerance becomes an all-pervasive belief system. Postevangelicals sacrifice the true message of the gospel to meaningless pluralism.

## Approaches to Postmoderns

Indeed postmodern cultural conditions make proclamation of truth difficult. However, rejection of exclusive trust in philosophy and science by non-Christian postmoderns is an advantage for evangelism because it opens the possibility of supernatural truth as a valid option. Philosophy and science are no longer autonomous and self-sufficient to the postmodern as they were with the modernist. Postmodernism undermines the presupposition that scientific materialism is autonomous; there is, therefore, something more than pure mechanism. This affords a wonderful opportunity to present the supernatural claims of the Bible.

Robert Webber believes that postmodern people are "not persuaded to faith by reason as much as they are moved to faith by participation in God's earthly community."[292] Community oriented "belief" is unadulterated ambivalence devoid of truth. Of course postmoderns are offended by truth as people were in Jesus' and Paul's day. There is an offense in the gospel, but this is exactly what postconservatives are trying to avoid. They can evade offense only by betrayal of truth. This presumes that somehow people will accept Christ by subjective experience rather than proclamation of the gospel. This muddles doctrine and mixes the objective gospel with subjective experience. A functional view of truth cannot perceive truth objectively but only subjectively.

Churches that offer spirituality without truth also betray the gospel. These churches reduce Christianity to idiosyncratic approaches and neglect powerful presentations of the Word. With this, we now have relationships without biblical principles for building relationships. These churches do not deem truth indispensable or effective in reaching postmoderns.

Another approach denies the need to change the method or the message to reach postmoderns. It says we can use the same methods used for reaching any other people at any other time. Thus, by simply presenting the message, people will come to Christ. Those who employ such an approach care nothing about how culture affects presentation of the gospel, but even the apostle Paul contextualized his method when approaching different people (1 Corinthians 9).

Postmoderns try to live without authority, so all that remains is their autonomous liberty whereby they must build their own construct for living. It is a disconnected and lonely philosophy without ultimate purpose or meaning. All that remains are communities of conflicting personal beliefs. Postmoderns place high value on freedom and want to live their lifestyles as they see fit without judgment or interference. They feel they have the right to hold any religious belief they choose. How then can biblical believers reach out to postmoderns if we accept their premises?

Surrendering the authority of biblical interpretation to individual subjective viewpoints will reduce God's Word to the personal preferences of autonomous man. That will invariably lead to radical pluralism and denial of the objective truth of Scripture. It will neuter the idea of a demand for repentance (Acts 17:30). All truth is not equal. Neither is it a tyrannical claim independent of reason.

Postmodernism changed the ground of debate in ministry today. Because non-Christians have given up the pursuit of finding truth with a clear worldview, how can evangelicals present the gospel message to them? There is a profound sense of despair out there. However, this affords a unique opportunity to present our wonderful good news.

The Bible accepts the reality that the unbelieving will view mutually exclusive truth of Christianity as "foolishness" (1 Corinthians 1:18, 23). This passage says that unbelievers deem the message, not the act of communication, as foolish. Jesus said that people would reject truth for vested interest in their dark lifestyles (John 3:19, 20). Christians should operate under no illusion that postmoderns will not hate them for claiming mutually exclusive truth (John 15:18; 16:2; 17:14). Many evangelicals would rather sacrifice truth for acceptance in society.

If we have enough gall to assert that Christ is the answer, that implies we are conveyors of truth. We cannot pretend that the Bible does not claim exclusive truth. Instead of flinching from God's truth, we should have confidence in its power.

> *For the word of God is living and powerful, and sharper than any two-edged sword, piercing even to the division of soul and spirit, and of joints and marrow, and is a discerner of the thoughts and intents of the heart. And there is no creature hidden from His sight, but all things are naked and open to the eyes of Him to whom we must give account.* (Hebrews 4:12, 13)

If we use pure Socratic method, people cannot come to the didactic message of the Bible. We must introduce didactics or we will not be able to share a clear message from God. The proclamation of the truth of God's message stands at the heart of evangelism.

## Courage to be Different

Contrary to popular opinion, evangelicalism grows by fearless conviction about the gospel rather than by accommodating the message to culture. Postconservatives value syncretism rather than the courage to be different. This attempt to make disparate beliefs similar will take the passion out of sharing the gospel. Christianity cannot grow without clear differentiation. There can be no battle for truth or souls without it. In this day when Christians are afraid to take a stand on the certainty of what they believe, evangelism is in grave danger of losing momentum.

Most approaches to reach postmoderns are about methodology or acculturation, not content of the gospel. Without content to believe, all talk of methodology and culture is empty. Without a solid biblical message, postmodern postconservativism wanders about aimlessly. It has sold its birthright for a bowl of cultural strategy. A message of truth by its very nature is confrontational, albeit in a kind and civil way. It challenges the validity of other belief systems, and especially the belief system that truth is entirely a private matter. It asserts the reality of heresy and apostasy. It will confront the idea that what is true for one might not be true for another.

The Bible does not allow for local truth, truth to a particular situation or culture. Truth is more than private perception; it is communication of the gospel with sufficient clarity that people can understand it. Subjective non-Christian postmoderns will accept certainty moved on their hearts by the Holy Spirit.

The Bible is not subject to endless change in interpretation; its interpretation does not rest in the individual psyche but is objective to the interpreter. The Word of God corresponds to what is real. Confrontation against what is not true is essential for a mutually exclusive message, but how we deliver that message is another matter. It is important to challenge people from their volitionally positive side (1 Corinthians 9); we approach people on their approachable side.

Even with this, postmodernism is not a neutral belief system operating on an arrangement of preference. It is a belief based on anti-Christian ideas, ideas that presume we cannot come to final certainty about the gospel.

All belief systems, even postmodernism, have a worldview. That worldview is subject to challenge and to comparison with Christianity. If we submerge Christianity into postmodernism, where is its distinctiveness? Where is its message? Is our message certain enough, separate enough, to strike non-Christians as a message of objective truth? Christianity cannot concede to pagan thinking.

At the heart of evangelism is a conviction that one holds truth as over against other claims. If evangelicals move into pluralism to the point that they cannot assert a metanarrative, or final answer, then they have no adequate message for those without Christ. They are left to wallow in subjectivity and uncertainty. This has far-reaching implications for evangelism.

The Christian assignment is to move the unbeliever from the view that there is no final meaning but only continuous interpretation to a belief in absolute truth, and from the belief that the individual is the final arbiter of truth to understanding the objective truth of the Word. We need to help them see beyond their cynicism to witness normative truth. They must do that in order to see that the secular viewpoint has heavy-laden assumptions (presuppositions) and that those assumptions carry loss of truth, meaning, and worth. The idea that the self is constantly in flux and without point or purpose needs to be seen for what it is.

## A Difficult Challenge

The most difficult challenge for evangelicals is our claim to exclusive truth. Postmoderns view such claims as oppression. At the heart of this problem is the autonomy of human beings who situate themselves as independent from an absolute God. Individuals deem themselves as final arbiters of truth. If that is so, they have no true place to stand.

Because postmoderns have a severe problem with certainty, they can know nothing for sure, making their despair protrude more than ever. Rejection of the Christian message is not an answer for those who desperately stand in need of truth; rather, acceptance of the Christian message is the answer for people who wallow in the despair of hopelessness. Although postmoderns are open to spirituality, it is a non-biblical spirituality that we can correct only by definitions from biblical propositions of truth.

The issue of message versus strategy is very difficult to balance. What is the justification for pre-evangelism? At what point does pre-evangelism come to assert an unambiguous message? All evangelism methodologies have some form of contextualization, but contextualization without message is a serious problem. If we have method without message or only a modest message, then we are not true to our mandate of preaching the gospel.

## Passion for Souls

Passion for souls comes from passion for truth. Evangelical fervor to reach those without Christ minus passion for truth will ultimately diminish passion for souls. Bankruptcy of belief produces bankruptcy of passion. One area that unites evangelicals is the call to world evangelism. If this call to evangelism does not rest on the conviction of a valid gospel, then no other motivation will support that conviction.

Evangelistic organizations grow by deep conviction that the gospel is true. For a movement to establish momentum, there must be (1) a widespread conviction of belief among believers, (2) a universally held goal among them, and (3) an *esprit de corps* (passion about the wonder of the gospel) that catalyzes the goal. Because evangelicalism has lost its passion for the gospel message, it is losing its goal of world evangelism. The *esprit* must have more than just a desire to evangelize; there must be a compelling reason to evangelize. The evangelical movement is losing its core of conviction and is fragmenting into a plurality of convictions. Wells points to this loss of core conviction among evangelicals:

> When we believe in nothing, we open the doors to believing anything. And the same is true within the precincts of Christian faith. As the body of common belief has shrunk and the importance has diminished within the evangelical world, there have arisen advocates for almost everything within the larger religious world. Who would have thought, for example, that *Christianity Today* would carry a proposal for the remaking of evangelical faith that scuttled one of the cardinal beliefs of the Protestant Reformation—justification by faith?[293]

Evangelical organizations such as Campus Crusade for Christ (with its rallying cry of "building spiritual movements everywhere") have made a huge, worldwide impact for the gospel. The reason for this is the burning conviction of their staff about the gospel. The catalyst for their evangelism is the conviction that they have the truth. This dynamic is not a tool such as *The Four Spiritual Laws* but rather the persuasion that Jesus is the only answer for eternal salvation, and it is the reason that tens of thousands have joined CCC staff. In other words, evangelicals trace their conviction to truth, not to tradition or personal experience or personal preference.

# *Conclusion*

Christians who fear that their message is not civil or irenic will negate the message. We cannot allow so-called undue civility, or irenic approach, to displace the gospel. Unadulterated civility is a code word for assault on the message. God ties salvation closely with clarity of the gospel. It is a false dichotomy to claim that God is not "generous" if he claims specificity in the way of salvation. Was Paul civil to Peter when he rebuked Peter "before them all?" Were scores of writers of the Bible uncivil when they rebuked false teaching? I think they were true to truth and not to prevailing opinion.

With so many evangelicals becoming happily uncertain about what they believe, it will not be long before we see significant decline of Christianity in the Western world. Evangelicals must awaken to the fact that this "uncertainty" is nothing more than unadulterated unbelief. It is a new wave of skepticism placing a pall on evangelicalism.

Self-styled, avant-garde evangelicals try to pawn off the idea that this new uncertainty is a new development, but it is simply old unbelief. These people are introducing skepticism in the name of reaching postmoderns.

It is one thing to use the postmodern method to reach postmoderns, but it is another thing to deny the gospel message by inference, which is denial of the faith cloaked in religious disguise. That disguise comes in the form of a phony humility that states we cannot have the arrogance to be certain about what we believe. Postconservatives fail miserably in coming to "sound doctrine" because their "itching ears" want to find some new truth.[294] Ever in protracted dialogue, they cannot come to finality of truth. Because they cannot come to final truth, they cannot present it with certainty.

Obviously, there is no place for an obnoxious approach to non-Christians. Peter says that we are to present the gospel with "meekness and fear" (1 Peter 3:15). Meekness is in-wrought grace. It is a sense of humility that we ourselves need the gospel. This has to do with treating others with a graceful attitude.

Christians should not look down their self-righteous noses at non-Christians. We cannot win people with a sense of arrogance. "Fear" means "respect, reverence." We respect perspectives of non-Christians.

Josh McDowell, in his 2005 commencement address to Dallas Theological Seminary, said that ninety-one percent of professing born-again, church-attending youth assert that there are no absolutes.[295] That figure was up from fifty-two percent in 1991, sixty-two percent in 1994, and seventy-eight percent in 1999. Of the ninety-one percent in 2005 "sixty-five percent of these same young people also say that we cannot know whether any religion is true or not, including Christianity. And today, fewer than four percent of these youth agree that the Bible is the infallible Word of God and true in every situation."[296]

Such erosion of Christianity will increase with postevangelical belief. Instead of facing down relativism with a counterculture position on absolutes, postevangelicalism caves into current culture, weakening our youth further. There is a great need to return to biblical Christianity, a Christianity that proclaims the objective, absolute truth of Christianity. Obviously, evangelicals should recognize the reality of postmodernism and develop strategies that will reach postmoderns, but this does not presume that we must believe their message to reach them with our message.

Certainty is essential for a passionate message. Otherwise, we are just passionate about passion. Let's accept for ourselves Paul's challenge to Timothy to protect the "pattern of sound words": "Hold fast the pattern of sound words which you have heard from me, in faith and love which are in Christ Jesus. That good thing which was committed to you, keep by the Holy Spirit who dwells in us" (2 Timothy 1:13, 14).

# Endnotes

1    [1] Brian McLaren, *A Generous Orthodoxy,* 293.

2    [2] Ibid., 198.

3    I highly recommend the book *Heresies: Heresy and Orthodoxy in the History of the Church* by Harold O. J. Brown (Peabody MA: Hendrickson Publishers, 1998).

4    One of the major writers on postconservatism is Roger E. Olson, *Reformed and Always Reforming: The Postconservative Approach to Evangelical Theology* (Grand Rapids, MI: Baker Academic, 2007). A conservative response to Olson is the book *Reforming or Conforming?* by Gary L. W. Johnson and Ronald N. Gleason (Wheaton, Il: Crossway Books, 2008).

5    *Evangelicals Engaging Emergent: A Discussion of the Emergent Church Movement* (Nashville TN: William D. Henard and Adam W. Greenway, eds., B & H Publishing Group, 2009) is a fair and balanced critique of the emergent idea in the evangelical church.

6    Brian McLaren's book *The Secret Message of Jesus—Uncovering the Truth That Could Change Everything* (Nashville: W Publishing Group, 2006) deals with this subject.

7    R. Albert Mohler, Jr., back cover of *Reclaiming the Center: Confronting Evangelical Accommodation in Postmodern Times,* by Millard J. Erickson, Paul Kjoss Helseth, and Justin Taylor, (Wheaton: Crossway Books, 2004).

8    Millard J. Erickson, Paul Kjoss Helseth, and Justin Taylor, 17.

9    McLaren, *A Generous Orthodoxy,* 19–20, 22–23.

10   David F. Wells, *No Place for Truth: Or Whatever Happened to Evangelical Theology?,* 104.

11   David F. Wells, *Above All Earthly Pow'rs, Christ in a Postmodern Word,* 265.

12   This is the issue of epistemology or the theory of knowing.

13   Brian McLaren in his book "*A New Kind of Christian*" (Jossey-Bass, 2001) undermines much of evangelicalism. It is what I call postevangelicalism because it is no longer evangelical.

14   Rationalism—the methodology that reason unaided by revelation can come to truth.

15   Wells, No place for Truth and God in the Wasteland: The Reality of Truth in a World of Fading Dreams (Grand Rapids: Eerdmans Publishing Co, 1994).

16   In his first chapter Bob DeWaay in *The Emergent Church: Undefining Christianity* (Saint Louis Park, IL: Bethany Press International, 2009) says that emergent church thinkers can be traced back to Jurgen Moltmann, and his thinking goes back to dialectical presuppositions. Some of these emergent disciples of Moltmann are Barry Taylor, Dwight J. Friesen, and Stanley Grenz. In chapter

nine DeWaay shows that Ken Wilber is the source for the emergent idea. Wilber roots his ideas in dialectical thought. It is striking that Wilber is a pantheistic Buddhist. His ideas are neo-pagan. McLaren reveals in Chapter 19 of *Generous* that Wilber had significant influence on him.

17    Contrary to popular thinking, Georg Wilhelm Friedrich Hegel did not believe in the dialectic model of "thesis, antithesis, synthesis." Gustav E. Mueller made this clear in "The Hegel Legend of 'Thesis-Antithesis-Synthesis,'" in *The Journal of the History of Ideas* (June 1958). Winfried Corduan also concurred with this understanding in "Transcendentalism: Hegel" in *Biblical Errancy, An Analysis of its Philosophical Roots*, Norman L. Geisler, ed. (Zondervan, 1981). Thanks to Drs. William E. Nix and Norman L. Geisler for calling my attention to this faulty understanding of Hegel.

18    Truth is not fixed but is constantly open to a new antithesis, which in turn forms a new thesis, which again forms a new thesis. Truth is always on the move; no one can find it for sure.

19    McLaren, "Emerging Values," *Leadership Journal* (Summer 2003), http://www.christianitytoday.com/le/2003/summer/3.34.html

20    Ibid.

21    Wells, *No Place for Truth*, 135.

22    Obviously, many verses describe the trinity or imply the trinity.

23    Most of society is not philosophically postmodern, but it is culturally postmodern. In other words, people do not know why they are postmodern but they accept the prevailing opinion.

24    This is what is called the *a posteriori* approach to truth. It is an inductive approach. However, if mankind is finite, there is no possibility of coming to an infinite truth because one would have to examine all reality of all time, both potential and actual, qualitatively and quantitatively equally. The only hope for certainty or absolute truth is an *a priori* approach.

25    That is, a presupposition. A presupposition is the most foundational, basic belief one has for finding truth.

26    "Americans Are Most Likely to Base Truth on Feelings," (February 12, 2002) www.barna,org.

27    David F. Wells, *Losing Our Virtue* (Grand Rapids: William B. Eerdmans Publishing Co, 1998), 3.

28    They are dialectical in method.

29    Note the writings of the recently deceased Robert E. Webber.

30    Erickson, Helseth, and Taylor, *Reclaiming the Center*, 53.

31    Stanley Grenz, *Renewing the Center: Evangelical Theology in a Post-Theological Era*, (Grand Rapids: Baker, 2000), 245.

32    D. A. Carson, "Faith a La Carte," *Modern Reformation Magazine* (July/August 2005, Vol. 14): 4.

33    Ibid.

34    Leonard Sweet, Brian D. McLaren, and Jerry Haselmayer, *A is for Abductive: The Language of the Emerging Church,* (Grand Rapids: Zondervan, 2003) 31.

35    D. A. Carson, *Becoming Conversant with the Emerging Church,* (Grand Rapids: Zondervan, 2005) 104–105.

36    Webber, *The Younger Evangelicals* (Grand Rapids, Baker Books, 2002) 68.

37    Ibid., 48, 49, 52, 185, 199.

38    McLaren, *Generous Orthodoxy,* Footnote, 147.

39    Ibid., 290.

40    Ibid., 291.

41    Ibid.

42    Ibid., 260.

43    Ibid.

44    Ibid., 291.

45    Ibid., 293.

46    Ibid., 293–294.

47    Ibid., 294.

48    Ibid., 295.

49    Ibid., 294, 295.

50    Ibid., 297.

51    Millard J. Erickson, Paul Kjoss Helseth, Justin Taylor (editors); *Reclaiming the Center* (Wheaton: Crossway Books, 2004), chapter by Stephen J. Wellum, *Postconservatism, Biblical Authority, and Recent Proposals for Re-Doing Evangelical Theology: A Critical Analysis* (Wheaton: Crossway Books, 2004) 192.

52    McLaren, *Generous Orthodoxy,* 278.

53    Ibid., footnote 282.

54    Ibid.

55    Ibid., 285.

56    Ibid., 286.

57    Ibid.

58    Ibid., 287.

59    Ibid.

60    Ibid., 289.

61    Ibid.

62    Ibid., 290.

63    Ibid., 290, 291.

64    McLaren, *Generous Orthodoxy*, 290.

65    Ibid.

66    Ibid., 291.

67    Ibid., 28, 29.

68    Ibid., 29.

69    Wells, *No Place for Truth*, 96.

70    Ibid., 117.

71    Ibid., 127, 128.

72    Ibid., 129.

73    Ibid., 130.

74    Ibid., 131.

75    Ibid., 188–189.

76    Ibid., 132.

77    Daniel Taylor, *The Myth of Certainty* (Grand Rapids: Zondervan, 1992).

78    D. A. Carson, *The Gagging of God* (Grand Rapids: Zondervan, 1996) 35.

79    Millard J. Erickson, *The Evangelical Left: Encountering Postconservative Evangelical Theology* (Grand Rapids: Baker, 1997) p. 86.

80    McLaren, *A Generous Orthodoxy*, 133.

81    Ibid., 133.

82    Ibid., 133–134.

83    Ibid., 134.

84    Ibid., 136.

85    Ibid.

86    Ibid., 294.

87    The battle is between the coherent view of truth and the correspondent view. (Facts must correspond to truth asserted.)

88    Dialectical reasoning.

89    R. Albert Mohler, Jr., "Standing Together, Standing Apart: Cultural Co-belligerence Without Theological Compromise," *Touchstone: A Journal of Mere Christianity*, (July/August, 2003) http://touchstonemag.com/archives/article.php?id=16-06-070-f.

90     Wells, *No Place for Truth,* 66.

91     Grenz, *Renewing the Center.*

92     Wells, *No Place for Truth*, 101.

93     Ibid., 259–60.

94     Grenz, *Renewing the Center,* 242.

95     McLaren, *A Generous Orthodoxy*, 19–20.

96     Ibid..

97     Ibid., 30.

98     Ibid., 198.

99     Ibid.

100   Ibid., 210.

101   Ibid.

102   Ibid., 24.

103   Ibid.

104   Ibid., 23.

105   Ibid., 210.

106   Carson, *Becoming Conversant with the Emerging Church*, 234.

107   McLaren, *Generous Orthodoxy*, 143.

108   Douglas Groothuis, *Truth Decay* (Downers Grove: Intervarsity Press, 2000),, 105.

109   Ibid., 108.

110   McLaren, *Generous Orthodoxy,* 11.

111   Ibid., 28.

112   Ibid.

113   Groothuis, *Truth Decay, 206.*

114   Erickson, Helseth, and Taylor, *Reclaiming the Center*, 77.

115   Douglas Groothuis, "Truth Defined and Defended, in *Reclaiming the Center,* 79.

116   McLaren, *A Generous Orthodoxy,* 254.

117   Carson, *Becoming Conversant with the Emerging Church,* 137.

118   Ibid.

119   Ibid., 138.

120   Ibid., 69.

121   Ted Koppel, 1987 commencement address at Duke University, Durham, North Carolina, May 10, 1987. *Time* in partnership with CNN website, Monday, June 22, 1987: http://www.time.com/time/magazine/article/0,9171,964745-1,00.html.

122    McLaren, *A Generous Orthodoxy,* 225.

123    Ibid.

124    Bob DeWaay, *The Emergent Church: Undefining Christianity,*
(Saint Louis Park, MN: Bethany Press International, 2009), 18.

125    Ibid., 162.

126    Ibid.

127    Ibid., 100.

128    Wells, *Above All Earthly Pow'rs,* 156.

129    Eddie Gibbs and Ryan K. Bolger, *Emerging Churches: Creating Christian
Community in Postmodern Cultures* (Grand Rapids, MI: Baker Academic,
2005), 131.

130    *The Merriam-Webster Dictionary of Quotations.* (Springfield, Mass.:
Merriam-Webster, 1992)

131    Brian McLaren, *A New Kind of Christian* (San Francisco: Jossey-Bass, 2001)
17, 52, 55.

132    McLaren, *A Generous Orthodoxy*, 22–3.

133    Ibid., 261.

134    Ibid., 293–4.

135    McLaren, *The Secret Message of Jesus,* 7.

136    John MacArthur, "Brian McLaren and the Clarity of Scripture,"
http://www.gty.org/resources.php?section=articles&aid=231584

137    McLaren, *A Generous Orthodoxy*, 155.

138    G. K Chesterton, "Orthodoxy," in *The Collected Works of G. K. Chesterton*,
David Dooly, ed. (San Francisco: Ignatius Press, 1986), vol. I, 211.

139    John R. Franke, preface to *A Generous Orthodoxy*, by McLaren, 10.

140    Ibid.

141    McLaren, *A Generous Orthodoxy*, 293.

142    Ibid.,, 87.

143    Ibid.

144    Ibid., 88.

145    D.A. Carson, "Domesticating the Gospel, A Review of Grenz's
Renewing the Center," in *Reclaiming the Center*, 46.

146    Ibid., 47.

147    Ibid.

148    McLaren, *A Generous Orthodoxy.*, 69.

149    Ibid.

150    Ibid., 76–77.

151    Ibid., 70.

152    Wells, *Above All Earthly Pow'rs*, 155.

153    Ibid., 152.

154    McLaren, *A Generous Orthodoxy*, 155.

155    Ibid., 151.

156    Ibid., 178.

157    DeWaay, *The Emergent Church*, 51.

158    David Wells, *Above All Earthly Pow'rs*, 133.

159    McLaren, *A New Kind of Christian*, 162.

160    Stanley Grenz, *Revisioning Evangelical Theology: A Fresh Agenda for the 21st Century* (Downers Grove, Ill.: InterVarsity, 1993), 94.

161    R. Albert Mohler, Jr., "The Integrity of the Evangelical Tradition and the Challenge of the Postmodern Paradigm," *The Challenge of Postmodernism,* David S. Dockery, editor, (Grand Rapids: Baker Book House, 2001) 67.

162    Ibid.

163    Groothuis, *Truth Decay,* 265.

164    Wells, *No Place for Truth*, 127.

165    Ibid., 127–128.

166    Ibid., 131.

167    D.A. Carson in Erickson, Helseth, and Taylor, *Reclaiming the Center*, 45.

168    Ibid., 45–46.

169    McLaren, *Generous Orthodoxy*, 155.

170    Ibid.,156.

171    Ibid., 157

172    Ibid.

173    Ibid., 162.

174    Ibid., 253.

175    Ibid., 160.

176    McLaren, *A Generous Orthodoxy*, 224.

177    Ibid.

178    Ibid., 225.

179    Ibid.

180    Ibid., 230.

181    Ibid., 32.

182    Ibid., 30ff.

183    Ibid., 61.

184    Ibid., 66.

185    C. F. H. Henry. *God, revelation, and authority.* (Wheaton, Ill.: Crossway Books, 199) 3:457.

186    McLaren, A *Generous Orthodoxy,* 286.

187    Wells, *No Place for Truth,* 131.

188    Robert P. Setters, "A Baptist View of Mission for Postmodernity," *Review and Expositor* 100.4.(2003; 2004) 645.

189    Doug Pagitt, *Church Re-Imagined: The Spiritual Formation of People in Communities of Faith* (Grand Rapids: Zondervan , 2005) 166.

190    Erickson, Helseth, and Taylor, *Reclaiming the Center,* 50.

191    Ibid., 130.

192    Ibid., 131.

193    McLaren, *Generous Orthodoxy,* 164.

194    Ibid., 165.

195    Ibid., 166.

196    Ibid., 166.

197    Ibid. 167.

198    Ibid., 170.

199    Ibid.,171.

200    Carl R. Trueman, *The Wages of Spin,* (Glasgow: Mentor Imprint, 2004), 92.

201    This is best represented Brian McLaren's *The Story We Find Ourselves In* (San Francisco: Jossey-Bass, 2003).

202    Carson, *Becoming Conversant with the Emerging Church,* 172.

203    McLaren, *Generous Orthodoxy,* 146.

204    Ibid.

205    McLaren, *Generous Orthodoxy,* 151.

206    Ibid.

207    Ibid., 152.

208    Rollan D. McCune, "The New Evangelicalism And Apologetics," *Detroit Baptist Seminary Journal,* Vol. 6, (2001; 2004): 100–102.

209    A. Duane Litfin, "1 Timothy" in *The Bible knowledge commentary:*

*An exposition of the Scriptures,* eds. J. F. Walvoord, R. B. Zuck, & Dallas Theological Seminary, Volume II, 729 (Wheaton, IL: Victor Books, 1983–c1985).

210    C. Ryan Jenkins, "Faith and Works in Paul and James," *Bibliotheca Sacra* Vol. 159 (2002; 2003): 65–66.

211    Erickson, *The Evangelical Left*, 58.

212    M. W. Holmes, *The Apostolic Fathers: Greek texts and English translations* (Grand Rapids, MI: Baker Books, 1999) 75.

213    McLaren, *Generous Orthodoxy* 261.

214    Most postmodern thinking rests on the dialectical method. Truth is always changing from a thesis to antithesis to synthesis. The new synthesis forms a new thesis, which forms a new antithesis and synthesis. On and on it goes without an ultimate conclusion or absolute.

215    Because God is absolute, he has sole authority for truth and knowledge. When humans try to find truth apart from God, we distort absolute truth (Romans 1:21–25; 1 Corinthians 1:18–25). The gravest epistemological error people make is to assert their autonomy for finding truth apart from God. Autonomy makes the individual the ultimate standard for finding truth. They will never find infinite truth as finite beings.

216    Cornelius Van Til, *The Defense of the Faith* (Philadelphia: Presbyterian and Reformed, 1975), 40.

217    Francis A. Schaeffer, *The God Who Is There* (Toronto: Hodder and Stoughton, 1968), 48.

218    Carson, *Becoming Conversant with the Emerging Church,* 122.

219    Incommunicable attributes have no analogy in mankind. God cannot share infinity or omnipresence. He can share love and mercy (communicable attributes).

220    Robert L. Reymond, *The Justification of Knowledge* (Phillipsburg, NJ: Presbyterian and Reformed, 1976) 30.

221    McLaren, *Generous Orthodoxy,* 133.

222    Ibid.

223    Ibid., 164.

224    Ibid., 153.

225    Dockery, *The Challenge of Postmodernism,* 86.

226    Reymond, *The Justification of Knowledge* 79.

227    Groothuis, *Truth Decay,* 109.

228    McLaren, *Generous Orthodoxy,* 152, 153.

229    Ibid., 152.

230 Ibid., 184, 185.

231 Ibid., 184.

232 Ibid., 191.

233 Ibid.

234 Ibid., 191, 192.

235 Ibid., 192.

236 Ibid., 193.

237 T. S. Eliot "The Rock," http://www.goodreads.com/quotes/show/28556.

238 John M. Frame, *Apologetics to the Glory of God, An Introduction,* (Phillipsburg: Presbyterian and Reformed Publishing Company, 1994) 80.

239 R. C. Sproul, "The Internal Testimony of the Holy Spirit," *Inerrancy,* Norman L. Geisler, Ed. (Grand Rapids: The Zondervan Corporation, 1979), 344–347.

240 John M. Frame, *The Doctrine of the Knowledge of God,* (Phillipsburg: Presbyterian and Reformed Publishing Company, 1987) 397.

241 Wells, *No Place for Truth,* 101–102.

242 Ibid., 481.

243 Postmodernism is rationalistic reductionism; therefore, the postevangelical view is that evangelicals are guilty of theological reductionism and uncritical biblicism. By the way, postevangelicals are in an epistemological reductionism themselves!

244 Roger Olson, "Reforming Evangelical Theology," in *Evangelical Futures: A Conversation on Theological Method,* ed. John G. Stackhouse, Jr. (Grand Rapids, MI: Baker, 2000) 201.

245 Erickson, Helseth, Taylor, *Reclaiming the Center,* 43.

246 Ibid.

247 Ibid, 45.

248 Wells, *No Place for Truth,* 134.

249 R. Albert Mohler, Jr., "Reformists Evangelicalism: A Center Without a Circumference," in *A Confessing Theology for Postmodern Times* (Wheaton: Crossway, 2000) 146.

250 D. A. Carson, *The Gagging of God* (Grand Rapids: Zondervan, 1999) 481.

251 R. Albert Mohler, Jr., "Standing Together, Standing Apart: Cultural Co-belligerence Without Theological," *Touchstone: A Journal of Mere* Christianity (http://www.touchstonemag.com/archives/article.php?id=16-06-070-f).

252 Ibid.

253 Ibid.

254 Jack Rogers and Donald McKim, *The Authority and Interpretation of the Bible: An Historical Approach* (New York: Harper, 1979).

255     John D. Woodbridge, *Biblical Authority: A Critique of the Rogers-McKim Proposal* (Grand Rapids: Zondervan, 1982).

256     Paul Jewett, *Man as Male and Female* (Grand Rapids: William B. Eerdmans, 1975).

257     Erickson, *The Evangelical Left,* 77.

258     Clark Pinnock, *The Openness of God: A Biblical Understanding of God* (Downers Grove: InterVarsity, 1994).

259     Carson, *Gagging of God,* 347–67.

260     Wells, *No Place for Truth,* 132.

261     This would include people such as Alister McGrath, Kwame Bediako (Ghanaian theologian), Thomas Oden, Michael Cooper, Wilbert Shenk, Lesslie Newbigin, Oliver Davies, David Cornick.

262     Alister McGrath, *Evangelicalism and the Future of Christianity* (Downers Grove, Il: Intervarsity, 1995) 55–56.

263     Kwame Bediako, *Theology and Identity: The Impact of Culture upon Christian Thought in the Second Century and Modern Africa* (Oxford: Regnum Books, 1992) 251–252.

264     "Q&A: Francis Beckwith," *Christianity Today,* http://www.christianitytoday.com/ct/2007/mayweb-only/119-33.0.html.

265     Ibid.

266     Associated Baptist Press, "Baylor prof Beckwith becomes Catholic, resigns as head of evangelical society," http://www.abpnews.com/content/view/2252/120/.

267     Evangelical Theological Society, "ETC Constitution," http://www.etsjets.org/about/constitution.

268     David S. Dockery, *Southern Baptists and American Evangelicals* (Nashville: Broadman, 1992).

269     Carl F. H. Henry, *Evangelicals at the Brink of Crisis* (Waco: Word, 1967) 111.

270     Wells, *No Place for Truth,* 209–210.

271     Wells, *Above All Earthly Pow'rs,* 5–6.

272     Wells, *No Place for Truth,* 217.

273     Ibid., 135.

274     Ibid., 136

275     Tim Keller, "The Gospel in All its Forms," *Leadership* Journal (2008), http://www.christianitytoday.com/le/2008/spring/9.74.html.

276     Wolfhart Pannenberg, "How to Think About Secularism," *First Things* 64 (June/July 1996): 27–32, http://www.leaderu.com/ftissues/ft9606/articles/pannenberg.html.

277   Erwin Raphael McManus, "The Global Intersection," in *The Church in Emerging Culture: Five Perspectives* Leonard Sweet, Ed. (Grand Rapids: Zondervan, 2003), 225.

278   Ibid. 248.

279   Carson, *Becoming Conversant*, 42, 44.

280   E. R. McManus, "The Global Intersection," 247.

281   Ibid.

282   Ibid.

283   E. R. McManus, *Soul Cravings*, (Nashville: Nelson Books, 2006) unnumbered page.

284   McManus, "The Global Intersection," 245.

285   Ibid.

286   Ibid., 256–57.

287   Al Sergel interview with Erwin Raphael McManus, "Soul Cravings, Q&A," *Relevant Magazine*, http://www.relevantmagazine.com/godarticle.php?id=7241.

288   E. R. McManus, *Barbarian Way* (Nashville: Thomas Nelson, 2005) 60–61, 109.

289   Mark Devine, "The Emerging Church: One Movement—Two Streams," in *Evangelicals Engaging Emergent: A Discussion of the Emergent Church Movement,* eds. William D. Henard and Adam W. Greenway (Nashville: B & H Publishing Group, 2009) 17, 20.

290   Ibid., 33.

291   Dean Kelley, *Why Conservative Churches Are Growing* (New York: Harper and Row, 1972).

292   Robert E. Webber, "Out with the Old," *Christianity Today* (February 19, 1990) 17.

293   Wells *No Place for Truth,* , 9–10.

294   Brian McLaren, in *A New Kind of Christianity,* tries to shift the paradigm of evangelicalism into a new social gospel, a kingdom that does not represent an accurate picture of the biblical kingdom. He picks and chooses verses for his own purposes. As well, he downplays the book of Romans and justifies it by an unjustified hierarchy of placing the gospels over the epistles.

295   Josh McDowell, "Teaching the Truth So Others Will Know and *Live* It," *Veritas*, Vol. 5, No. 3, (July 2005): 1–2.

296   Ibid., 2.